MODERN STUDIES IN PHILOSOPHY

PLATO

D0905621

Modern Studies in Philosophy is a series of anthologies presenting contemporary interpretations and evaluations of the works of major philosophers. The editors have selected articles designed to show the systematic structure of the thought of these philosophers, and to reveal the relevance of their views to the problems of current interest. These volumes are intended to be contributions to contemporary debates as well as to the history of philosophy; they not only trace the origins of many problems important to modern philosophy, but also introduce major philosophers as interlocutors in current discussions.

Modern Studies in Philosophy is prepared under the general editorship of Amelie Oksenberg Rorty, Livingston College, Rutgers University.

Gregory Vlastos is Stuart Professor of Philosophy at Princeton University. He had previously taught philosophy at Queen's University, in Kingston, Ontario, and at Cornell University.

MODERN STUDIES IN PHILOSOPHY

Amelie Oksenberg Rorty, General Editor

PLATO

A Collection of Critical Essays

II: ETHICS, POLITICS, AND PHILOSOPHY
OF ART AND RELIGION

EDITED BY GREGORY VLASTOS

UNIVERSITY OF NOTRE DAME PRESS
Notre Dame, Indiana

University of Notre Dame Press edition published 1978
Copyright © 1971 by Gregory Vlastos
Published by arrangement with Doubleday and Company

Library of Congress Cataloging in Publication Data

Vlastos, Gregory, comp.
  Plato: a collection of critical essays.

  Reprint of the ed. published by Anchor Books,
Garden City, N.Y., in series: Modern studies in
philosophy.
  Bibliography: v. 1, p.   ; v. 2, p.
  Includes indexes.
  CONTENTS: 1. Metaphysics and epistemology.
—2. Ethics, politics, and philosophy of art and
religion.
  1. Plato—Addresses, essays, lectures. I. Title.
B395.V57 1978   184'.08   77-19103
ISBN 0-268-01530-9 (v. 2)
ISBN 0-268-01531-7 pbk. (v. 2)

CONTENTS

ABBREVIATIONS USED IN THIS BOOK

Aristotle (Arist.)
APo. = Posterior Analytics
APr. = Prior Analytics
de An. = de Anima
EE = Eudemian Ethics
EN = Nicomachean Ethics
GA = de Generatione Animalium
GC = de Generatione et Corruptione
Int. = de Interpretatione
Metaph. = Metaphysics
MM = Magna Moralia
Ph. = Physics
Pol. = Politics
Rh. = Rhetoric
SE = de Sophisticis Elenchis
Top. = Topics

Isocrates (Isoc.)
Areop. = Areopagiticus

Plato (Pl.)
Alc. = Alcibiades
Ap. = Apology
Chrm. = Charmides
Cra. = Cratylus
Cri. = Crito
Criti. = Critias
Def. = Definitions
Ep. = Epistles
Epin. = Epinomis
Euthd. = Euthydemus
Euthphr. = Euthyphro
Grg. = Gorgias
Hp. Ma. = Hippias Major
Hp. Mi. = Hippias Minor
Ion

La. = Laches
Lg. = Laws
Ly. = Lysis
Men. = Meno
Phd. = Phaedo
Phdr. = Phaedrus
Phlb. = Philebus
Plt. = Politicus
Prm. = Parmenides
Prt. = Protagoras
R. = Republic
Symp. = Symposium
Sph. = Sophist
Tht. = Theaetetus
Ti. = Timaeus

Plotinus (Plot.)
Enn. = Enneads

Xenophon (X.)
Cyr. = Cyropaedia
Mem. = Memorabilia

Thucydides (Th.)

INTRODUCTION

The last three decades have witnessed a renaissance of interest in Plato among philosophers throughout the world. This interest is still growing. Plato is being studied and argued over with greater vigor than ever before. The philosophical and even the classical journals of English-speaking countries have reflected this development. More articles and discussions of Plato have appeared in them than of any other of the great thinkers of the past. And the number of books and commentaries on Plato is also impressive, as one can see by glancing at the bibliographies at the back of each of the two volumes in this anthology.

Much of this new zeal for platonic studies has been generated by the importation of techniques of logical and semantic analysis that have proved productive in contemporary philosophy. By means of these techniques we may now better understand some of the problems Plato attempted to solve and we are, therefore, better equipped to assess the merit of his solutions. The result has been a more vivid sense of the relevance of his thought to the concerns of present-day ontologists, epistemologists, and moralists. He has become for us less of an antique monument and more of a living presence than he seemed to be in the twenties and the thirties.

With this has come a higher appreciation of his stature, in spite of the fact that the more rigorous canons of criticism by which we now judge his claims have shown errors in his thought which had not been seen, or seen clearly, by earlier scholars. Only a puerile critic would make immunity to logical error the measure of a philosopher's greatness. Can one read through a chapter in any acknowledged philosophical masterpiece—Spinoza's *Ethics*, Hume's *Treatise*, the First or the Second of Kant's *Critiques*—without spotting some error, often enough a big one? I agree with Richard Robinson that "greatness in science consists mainly in leaving the subject much more advanced than when you entered it."[1] Plato has no difficulty passing this test. He was a pioneer moving through *terra incognita*. Even a formal logic had yet to be created; Aristotle was Plato's pupil.

Extravagant claims have been made for the gains in insight

[1] *Plato's Earlier Dialectic*, 2nd Ed. (Oxford, 1953), p. vi of the Preface.

which have resulted from the use of more sophisticated methods of conceptual analysis in platonic exegesis. One of the distinguished advocates of this new approach once startled a seminar by declaring that these methods now enable us to understand Plato better than he was ever understood by anyone in history—better than by any of his own contemporaries, even better than by himself! One need not share the euphoria that produced this boast to insist that there is an element of truth in it after all. Take two statements, S and S′, expressed by Greek sentences so similar in vocabulary and superficial syntax that they could be read in either of two different ways, the resulting difference to the sense being so great that S would, and S′ would not, be consistent with major platonic theses. Alerted by our analytic tools to the ambiguity and the resulting consequences, we can tell that in a given context, where it is clear that Plato has no interest in asserting anything but S, this is the only thing he must be understood to mean. One who lacked the means to block out as clearly the difference in sense between S and S′ would not be as aware of the enormous risks taken in using sentences of that form; he might, therefore, use them in cases where the context does not of itself suffice to rule out the S′ reading, thereby courting grave misunderstanding by others and even by himself. Coming across such sentences in Plato, it would be plainly true to say that we can understand them better than he did and even to add that we can, therefore, understand *him* better, since we can see both what he meant to say and the logical liabilities of his incautious statements. "Self-predication" is a fair example. Had Plato known the Russellian paradox,[2] he would have seen instantly the absurd consequences of "The *F* is *F*" for most values of *F*,[3] for example. The increment in self-understanding would have altered the texture, indeed the very substance of his metaphysics.

Once we have made full allowance for what modern semantics and logic can do to make Plato more intelligible and alive for us today, we should be quick to concede that borrowings from this quarter must be used with economy and discretion, and that con-

[2] Bertrand Russell, *Principles of Mathematics* (London, 1903), Chapter X, "The Contradiction." For a succinct recent discussion see the article on the Logical Paradoxes by J. van Heijenoort in the *Encyclopedia of Philosophy* (New York, 1967).

[3] Cf. G. Vlastos, "The Third Man Argument in the *Parmenides*," *Philosophical Review* 63 (1954), 319–49 at 337–38; "Self-predication in Plato's Later Dialogues," *Philosophical Review* 78 (1969), 74–78.

tinuing reliance on older linguistic and historical disciplines is as essential now as it has ever been in the past if the object of our inquiries is *Plato* himself, instead of some mock-up more pleasing to current taste. The man we have to deal with, the flesh-and-blood person whose thought we seek to comprehend, is the one who, as a young man, was the companion and admirer of Socrates, but was influenced at the same time by that bizarre metaphysician, Cratylus, and was exposed to many other philosophical currents swirling in and out of Athens. He must have fought against Sparta during the war years, even though admiring Spartan discipline and hating Athenian liberty. Although his hatred of democracy abated in his later years, he continued to oppose it on principle and tolerate it only as a lesser evil to lawless despotism. A great artist, he nevertheless feared art and clamped a moralistic strait-jacket on it in his utopias. He undertook to refute not only the Sophists, like Protagoras, whom he scorned, but the greatest of his predecessors, like Parmenides, whom he revered. He was fascinated, but not mesmerized, by number theory and geometry. He did not think that empirical science deserved serious study, but he studied and wrote it just the same. He projected a physical theory which owed no less to the materialistic atomists than to Pythagorean numerological mystics. He shared Pythagoras' faith in a divine, transmigrating, soul, but his own mysticism was obstinately intellectual—for him the beatifying, immortalizing experience came through a discipline in which mind and heart were partners.

What is the bearing of these facts on the interpretation of his metaphysics and theory of knowledge, not to speak of their even more urgent import for his ethics, his moral psychology, his political theory, his theory of art? And what other facts can we extract from our textual and historical data which will make our ideas on these diverse phases of his thought more exact? Here the philosopher must look for help to the classical scholar: to the philologist, who is best fitted to recover Plato's text and to capture its sense, reading it with scrupulous care for detail, but knowing so well its entirety that he can bring to bear on the interpretation of a single sentence parallels and contrasts culled from a thousand pages of platonic text; to the historian of Greek philosophy, who has the broadest as well as the most carefully sifted knowledge of those earlier thinkers from whom Plato learned so much, and has also knowledge of the work of Aristotle, whose metaphysics, philosophy of science,

cosmology, psychology, ethics and politics were formed in nearly
two decades spent in the Academy and whose criticisms of Plato are
instructive even when they are demonstrably tendentious in their
form; and, finally, to the historian of Greek culture, who is in the
best position to ascertain what it was in the science, morality,
politics, art and religion of his people which presented Plato with
the problems he tried to solve.

The essays in this anthology should give the reader a good idea of
the variety of approaches represented in current contributions to
the interpretation of Plato. Volume One is heavily weighted on the
"analytical" side. All but one of its essays were written by men
whose academic training was strongly philosophical (though
several of them are also accomplished classicists). Volume Two is
weighted on the other side, though not as heavily. There are
several essays in it by distinguished hellenists, writing as pure
historians, making no effort to line up platonic doctrines with their
counterparts, if any, in present-day philosophizing; some of them
would object on principle to this kind of effort as more likely to
distort than clarify what we find in Plato. Glad though I am to
illustrate this diversity of point of view, I did not make the selections with this in mind. My one concern was to bring together
significant contributions to the interpretation of those aspects of
Plato's thought which could be covered in this volume. Since my
space was all too limited, compactness of presentation became a
primary desideratum. Some fundamental work could not be represented here because it was not available in this format. For the
material I looked to the classical, no less than the philosophical,
books and journals, and I solicited essays from classicists as well as
philosophers. It is my strong conviction that each of these two
disciplines has its own indispensable place in the elucidation of
Plato's thought, and I am proud that outstanding work from both
appears in this anthology.

Though my policy favored the more recent publications over
older ones, I have made an exception in the case of an earlier
classic: the chapter on Plato's ethics in Paul Shorey's *Unity of
Plato's Thought* (1903). This seems to have fallen into undeserved
oblivion. I cannot recall a single reference to it in current discussions of its theme. Yet no later essay can compete with it in
giving in so brief a compass an incisive, comprehensive, and richly

documented account of Plato's ethical doctrines. Readers will find it a useful preliminary to the next six pieces, which focus sharply on special issues in Plato's moral philosophy and psychology.

For the privilege of including the selected material in this volume I wish to express my warmest thanks to those whose cooperation has made the venture possible: to Professor Penner, for his essay written especially for this volume; to Mr. J. D. Mabbott for revising an early essay of his for its inclusion here; to Professors Bambrough, Cherniss, Dodds, Guthrie, Leys, Markus, Morrow, Sachs, Sparshott, Verdenius, for authorizing me to reprint their papers.

My warmest thanks are due to Amelie Rorty, under whose general editorship the Modern Studies in Philosophy have been prepared, and to Kay Scheuer and Paul H. Drymalski without whose help and advice I could not have carried out the commitment. And I must not forget Gregory Zeigler, who gave up most of his Christmas holiday to prepare the *index locorum;* he has earned the thanks of those who will be using it, as well as mine.

GREGORY VLASTOS

Princeton, New Jersey

1

PLATO'S ETHICS

PAUL SHOREY

The chief topics of the Platonic ethics are these: (1) the Socratic paradoxes; (2) the definition of the virtues, and, more particularly, the determination of their relation to a postulated supreme science or art, to happiness, to the political or royal art, to the idea of good; (3) the problem of hedonism; and (4), associated with it, the attempt to demonstrate the inseparability of virtue and happiness.[1]

1. Plato always formally maintained that all wrongdoing is involuntary;[2] that virtue is insight or knowledge, is in its essence one, and can in some sense be taught.[3] Sometimes he merely dramatically illustrates the conflicts that arise between these paradoxes and common-sense. Elsewhere, most explicitly in the *Laws*,[4] but by implication even in the minor dialogues, he reveals his perception that these propositions can be reconciled with experience only by the conscious employment of words in a special sense.[5] Wrongdoing is involuntary (1) because all men will the good or what they deem the good;[6] (2) because no man who knows the right will do the wrong, if we take knowledge in the highest sense, or refuse the term to any cognition that does not control the will;[7] (3) because the conditions that shape conduct lie far more in heredity, education,

---

[1] These are, as a matter of fact, the chief topics of the ethical dialogues. If we base Plato's ethics on the idea of good, or on any other metaphysical principle or schematism, we shall distort his meanings.

[2] Xen., *Mem.*, 3, 9, 4; 4, 6, 6; *Ap.*, 26A; *Prt.*, 345D, 358C–D; *Meno*, 77, 78; *Grg.*, 466E, 467B = *R.*, 577E = *Laws*, 688B; *R.*, 382A (?), 413A (?), 492E (?), 589C; *Phlb.*, 22B; *Sph.*, 228C, 230A; *Ti.*, 86D; *Laws*, 731C, 734B, 860D.

[3] *Euthd.*, 282C; *Laws*, 644A.

[4] 689D, 696C, 710A, ἤν τις σεμνύνων ἂν λέγοι, φρόνησιν προσαναγκάζων εἶναι τὸ σωφρονεῖν.

[5] *Laches*, 196E; *Laches*, 191E, ἀνδρεῖοι . . . ἐν ἡδοναῖς, cf. *Laws*, 633D–E, and *R.*, 429D; *R.*, 443E, 444A; *Th.*, 176C; *Plt.*, 306A.

[6] *Meno*, 77; *Euthd.*, 279; *Symp.*, 205A; *Grg.*, 468.

[7] *Prt.*, 352B; *Laws*, 689; *Tht.*, 176C.

and environment than in our conscious wills.[8] The contradiction noted by Aristotle between this charitable principle and the edifying proclamation "virtue is free,"[9] is emotional rather than scientific.[10] The modern free-will controversy arises out of two conceptions not connected with this problem by Plato: the infinite foreknowledge of God, and the absolute continuity of physical causation. It is, then, unprofitable to inquire whether Plato taught free-will or determinism.[11] But it should be distinctly noted that in the *Laws* he employs precisely the logic of modern determinism to prove that the involuntary character of wrongdoing is compatible with the distinction for legal purposes of voluntary and involuntary acts.[12]

Virtue is knowledge because it must be assumed to be a good, and the only certain good, the only sure guide to the good use of what the world calls good, is knowledge.[13] Opinion and habit may often suffice to regulate action, but persistent right opinion presupposes knowledge in its teachers, and the highest rule of conduct must be deduced from and referred to a rational apprehension of ultimate good.[14] Virtue is one because each of the virtues is a form of knowledge,[15] or because each, when taken in the highest sense, involves all the others.[16] Virtue is teachable in the senses in which knowledge and right opinion may be taught. The capacity for knowledge, the divine faculty, is innate, but teaching and guidance may direct it toward the good.[17] The ordinary virtues of habit and

[8] *Ti.*, 86D.   [9] *R.*, 617E.

[10] *Cf.* my note in *A. J. P.*, Vol. X, p. 77.

[11] Zeller, *Philosophie der Griechen*, 4th ed., Vol. II, No. 1, p.853; Jowett, Vol. III, pp. 408, 425.

[12] 861–864C. The meaning of the passage, though often misunderstood, is perfectly clear, and Plato warns us, 864B, not to cavil about the terminology.

[13] *Euthd.*, 281, 289; *Meno*, 88C. *Cf.* from another point of view *Phaedo*, 69 A–B; *Prt.*, 356, 357, with *Phlb.*, 41E.

[14] *Meno*, 97B; *Meno*, 100A οἶος καὶ ἄλλον ποιῆσαι, etc. *Cf. Euthd.*, 292D; *infra*, p. 16: *Laws*, 951B.

[15] *Laches, Prt., Phaedo*, 69A–B. *Meno*, 71 D ff., is logical rather than ethical. The unity of ἀρετή is postulated, like that of any other abstract idea, as a precondition of a definition.

[16] *Grg.*, 507A; *Laws*, 696C. There is a suggestion of this also in the (of course intentional, Bonitz, *Platonic Studies*, p. 265) fallacies of *Prt.*, 330, 331.

[17] *R.*, 518B, 519A. This apparently contradicts the statement of the *Meno*, 99A, and *Prt.*, 361B, that ἐπιστήμη (knowledge) alone can be

opinion may fairly be said to be taught when they are systematically inculcated by superior wisdom enlisting all the forces of
society in its service.[18] This is not the case at Athens,[19] and therefore
the Platonic Socrates alternately affirms and denies the possibility
of teaching "virtue,"[20] and at the close of the *Meno* declares that
under present conditions it comes by a grace divine which is
equivalent to chance.[21]

Plato uses, but is not himself confused by, the Socratic analogy
between the virtues and the arts and sciences.[22] That comparison,
though it ignores the distinctively ethical element, contains a
certain measure of truth. In a sense, each of us is good in that
which he knows.[23] Knowledge as ordinarily understood is not
virtue, but it does away with many forms of wrongdoing. It is not
courage, but the man who knows how is less likely to be afraid.[24]
It is not σωφροσύνη (temperance), but it is incompatible with many
forms of ἀφροσύνη (intemperance). The wise man knows his own
limits, and will undertake only what he can perform.[25] Partly for
these reasons, and partly because he did not or, in ironical assump-

---

taught. But the objection is captious. The *Republic* is satirizing the
exaggerated claims of the Sophists and is speaking of the faculty, not
the content, of knowledge. The whole higher education is a teaching of
knowledge in a sense. And, on the other hand, though both Plato and
Aristotle limit teaching in the strict sense to knowledge, opinion is
imparted ἐν τῇ παιδείᾳ, 429C, *i. e.*, is virtually taught.

[18] *R.*, 500D, 429C–D; *Plt.*, 309D; *Laws, passim.*

[19] *R.*, 492E; *Ti.*, 87B; *Meno*, 93B ff.; *Prt.*, 320; *R.*, 520B; *Euthyphro*,
2 C–D; *Grg.*, 521D; *Ap.*, 24, 25; *Laches*, 179C–D.

[20] *Prtg.; Meno; Euthd.*, 282C (274E).

[21] *R.*, 492, 493. At present good men spring up αὐτόματοι (*R.*, 520B;
cf. Prt., 320A; *Euthd.*, 282C); *Laws*, 951B.

[22] The lesser *Hippias* (certainly by Plato) presents the fallacy in its
most paradoxical form (the voluntary lie better than the involuntary)
and by its obvious irony (372D–E, 376C) shows that Plato "already"
in the Socratic period does not take it seriously, but merely uses it for
dramatic or propaedeutic purposes. Zeller, p. 597, takes this as Plato's
real opinion, citing *R.*, 535D and 382, which merely use the paradoxical terminology to emphasize the thought, acceptable to Mill or
Huxley, that the mere intellectual love of truth (knowledge) ought to
be counted a virtue as well as the ordinary virtue of truthfulness.

[23] *Laches*, 194D; *Lysis*, 210D; *R.*, 349E.

[24] *Laches*, 193; *Prt.*, 350.

[25] Xen., *Mem.*, 2, 2, 24; *Chrm.*, 171D–E; *Alc.*, I, 117 D–E; *Sophist*,
229C; *Laws*, 732A.

tion that others were even as himself, would not recognize that men know the right and yet the wrong pursue, the Platonic Socrates seems to ignore the chief ethical factor, a virtuous will, and argues that he who knows justice is just.[26] But such "fallacies" are for Plato merely the starting-point of a fuller analysis. All knowledge is good and commendable,[27] but the supreme knowledge that may be identified with "virtue" is plainly something different from the specialties of the arts and sciences.[28] Courage, for example, apart from mere animal and temperamental fearlessness, may be defined as knowledge of what is and is not to be feared. But this involves real knowledge of good and evil, a complete ideal of life, either that of the Sophists and average Athenian opinion, or that unfolded by Plato himself in the *Republic*. The attempt to define courage in the absence of these distinctions merely illustrates the inadequacy of conventional ethical thought.[29]

The effective application to these problems of the obvious distinction between science and right opinion requires the larger canvas of the *Republic*. And even then it remains true that the courage most worthy of the name implies a complete philosophic mastery of the conception of life that educates the masses in such right opinion.[30] Plato tacitly assumes that this supreme knowledge

---

[26] *Grg.*, 460B. The fallacy, so far as it is one, is intentional. Observe κατὰ τοῦτον τὸν λόγον, and the explanation in *R.*, 438D–E, that the knowledge of health, though differentiated from knowledge in general, is not necessarily healthful. But for the broad purposes of the argument of the *Gorgias* it is true (460E) that rhetoric, if really the science of the just, could not be the instrument of injustice which Gorgias with unconscious immorality complacently represented it to be. Socrates is "the sort of man who assents to nothing in him except to argument," *Crito*, 46B; *cf. Laches*, 188D–E; *Grg.*, 488A. Hence, as Aristotle (*E.N.*, 7, 2, 1), quoting *Prt.*, 352B, says, he thought it monstrous that any other impulse in man should prevail over his better knowledge. And Plato in his latest work refuses the term "knowledge" to any belief that does not control the will, and pronounces discord between the desires and the ethical convictions the grossest form of "ignorance."

[27] *Prt.*, 318B; *Laches*, 182D.

[28] *Chrm.*, 165C; *Euthd.*, 282E, 290; *Prt.*, 311, 312, 319A; *Laws* 961E ff.

[29] *Laches; Prt.*, 349, 350, 360D; *R.*, 429, 430.

[30] The courage defined in 429C is only "political." *Cf.* δημῶδη γε, *Laws*, 710A; *Plt.*, 309E; *Phaedo*, 82A. There are, strictly speaking, three or four grades: brute animal courage, the courage of soldiers and citizens in ordinary states, the citizen courage of the Platonic state, the philosophic courage.

will be inseparable from the virtuous will in his philosophic statesmen as it is in Socrates.[31] And thus on this higher plane the Socratic
paradox becomes true again.

It matters little to the consistency and unity of Plato's thought
whether we regard this harmony of the intellect and the will as a
mere ideal or as a practicable postulate realized in Socrates and to
be fulfilled by others in a reformed society. The distinction once
drawn, the ideal once affirmed, Plato can afford to make concessions to common-sense. He can admit that in present experience
a kind of bravery is found dissociated from the other virtues.[32] He
can allow the word σωφροσύνη to be used merely for the instinctive
temperamental moderation in appetite that is the fortunate endowment of some children and animals.[33] He can recognize that
knowledge, or at least quickness and acumen of thought, is not in-
frequently associated with intemperance and injustice.[34] But he
prefers to translate the facts into a more edifying terminology.
Conventional virtue is a worthless currency unless redeemable and
redeemed by and in the coin of wisdom.[35] And, on the other hand,
we will refuse the name of wise to him whose will does not follow
his judgment of right; and we will grant it to the man who knows
enough to obey his acquired belief in the good rather than the
innate promptings of appetite, though he know not how to swim or
recite the alphabet.[36]

2. Plato found the suggestion of the cardinal virtues and of the
predominance of justice in the poets. He also mentions ὁσιότης

---

[31] This harmony is the chief point in the selections and tests applied
to them; *R.*, 485, 486, 539D ff. *Cf. Plt.*, 309A–B. The *Laws* emphasize
character, as compared with intellect, still more, and preserve the
identity of the moral and the intellectual "which are ever dividing, but
must ever be reunited" (Jowett), by reserving the word "wise" for the
virtuous, 689D.

[32] Protagoras maintains this view, *Prt.*, 350, and is not answered by
Socrates, who refutes him only indirectly by the proof that all virtue is
one—the science of measuring pleasure and pain. But the obvious fact
of experience is presumably as clear to Plato when he allows Protagoras
to state it as when it is enunciated more explicitly in the *Politicus*, 306B,
or the *Laws*, 631C. Zeller (p. 599) incomprehensibly affirms that the
plurality in unity of virtue is found only in the *Republic!*

[33] *Laws*, 710A–B.

[34] *R.*, 519A; *Laws*, 689D, ὅσα πρὸς τάχος τῆς ψυχῆς; *Tht.*,176C.

[35] *Phaedo*, 69B.

[36] *Laws*, 689D. *Cf. Tht.*, 176C. The whole passage is in the mood and
temper of the *Laws*.

(piety)[37] and μεγαλοπρέπεια (dignity), the latter sometimes with irony.[38] But the number four was consecrated by its incorporation in the scheme of the *Republic*. This implies no change of doctrine. Even in the *Republic* other virtues are mentioned.[39] And in the *Euthyphro* it is hinted that piety is a form of justice.[40]

Plato would always recognize piety as one of the chief virtues, or perhaps as a synonym of all virtue,[41] and he would always shrink from giving so problematical a concept a place in a scientific scheme.[42]

Several of the minor dialogues turn on the attempt to define the virtues and allied notions. The *Laches* and *Charmides* are both Socratic quests for definition—of courage in the one case, of temperance in the other. Both involve the antithesis of the quiet and the energetic temperament.[43] Both terminate in perplexity—in the puzzle that, if any one virtue is identified with the supreme knowledge that will make us happy, the distinction between the virtues

[37] *Prt.*, 329C; *Meno*, 78D; *Laches*, 199D.

[38] *Meno*, 74A; *R.*, 560E. In *Meno*, 88A, εὐμάθεια (quickness of mind) and μνήμη (retentiveness) are included.

[39] 402C, ἐλευθεριότης, μεγαλοπρέπεια (liberality, dignity), 536A.

[40] *Cf.* also *Prt.*, 331A.

[41] If it were desirable to produce a Platonic definition of piety, I should accept that of Bonitz as formulated by Professor W. A. Heidel (introduction to his edition of *Euthyphro*, p. 24). It is the endeavor to realize the good felt as the service of God, and as a willed co-operation with Him. But this is a mood in relation to, or an emotional synonym of, all virtue. It is not one aspect of virtue which it is necessary to distinguish in relation to a special field of conduct or a particular classification of the faculties of the soul.

[42] The suggestion that the *Euthyphro* "eliminates" piety, and that the *Meno* may be dated by its recognition of ὁσιότης (78D) is utterly fantastic.

[43] *Cf. Chrm.*, 159B ff., with *Plt.*, 307A–B. Temperament is not virtue, but is the basis of the seeming opposition between bravery and temperance (*Plt.*, 306, 307; *R.*, 410D–E, 503C–D; *Laws*, 735A, 681B, 773B, 831E; *Prt.*, 349E). Nicias and Laches, for want of this distinction, maintain opposite paradoxes. Socrates calls our attention to this by attributing to Nicias the doctrine ὁμοίως λέοντα καὶ ἔλαφον .... πρὸς ἀνδρείαν—πεφυκέναι, "that a lion is not naturally more disposed to courage than a deer" (196E). In the *Republic* (430B), Plato chooses to deny the term "bravery" to mere animal courage. In the *Laws*, 963E, he attributes a kind of courage to children and animals. But ὁμοίως πεφυκέναι pointedly ignores the distinction of temperament.

vanishes,[44] or in the tautology that the knowledge that is good is knowledge of the good.[45]

It is often assumed (1) that Plato was serious in these attempts to express by a phrase or a substituted synonym the essence of a virtue and the various and contradictory meanings of its conventional name; (2) that the failure and pretended perplexity of Socrates at the close mark the point reached by Plato's own thought at the time. This is *a priori* conceivable. But the following considerations make it highly improbable:

a) Plato, in this unlike Xenophon,[46] always proceeds as if he were aware of the true theory and use of the definition and of the multiple meanings of ethical terms. All attempts in his writings to work out absolute and isolated definitions fail.[47] His own definitions, when not mere illustrations,[48] are always working hypotheses[49] or epigrammatic formulas, subordinate to and interpreted by the argument of which they form a part, and recognized as imperfect, but sufficient for the purpose in hand.[50] The definitions of the virtues in *R.*, 429 ff. cannot be understood apart from their context, and are never used again. They are declared to be a mere sketch— ὑπογραφήν, 504D.[51] How shall we explain this on the supposition that he was under any illusion as to the value of absolute and isolated definitions?

b) Plato repeatedly refers in a superior way to eristic, voluntary

---

[44] *Laches*, 199E.

[45] *Chrm.*, 174B; *cf. R.*, 505B–C—a connection generally missed.

[46] The Xenophontic Socrates perceives no difficulties, is never in doubt, and propounds dogmatically such definitions as νόμιμον = δίκαιον, *Mem.*, IV, 4, 12.

[47] Except the not quite serious definitions reached by dichotomy in the *Sophist* and *Politicus*. *Cf. Charmides, Laches, Lysis, Meno, Theaetetus, Euthyphro, Hippias Major*.

[48] τάχος, *Laches*, 192B; σχῆμα, *Meno*, 75, 76; πηλός, *Tht.*, 147C; ἥλιος, *ibid.*, 208D.

[49] *Phdr.*, 237D, ὁμολογίᾳ θέμενοι ὅρον. *Cf.* 263D–E.

[50] *E.g.* ῥητορικὴ = πολιτικῆς μορίου εἴδωλον, *Grg.*, 463D, but in *Phdr.*, 261A, ψυχαγωγία τις διὰ λόγων. *Cf.* the definitions of σωφροσύνη, *Phdr.*, 237E.

[51] The *Laws* repeats the substance of the definition of justice, 863E: "the domination of passion . . . and desire in the soul I call 'injustice'." *Cf.* 689A–B. *R.*, 442A.

and involuntary,[52] and more particularly to the confusion, tautology, and logomachy into which the vulgar fall when they attempt to discuss abstract and ethical problems.[53] Some of these allusions touch on the very perplexities and fallacies exemplified in the minor dialogues.[54] They do not imply that Plato himself had ever been so confused.[55] Why should we assume that he deceives us in order to disguise his changes of opinion, or obliterate the traces of his mental growth? Have we not a right to expect dramatic illustration of so prominent a feature in the intellectual life of the time, and do we not find it in the *Laches, Charmides, Lysis*, and the corresponding parts of the *Protagoras?* In brief, the *Euthydemus*, 277, 278; *Phaedrus*, 261, 262; the *Theaetetus*, 167E; the *Republic*, 454, 487B–C; the *Sophist*, 230B, 251B, 259C, and *Philebus*, 20A, 15E, show a clear consciousness of dialectic, not merely as a method of truth, but as a game practiced for amusement or eristic, to purge

[52] *R.*, 454A; *Phlb.*, 14C; *Tht.*, 206B; *Tht.*, 167E; *Sophist*, 259D; already in *Lysis*, 216A–B. *Cf. infra*, p. 19.

[53] *Phdr.*, 237C, 263 and, from a slightly different point of view, *R.*, 538D; *Phaedo*, 90C. This is largely due to a false conceit of knowledge, *Phdr.*, 237C, which the Elenchus as described in *Sph.*, 230B, and practised in the minor dialogues cures. *Cf. Meno*, 84A–B. So *Sph.*, 232A–B, gives the *raison d'être* of passages (*Gorgias, Prt., Ion*) in which a pretender to universal knowledge is pressed for a specific definition of his function which he naturally is unable to give.

[54] *Plt.*, 306 ff., especially 306A. *Cf. Laws*, 627D; *R.*, 348E, with reference to the arguments of *Grg.*, 474C ff. *Cf. Laws*, 837A, with reference to the problem of the *Lysis; Laws*, 661B, 687, 688, 688B, where the paradox of *Grg.*, 467, is reaffirmed; *Republic*, 505B, with *Chrm.*, 173E–174B; *R.*, 505C, with *Grg.*, 499B, where Callicles is forced to admit that some pleasures are bad. Zeller (p. 604) thinks that *R.*, 505C, refers to the *Philebus*. But the advocates of late date for the *Philebus* rightly deny any specific parallel.

[55] Even after the *Republic* and *Politicus*, Plato in *Laws*, 963 ff., approaches the problem of the "political art" and the unit of virtue precisely in the manner of the tentative dialogues. There is no reason for taking seriously Socrates's dramatic bewilderment as to the "political art" in *Euthd.*, 292D–E, that would not apply equally to the avowal of ignorance in *Laws*, 963B, or in the *Politicus* itself, 292C. The political art, *i.e.*, ultimate ethical and social "good," was always a problem to Plato, as it must be to any thoughtful, conscientious man (*R.*, 451A). In the *Laws*, 964 ff., as in the *Republic*, he finally limits himself to indicating the kind of training that will prepare the mind to apprehend it best. But as against the ideals of Athenian sophists and politicians, his beliefs were defined "already" in the *Euthyphro*, 2C, and the *Gorgias*, 463D ff., 521D.

the conceit of ignorance or awaken intellectual curiosity. When we find this game dramatically illustrated why should we assume naïve unconsciousness on Plato's part?

c) The *Republic*, in which Plato explicitly states his solution of these problems, is a marvelous achievement of mature constructive thought. But the ideas and distinctions required for the solution itself are obvious enough, and it is absurd to affirm that they were beyond the reach of a thinker who was capable of composing the *Protagoras*,[56] the subtle *Lysis* and *Charmides*, or the eloquent and ingenious *Gorgias*. That the highest rule of conduct must be based upon complete insight and is the possession of a few; that the action of the multitude is determined by habit and belief[57] shaped under the manifold pressure of tradition and public opinion; that the virtues may be differently defined according as we refer them to knowledge or to opinion and habit; that opinion in the Athens of the Sophists and of the Peloponnesian war was not guided by true philosophy, and therefore was not the "right opinion" which should become the fixed habit of the populace in a reformed society; that the Sophists who professed to teach virtue taught at the best conformity to the desires and opinions of the many-headed beast, and that therefore in the proper sense virtue was not taught at all at Athens;[58] that virtue is one regarded as knowledge, or as the spiritual harmony resulting from perfect self-control (443E), but many as expressing the opposition of contrasted temperaments and different degrees of education; and that endless logomachies result from the inability of the average disputant to grasp these and similar distinctions[59]—these are reflections that might present themselves to any intelligent young man who had listened to Socrates, and surveyed the intellectual life of the time, though only the genius of Plato could construct a *Republic* from them. They could occur to Plato at the age of thirty or thirty-five as well as at forty or forty-five; and it is extremely naïve to assume that so obvious a distinction as that between science and opinion, familiar to every reader of *Parmenides*, and employed to bring the *Meno* to a

---

[56] "One of the finest specimens of analysis in all his writings," John Stuart Mill, *Dissertations and Discussions*, Vol. IV, p. 250.

[57] *Phaedo*, 82A; *R.*, 522A, 619C; *Laws*, 966C.

[58] *R.*, 492, 493.

[59] *Laws*, 964A.

plausible dramatic conclusion, was a great scientific discovery, marking an epoch in Plato's thought.[60]

d) Lastly the structure and logic of the minor dialogues are indicative of dramatic design rather than of tentative inquiry. The systematic evolution of the argument and of the antitheses which it involves;[61] the emphasis laid on the very difficulties elucidated by the latter theory;[62] the reserves and qualifications of the argument

---

[60] Not to dwell on the resemblance of *Meno*, 99C, and *Apology*, 22C (*cf.* also the *Ion*), why, if Plato has no dramatic reserves, is true opinion ignored in the *Euthydemus?* Or is the *Euthydemus*, with its mature logic and its assumption that virtue can be taught, earlier than the *Meno?*

[61] In the *Charmides* σωφροσύνη is first defined by the quiet temperament, 159B, then by the associated modesty, αἰδώς, 159E, which is elsewhere its virtual synonym, *Prt.*, 322C–E; then by τὰ ἑαυτοῦ πράττειν ("doing one's own") 161B, another rhetorical equivalent, *Ti.*, 72A, which, however, requires an interpretation that Critias is unable to give, even though assisted by a hint from Socrates (161E). He cannot generalize minding one's own business, and distinguish (1) the economic, (2) the social and political, (3) the psychic division of labor; *R.*, 443C. The formula is allowed to drop, and the equally ambiguous expression "self-knowledge" is substituted (164), which is found to involve puzzles that Critias can neither untie nor cut (*cf.* 167A with *Meno*, 80E; *Tht.*, 188A).

In the *Laches*, Laches insists exclusively on the temperamental aspect of bravery which opposes it to other virtues, Nicias on the cognitive element which identifies it with them. Laches's theory tends to show how the virtues are many, that of Nicias how they are one (*Laws*, 963E ff.). But neither can expound his own view completely, still less reconcile it with the truth of his adversary. They exemplify the logomachy described in *Plt.*, 306, 307.

In the *Lysis* we begin with purely verbal quibbles, pass to the suggestive antithesis of the attraction of like and unlike in nature and man (214, 215), and conclude with the problem of good and evil, and the ultimate nature of desire and the good.

[62] Note the repeated demand that it be shown how σωφροσύνη is a good, *Chrm.*, 159C, 161A, 165D, 172D, 174B, with *R.*, 50. *Cf. infra*, p. 17. Also *Laws*, 710, when, even after the *Republic*, it is recognized that σωφροσύνη as the mere passive *conditio sine qua non* of the usefulness of the active virtues would be of little value. Again, *cf.* the association of τὰ ἑαυτοῦ πράττειν in 161 with the division of labor, and *R.*, 370A, 432A, 434C, 443D. So in the *Laches*, Nicias is driven to admit that the knowledge of things really terrible and the reverse is not the property of any craftsman even in his own field, but is some higher knowledge of final ends which he cannot define—*i.e.*, obviously the "political art" or the idea of good.

and the hints of dramatic purpose[63]—all point to Plato's possession of the clue. The argument based on the absence from the "Socratic" dialogues of certain features of the longer works begs the point at issue.

Assuming that Plato undertook to illustrate in brief dramatic discussions the ethical logomachies of the day, he would by hypothesis as a rule abstain from Pythagorean myths, criticism of pre-Socratic thinkers, demonstrations of immortality, psychological or physiological digressions, and dogmatic developments of his own philosophy. It may be argued that such dramatic dialogues form as a whole an earlier group. It cannot be maintained that they mark the stages of Plato's own progress.[64] The definitions of the virtues proposed in the fourth book of the *Republic*, interpreted by their context, meet the dramatic difficulties of the *Laches, Charmides, Protagoras,* and *Meno.* Courage is not animal fearlessness, neither is it precisely knowledge of things terrible and the reverse. But the courage to be expected of the masses in a reformed state is the conservation by disciplined feeling of the opinion about things terrible or not terrible inculcated by the possessors of such knowledge.[65] Σωφροσύνη is not precisely quietness, nor doing one's own business, nor self-knowledge, though each of these definitions emphasizes one of the shades of meaning which Greek usage assigned to this "mixed mode." It is in man and state the willing acceptance by all the psychic faculties and the corresponding classes in the population of a harmonious scale of subordination from higher to lower.[66] It is thus the precondition and obverse aspect of justice which is the fulfilment of its own function by each faculty and class—a higher

[63] *Chrm.*, 160B; the obvious design of humbling Critias, 162C–D; Charmides's disbelief in Socrates's ignorance, 176B. *Cf. Phdr.*, 262D. Laches's unfamiliarity with dialectic and the awakening effect of the Elenchus upon him; 194A–B.

[64] As Ueberweg says (*Untersuchungen*, p. 280): "Für das Verständniss des Platonismus ist kaum ein anderer Irrthum gefährlicher, als der, eine Zurückhaltung, die Plato aus methodischen Gründen übte, mit einem Nochnichtsein zu verwechseln."

[65] *R.*, 429C–D, 442C.

[66] 432A, 442D. This definition is adapted to the literary machinery of the *Republic*. It does not stop Plato from employing the word in its normal Greek sense (*R.*, 389D–E, ὡς πλήθει, etc.), or from recognizing that it is a condition of virtue rather than an active virtue; *supra*, p. 12.

than the economic division of labor in the soul and in society.[67] These definitions are stated in terms of being rather than of doing, and Plato preferred this form of statement to the end.[68] But he is careful to add that the one includes the other and that the justice within the soul will express itself in just action.[69]

3. These definitions, then, meet the chief difficulties of the minor dialogues and fill their place in the literary economy of the *Republic*. But Plato warns us that they are not the final definitions of a complete philosophy.[70] It is not enough to define the virtues psychologically on the assumption that their sum is good.[71] A final definition must relate virtue to, and deduce its utility from, an ultimate

[67] Allowance once made for the literary schematism of the four virtues, the three faculties, and the analogy between the man and the state, and account once taken of *Laws*, 696C, 710, and *Politicus*, 306 ff., it becomes a little naïve to complain that the distinction intended between σωφροσύνη and δικαιοσύνη is not clear, and a little pedantic to institute a learned philological inquiry to ascertain it.

[68] *Laws*, 864A.

[69] 442E, 443A.

[70] Grote, followed by many others, denies this. But that is because he persists in attributing to Plato the doctrine that ethical abstractions ("mixed modes") have one meaning only which can be expressed in an absolute definition; *cf. supra*. But, on the contrary, the very cause of the confusion, according to Plato, is that men fail to take notice of the different meanings and sub-species covered by one generic term (*Phdr.*, 161, 162; *Euthd.*, 277, 278; *Laws*, 837A; *Phlb.*, 12E ff.; *Euthyphro*, 7D, with *Phdr.*, 263B, and *Plt.*, 285E; *Plt.*, 306A). Laches, Nicias, Charmides, Critias, discuss the virtues without distinguishing temperament, convention, habit, systematic discipline, opinion, and complete insight. They are unable to attach any precise meaning to the conventional phrases "know thyself" and "minding one's own business." There is not one temperance or bravery, but three or four. There is no incompatibility between this view and Plato's insistence on the necessity of the definition and the final unity of virtue. If the word has many meanings, the first step in rational argument is to define the one intended. And the unity of virtue is to be sought, not in a verbal definition, but in the unity of the moral life, the idea of good, the political art, (*cf. infra*, n. 102). The definition is a hypothesis at the beginning, or a stage in the progress of the argument (*Chrm.*, 163A; *Euthyphro*, 9D, 11C; *Phdr.*, 237D, 263D–E). It cannot be an end, and for this reason dialogues that seek a definition fail. This dialectical relativity of the definition, of course, does not preclude Plato from arguing that his ideal of the moral and social life is better than that of average Athenian opinion, and that the definitions which embody it are right as against formulas that express some aspect of the traditional belief.

[71] *R.*, 427E.

standard or ideal of good.[72] Such a definition is rather a regulative conception than a practical possibility. The Platonic Socrates is always prepared to silence by dialectic or overwhelm by his eloquence those who deny that "virtue" is a real good.[73] But a formal, positive enumeration of the reasons why courage and justice are good and desirable can never be complete, and will always prove unedifying: "Does law so analyzed coerce you much?" Plato wisely attempts nothing of the kind. He merely describes the discipline and education[74] that will enable his philosophic rulers to prove, if required, the coincidence of virtue and happiness, and systematically inculcate efficacious right opinion, thus teaching virtue and molding character and institutions in the light of a reasoned and unified conception of the true scope and good of individual and public life. The attainment of this mastery he poetically describes as the vision of the Idea of Good. But it must never be forgotten that all this mysticism culminates in the precise and purely logical statement of 534 B-C, which affirms little more than *Phaedrus*, 278C, or than Mill when he says: "There is no knowledge, and no assurance of right belief, but with him who can both confute the opposite opinion and successfully defend his own against confutation.[75] Many secondary suggestions attach themselves to the phrase by association with the goodness of God, the universal cause, in the *Timaeus*,[76] the vision of the absolute ideas in the *Phaedrus* and *Symposium*, the fantastic enumeration in the *Philebus* (66) of the elements of "good" conceived at once as an ethical and a cosmical principle.[77] Its chief logical and ethical significance for the *Republic* has been hopelessly misunderstood, owing to the failure to connect it rightly with the

[72] *Ibid.*, 504B–D, 505A.

[73] *Gorgias*; *R.*, I.

[74] The "longer way," *R.*, 504C, is for the guardians, not for us who are reading the *Republic*. See *Laws*, 964, 966C. Neglect of this point has caused much misinterpretation. See *Idea of Good*, in "University of Chicago Classical Studies," Vol. I, p. 190.

[75] *Dissertations and Discussions*, Vol. IV, p. 283.

[76] 29E, ἀγαθὸς ἦν. On the identification of the good with God see *Idea of Good*, pp. 188, 189.

[77] Fantastic because due (1) to the wish to depress ἡδονή to the fifth place; (2) to the neo-Platonic device of extending the intelligible hierarchy by the interpolation of new members between the highest and the lowest. It belongs to rhetoric or religious emotion, then, not to Plato's scientific ethics.

problem of the "good" as presented in the minor dialogues.[78] In these dialogues Socrates repeatedly tests definitions of the virtues by demanding that they be related to happiness, the political or royal art, or the good. A virtue by hypothesis must be a καλόν (beautiful) and ἀγαθόν (good).[79] The definitions proposed repeatedly break down because Socrates is able to instance cases in which the rule prescribed does not conduce to happiness—is not good.[80] Similarly the rhetorician, the sophist, and other pretenders to some supreme knowledge are confounded by Socrates's demand that they shall sharply discriminate their art and science from all merely instrumental and technical specialties which effect good or evil according as they are rightly or wrongly used, and show its identity with the art of arts, the art of final ends, the political art, the good.[81]

In some of the minor dialogues the negative dialectic seems to go too far, and Socrates makes demands that neither Platonism nor any other doctrine can meet. Thus in the *Charmides* the familiar expression "knowing one's self," "knowing one's limits," "knowing what one can or cannot do," is made a puzzle by confounding it with the psychological question of self-knowledge or self-consciousness, and the fallacy or problem about knowing and not knowing the same thing;[82] and, waiving this point, Socrates demands proof that knowing the things one cannot do and intrusting them to experts is a good—a fundamental axiom of Platonism.[83] The explanation is that the phrase, like τὰ ἑαυτοῦ πράττειν ("doing one's own") above, is taken externally of adminicular and mechanical arts and sciences, not as in the *Republic*, with reference to the division of labor or function in the soul and the supreme arts of life and

---

[78] *E.g.*, one hundred and fifty pages separate Zeller's treatment of the idea of good (p. 707) from his discussion of the ethical good (p. 867). In elucidation of the former he quotes little or nothing from the ethical dialogues and cites neither *Phaedo*, 99A, nor any other passage in which the "opinion of the best" is treated as a potent cause. Finally he identifies the idea of good with God by a sophistical interpretation of παραπλήσια ἑαυτῷ (*Ti.*, 29E) and a false construction of (92B) εἰκών τοῦ νοητοῦ (*sc.* ζῴου, not θεοῦ, *cf.* 38C–D).

[79] *Meno*, 87D; *Laches*, 192C, 193D; *Prt.*, 349E; *Hp. Ma.*, 284D; *R.* 332, 333.

[80] See *Idea of Good*, pp. 200–4.

[81] *Euthd.*, 282E, 290, 291C; *Chrm.*, 170B; *Prt.*, 319A ; *Grg.*, 501A–B, 530D; *Plt.*, 289C, 293D, 309C; *R.*, 428D.

[82] *Cf. Meno*, 80E; *Euthd.*, 286D., *Tht.*, 191B, 196C.

[83] *Cf.* X., *Mem.*, 4, 2, 24; *Alc.*, I, 117D–E; *Laws*, 732A.

government. To ask why Critias is allowed to be baffled for lack of this distinction is to ask why Plato wrote short dramatic dialogues at all—why he did not incorporate the fourth book of the *Republic* in the *Charmides*. So in *Euthydemus*, 292E, the suggestion that the good achieved by the possessors of the political art will be the training up of successors to know it is treated as a vicious circle or an infinite regress, although, when accompanied by the fuller explanations of the *Republic*, it is evidently in part the true Platonic doctrine.[84] And similarly in the *Lysis* the theory, virtually repeated in the *Symposium*, that that which is intermediate between good and evil desires the good as a remedy against evil, is rejected because it makes the good a mere means to an end.[85] But the general meaning that emerges from the puzzles of the minor dialogues, and the answer to them given in the *Republic*, is as simple as it is sound. A philosophic ethics must systematically relate its definitions and prescriptions to some consistent conception of final ends and good —be it the realization of spiritual health and order in a reformed society, the development of personality, the greatest happiness of the greatest number, the fulfilment of the will of God, the renunciation of the will to live, or the survival of the fittest. The statesman rises above the politician, the thinker and artist above the rhetorician, the true teacher above the charlatan, by his possession of an aim and a standard, his apprehension of a type of perfection toward which all his thoughts, and words, and acts converge.[86]

Plato's own ethical and social conceptions were thus co-ordinated and unified. Those of the brilliant sophists and rhetoricians who figure in his pages were not. They may have been very estimable and ingenious men. They could not in Plato's judgment be true philosophers, statesmen, or teachers of statesmen, because they lacked both the "idea of good" and the synoptic and unifying dialectic required for its systematic application in ethics and politics, and in the education of the masses to "virtue." This recognition of the logical significance of the idea of good for the *Republic* and the Socratic dialogues does not commit us to an acceptance of all Plato's social ideals. It does not even require us to admit that the doctrine of the *Republic* really solves all the difficul-

[84] *Cf. Meno*, 100A; *R.*, 412A–B, 497C–D; *Laws*, 950B ff.; *Plt.*, 309D.
[85] *Cf. Lysis*, 218A, with *Symp.*, 203E.
[86] *Grg.*, 503E, 501C, 517, 518; *R.*, 484C, 500D–E, 520C; *Laws*, 625E, 630C, 688B, 693B, 706A, 717A, 733C–D, 962A.

ties suggested by Plato's "negative dialectic." But it creates the strongest presumption that it was present to his mind when he wrote the *Laches*, *Charmides*, and *Euthydemus*.

Parallel to the quest for the definition of the cardinal virtues leading to the idea of good is the study of friendship, love, passion, culminating in the apprehension of the idea of beauty at the point where it is hardly to be distinguished from the good.[87] No complete philosophy can ignore these things. Plato's reflections upon them have become the commonplaces of the philosophy and poetry of modern Europe: the strange antinomy between the love of like for like and the attraction of dissimilars in man and nature; the exaltation of character and mood in passionate love and friendship; the transfiguration of the passion in the love of aesthetic, moral, and intellectual beauty;[88] the overloading of the instinct to achieve the ends of nature—the immortality of the species.[89] The student of the *Lysis*, *Phaedrus*, *Symposium*, *Republic*, and *Laws* will find it impossible to fix a date at which these ideas first presented themselves to Plato's mind.[90] The mood, the treatment, the emphasis varies. Some of the thoughts are omitted in each dialogue, none are treated in all, and contradictions and developments may be "proved" by uncritically pressing the language and the imagery. But the differences between the *Symposium* and *Phaedrus*, both presumably works of the middle period, are as noticeable as those found in any other works that touch on the theme. The *Symposium* mentions one idea, the *Phaedrus* several; the former ignores immortality and ἀνάμνησις (recollection), the latter is one of the chief sources for both.[91] The *Phaedrus* ignores the thought that love is the yearning of the mortal for immortality, the *Symposium* virtually omits the doctrine of μανία (madness) and enthusiasm. In the *Symposium* love is not a god, but a demon; in the *Phaedrus* he is "a God" or (to escape explicit contradiction) "something divine".

---

[87] *Lysis*, 219, 220; *Symp.*, 205D, 210, 211; *Phdr.*, 250D ff.; *Phlb.*, 64E.

[88] Zeller's theory that Eros is *der philosophische Trieb* is a somewhat rigid and matter-of-fact interpretation of this poetry.

[89] *Symp.*, 207D; *Laws*, 721, 773E.

[90] Cf. *R.*, 402, 403, with *Symp.*, 210C; *R.*, 490A–B; *Laws*, 688B; *R.*, 499C, with *Laws*, 711D. *Laws*, 841D,633C, παρὰ φύσιν (contrary to nature), with *Phdr.*, 251A; *Laws*, 837; *Grg.*, 474D–E, generalization of καλόν as in *Symp.*

[91] Lutoslawski (*Origin and Growth of Plato's Logic*, p. 242) fails to tell us where ἀνάμνησις is "alluded to in the speech of Aristophanes."

These and other differences present no difficulties to a rational literary interpretation. On no reasonable theory of Plato's development can they signify real changes in Plato's beliefs in the interval between the composition of the two dialogues.

The *Lysis*, though a slight Socratic dialogue, displays extreme subtlety of dialectic,[92] and implies some of the most characteristic thoughts of the *Symposium*.[93] The failure to establish a formal definition, and the Socratic avowal of ignorance at the end prove nothing. There is a plain hint that Menexenus is an "eristic," and Socrates's treatment of him, so different in tone from the edifying little conversation with Lysis, is a mere dramatic illustration of the perplexity that results from failure to discriminate the different meanings of an ambiguous term. Love, as the *Phaedrus* tells us, is such a term—including subordinate and contradictory species.[94] For, as the *Laws* say, 837A "what causes the utmost perplexity and obscurity is the fact that this simple term embraces these two, and also a third compounded of both." How familiar the two kinds were to Plato appears from the almost technical use of the phrase δι' ὁμοιότητα φιλίαν (love in virtue of similarity) in *Phdr.*, 240C. Menexenus's bewilderment is precisely on a par with that of Kleinias over the two meanings of μανθάνω in the *Euthydemus*.[95] Plato is no more confused in the one case than in the other. The mood of the *Symposium* and *Phaedrus* is compatible with youth or maturity, hardly with old age. The thoughts are naturally not repeated in their entirety, but many of them appear in the *Republic*,

---

[92] The conception of eristic, 216A–B, arguing to the word, not the meaning, is as clear as it is in *R.*, 454A, or *Euthd.*, 295B–C, and the fallacy by which it is illustrated, the identity of opposites as such, recurs in substance in *Prm.*, 148A–B, and belongs to the same class as the quibble on ἕτερον, *Euthd.*, 301B; *Tht.*, 190C; *Prm.*, 147E. *Cf.* also ἀνομοιότατον, *Phlb.*, 13D; *Prm.*, 127E, 148B–C.

[93] *E.g.*, θεῶν οὐδεὶς φιλοσοφεῖ, etc., *Symp.*, 203E, which Lutoslawski (p. 239) thinks an important new point, in advance even of the *Cratylus*, is "already" in *Lysis*, 218A. Zeller, who is "unable to suppose" that Plato had "already" attained the guiding thoughts of his later system (p. 614), argues that in the *Lysis* the psychological analysis is carried as far as is possible on a Socratic basis, but that the metaphysical explanation was revealed later. If Plato must tell all he knows in every dialogue, why is ἀνάμνησις not associated with ἔρως in the *Symposium* and *Republic?*

[94] 263C, 265E.
[95] 277E.

or are suggested elsewhere. They are nowhere contradicted,[96] and
there is no reason to doubt that they were essential permanent elements of Plato's criticism of life. But he was not always in the mood
to dwell upon them.

4. In another aspect the Platonic ethics is a polemic against
hedonism. This must not be confounded with the modern utilitarian controversy. The modern opponent of utilitarianism is chiefly
concerned to prove that the moral law cannot be deduced from
experiences of utility, but has an *a priori* origin and requires a
supernatural sanction. Plato does not directly discuss the origin of
morality, but he explicitly disclaims the necessity of the sanction
derived from the hope of immortality,[97] affirms with great emphasis
that the useful is the right,[98] and bases all virtue on the supremacy
of the λογιστικόν or calculating reason.[99] In the *Protagoras* Socrates
is represented as maintaining against Protagoras by purely Benthamite arguments the identity of pleasure and the good.[100]

The seeming contradiction between this and the anti-hedonism
of the *Gorgias* and *Philebus* demands explanation. It has sometimes
been argued that Plato's own opinions on this point were reversed
between the composition of the *Protagoras* and that of the *Gorgias*.
Another explanation is that Socrates merely develops a paradox for
the bewilderment of the Sophist. And it is true that in some parts of
the dialogue Socrates is obviously jesting,[101] and that we are warned

---

[96] Grote says that in the *Theaetetus* the spectacle of a beautiful youth
is not required as the indispensable initiatory stimulus to philosophy.
But the *Symp.*, 210C and the *R.*, 402D, emphasize the unimportance of
the beauty of the body as compared with that of the mind. The Platonic
Socrates is still the erotic as he was in the *Lysis*, nor can we suppose that
he would ever have found the beautiful *Meno* as helpful an "initiatory
stimulus to philosophy" as the snub-nosed Theaetetus.

[97] *R.*, 363B–D, 367E, 612B–C. The *Gorgias* does not differ herein
from the *Republic*. The argument is complete without the myth, and the
phrases at the end about living justly in order to prepare for the judgment of Minos prove no more than the ἵνα of *R.*, 621C.

[98] καλόν, *R.*, 457B.   [99] *R.*, 440E, 571C,605B.

[100] *Prt.*, 353–58.

[101] 340 ff. In 341D, Protagoras, anticipating *Philebus*, 12E, and in
language suggesting the protest against eristic in *Sophist*, 259D, points
out that (generic) resemblance is compatible with difference and even
contrariety (*cf.* also *Meno*, 74D). He does not explain himself fully,
however, and Socrates, ignoring the point, proceeds to trip him up by a
fallacious use of the principle that one thing can have only one opposite. Whatever the date of the *Euthydemus*, its author was aware that a
word used in two senses may have two opposites, quite as early as he
was capable of writing the *Protagoras*. The passage is merely a dramatic

against accepting the result too seriously by the reminder that both Socrates and Protagoras have maintained theses incompatible with the positions from which they started.[102] But the full explanation lies deeper. In the *Republic* Plato undertakes to demonstrate the intrinsic desirability of virtue against two forms of disbelief—the explicit skepticism of the cynic, who affirms that natural justice is the advantage of the stronger and human justice an artificial convention, and the unfaith of the ordinary man, who virtually admits this theory by commending justice solely on external and prudential grounds.[103] The Callicles of the *Gorgias* represents the former view, Gorgias himself and (less obviously) Protagoras the latter. Like other Sophists, he is the embodiment of average public opinion which his teaching reproduces.[104] He himself says that all men teach virtue. He modestly claims at the most only to teach it a little more effectively and persuasively than the layman.[105] Plato would admit both assertions, with the reservation that the virtue so-taught hardly deserves the name, and that the teaching is neither systematic nor philosophical.

The molding power of public opinion, operating through countless social and educative agencies, is admirably depicted in the myth attributed to Protagoras, the main thought of which is repeated in the *Republic*.[106] There, however, the philosophic rulers are

---

illustration of Socrates's superiority in the game of question and answer. Again in 350B–351A, when it is argued that bravery is knowledge because knowledge imparts confidence, Protagoras points out that we cannot convert the universal affirmative proposition, "all bravery is confidence," and distinguishes as bravery the confidence that arises from nature and training. Though not a match for Socrates, Protagoras is a far better reasoner than Laches or Nicias, and again Socrates refutes him only by taking up a new line of argument—the identity of pleasure and good, and the consequent unity of the virtues in the "measuring art." Plato of course was aware here, and in the *Euthyphro* (12), and everywhere, that a universal affirmative cannot be directly converted. But it is a part of the scheme of the dialogue that Protagoras should make some good points, though defeated in the end. And Socrates is baffled in or fails to complete other proofs of the unity of virtue, and so is driven to rely on the proof from hedonism, which is the chief feature of the dialogue.

[102] *Prt.*, 361.

[103] *R.*, 362E ff. *Cf.* Zeller, p. 603, n. 1.

[104] *R.*, 492 ff.   [105] *Prt.*, 328B.

[106] Ritchie, *Plato* (New York, 1902), p. 156, says: "The argument of the Sophist Protagoras . . . . is not fully accepted by Plato," etc., as if Plato was not the author of the *Protagoras*.

to employ this irresistible force for the inculcation, not of average Greek opinion, but of Platonic virtue. The *Protagoras* dramatically illustrates the dialectic incapacity and philosophic superficiality of the great popular teacher. His ethical teaching is spiritually and logically on a level with the precepts of the worthy sires and guardians satirized by Adeimantus.[107] However unlike in temper and practical effect, it is philosophically akin to the individual hedonism of Callicles and Thrasymachus who reject all morality as an unreal convention. Protagoras is naturally unaware of this. Like the populace, he recoils from the naked exposition of the principles implied in his preaching and practice. He accepts the terminology of individual hedonism only under compulsion of Socrates's superior dialectic. But Socrates's explicit challenge to him and the assembled Sophists to name any other final good than ἡδονή is a proof that one of Plato's objects was to identify the Sophistic ethics with hedonism.[108] But neither this nor the demonstration of Protagoras's inability to cope with Socrates in dialectic exhausts the significance of the dialogue.

Plato, however reluctantly, always recognized a certain measure of truth in the Benthamite analysis here attributed to Socrates. He knew that "act we must in pursuance of that which (we think) will give us most pleasure." Even the *Gorgias* contains phrases of utilitarian, if not hedonistic, implication.[109] The Eudaemonism of the *Republic* has often been pointed out,[110] and in the *Laws* Plato explicitly declares, in language recalling that of the *Protagoras*, that it is not in human nature to pursue any course of action that does not promise a favorable balance of pleasure.[111] But the inference which he draws is not that it is safe or desirable to proclaim that pleasure is the good, but that it is necessary to demonstrate that the good—the virtuous life—is the most pleasurable.

To a Benthamite this will seem a purely verbal or rhetorical distinction. And Aristotle himself hints that Plato's aversion to the name of pleasure cast a suspicion of unreality over his ethical teaching.[112] But Plato is not alone in his aversion to the word. Matthew Arnold acknowledges a similar feeling. And Jowett, in his

---

[107] *R.*, 362E.   [108] 354D, 358A.

[109] 499D. Ritchie (p. 155) strangely says that in the *Republic* Plato recognizes, in marked advance upon the position of the *Gorgias*, that there are good pleasures as well as bad!

[110] 357B, "harmless pleasures" are goods *per se*, 457B, 458E, 581E (with *Laws*, 732E).

[111] *Laws*, 733, 734; *cf.* 663A.   [112] *EN*, X, 1.

admirable introduction to the *Philebus*, has once for all set forth the considerations by which many clear-headed modern thinkers, who perfectly understand the utilitarian logic and accept whatever is true in its psychology, are nevertheless moved to reject its language. The Greek word ἡδονή is much more closely associated with a low view of happiness than the English word "pleasure"; and Plato had, or thought that he had, much stronger reasons than the moderns have, for identifying hedonism with the negation of all moral principle.

The *Gorgias* and *Philebus* nowhere explicitly contradict the thesis of the *Protagoras* that a preponderance of pleasure, rightly estimated and abstracted from all evil consequences, is good.[113] The doctrine which they combat is the unqualified identification of pleasure and good, coupled with the affirmation that true happiness is to be sought by developing and gratifying the appetite for the pleasures of sense and ambition.[114] Plato represents Callicles and Philebus as unable or unwilling to limit these propositions even by the qualifications of the *Protagoras*.[115] It is he, not they, who introduces the distinction of pure and impure,[116] true and illusive,[117] wholesome and unwholesome,[118] necessary and unnecessary pleasures.[119] The modern critic may object that Plato was not justified in attributing to any contemporaries either this dialectical incapacity or this cynical effrontery. Plato thought otherwise. It is a question of historical evidence. But it is not legitimate to attribute to the Callicles and the Philebus of the dialogues the utilitarianism of Grote or John Stuart Mill, or even that of the *Protagoras*, and so convict Plato of self-contradiction.[120]

With these remarks we may dismiss so much of the *Gorgias* and *Philebus* as is merely dialectical, dramatic, or rhetorical, directed against the crudest form of hedonism which Plato chooses to bring

---

[113] *Phlb.*, 60A–B, is verbally a direct contradiction of *Prt.*, 355B.

[114] *Grg.*, 495A, 492D–E; *Phlb.*, 12A, 12D, 27E.

[115] The verbal identification of pleasure and good in 355 has been preceded by such phrases as "insofar as they are pleasant", 351C, and the explanation that some painful goods are medicinal (354A = *R.*, 357C), and is checked by the calculus of all consequences, all of which is ignored by Callicles and Philebus.

[116] *Phlb.*, 51, 52.   [117] *Ibid.*, 36C ff.

[118] *Ibid.*, 41A; *Grg.*, 499D–E.   [119] *R.*, 558D.

[120] Plato, as Jowett says, is "playing both sides of the game . . . but it is not necessary in order to understand him that we should discuss the fairness of his modes of proceeding."

upon the stage before grappling with the problem in earnest.[121] The real arguments which he employs, not so much to refute the thesis of the *Protagoras* as to limit its practicable application and justify his repudiation of its terminology, may be summed up as follows: The distinction between good and bad pleasures once admitted, the statement that pleasure as such is the good, becomes an unreal abstraction.[122] The reality is specific kinds of pleasure and the principle of distinction, whether intelligence, measure, or the will to obey the "opinion of the best,"[123] becomes more important than the bare name of pleasure, and more nearly allied to the good.[124] The "measuring art" postulated in the *Protagoras* is impracticable. Pleasure and pain are, like confidence and fear, foolish counselors;[125] either deprives the mind of the sanity required for a just estimate.[126] No scale of human judgment can be trusted to weigh the present against the future, and make allowance for all the illusions of memory, hope, and contrast.[127] The most intense pleasures and pains are associated with a diseased condition of mind and body.[128] And the habit of pursuing pleasure, of thinking and speaking of it as the good, tends to make the world of sense seem more real than that of thought and spirit.[129] The contrary is

[121] *Phlb.*, 55A–B, and *Grg.*, 495C, 499B, show that the arguments of *Grg.*, 495C–499B, are, in the main, a conscious dialectical sport. I recur to this point so often because the *Gorgias* and the first book of the *Republic* are the chief source of the opinion, widely spread by Grote, Mill, and Sidgwick, that Plato is a magnificent preacher, but often a weak reasoner. *Cf.* Mill, *Diss. and Discuss.*, IV, 291: "This great dialogue, full of just thoughts and fine observations on human nature, is, in mere argument, one of the weakest of Plato's works." *Cf. Idea of Good*, pp. 213–15.

[122] *Phlb.*, 12D–E. In answer to the question, "how could pleasure be opposite to pleasure?", Socrates shows that generic (verbal) identity is compatible with specific difference or even opposition, a logical principle "already" glanced at in the *Prt.*, 331D, with the same illustration of *black* and *white*.

[123] *Phdr.*, 237D. *Cf. Laws*, 644D, 645A. *Phaedo*, 99A.

[124] *Phlb.*, 64C, with the context.

[125] *Cf. Ti.*, 69D, with *Laws*, 644C.

[126] *R.*, 402E; *Phlb.*, 63D; *Phaedo*, 66B.

[127] *Cf. Phlb.*, 41E ff., with *Prt.*, 356, 357; *Gorgias*, 500A, *Laws*, 663B, and the rhetorical repudiation of the whole hedonistic calculus, *Phaedo*, 69A–B.

[128] *Phlb.*, 45B–E.

[129] *Cf. Phaedo*, 83D, with James's *Psychology*, Vol. II, p. 306: "Among all sensations, the *most* belief-compelling are those productive of pleasure or pain."

the truth. The world of sense is a pale reflex of the world of ideas,[130] and the pleasures of sense are inherently unreal, illusory, and deceptive, and may in sound logic be termed false, as fairly as the erroneous opinions that accompany them.[131] They are false because composed of hopes and imaginations not destined to be fulfilled;[132] false, because exaggerated by the illusions of distance in time or contrast;[133] false, because what we mistake for positive pleasure is usually the neutral state, the absence of uneasiness, the cessation of pain.[134]

This doctrine of the negativity of what men call pleasure is the fundamental basis of Plato's ethics, as it is of Schopenhauer's. On this, in the last instance, rests his refutation of hedonism, and, as we shall see, his demonstration that virtue and happiness are one.[135] Sensuous pleasures are in their nature impure and illusory. They are preconditioned by, and mixed with, desire, want, pain. "Surgit amari aliquid" is ever true of them. They are the relief of an uneasiness, the scratching of an itch, the filling of a vacuum.[136]. To

---

[130] *R.*, 509, 510, 514 ff., the allegory of the cave.

[131] *Phlb.*, 36C ff. As Berkeley and Huxley argue from the subjectivity of pain to that of sensations and ideas; as Epicurus proceeds from the reality of pain to that of the other secondary qualities; so, reversing the order, Plato infers the falsity of pleasures and pains from that of the associated perceptions and beliefs. Grote, Jowett, Horn, and others pronounce the whole train of reasoning fallacious. But it is to be observed: (1) that their objections as usual are anticipated by Plato (*Phlb.*, 38A), who has a right to use his own terminology provided his meaning is unambiguous (*Charmides*, 163D); (2) that the epithet "false" is used either with reference to a postulated objective judgment of life as a whole, or as a mere rhetorical expression of the disdain or pity felt by an onlooker. In the first sense it is justified by the argument, in the second by the usage of the poets—*falsa licet cupidus deponat gaudia livor* (*Propert.*, 1, 8, 29); (3) having demonstrated against Sophistic negations that "false" applies to beliefs, Plato was naturally tempted to extend it to pleasure.

[132] *Phlb.*, 39E, 40C. *Cf.* "we are all imaginative, for images are the brood of desire" (George Eliot).

[133] *Ibid.*, 41, 42B; *Laws*, 663B.

[134] *Phlb.*, 42C ff.; *R.*, 583D.

[135] The argument that pleasure is γένεσις (becoming), not οὐσία (being), is not, as Zeller says (p. 604), the nerve of the proof. It is obviously, as the language of 53C implies, one of those half-serious metaphysical and rhetorical confirmations used to make a strong case where Plato's feelings are enlisted. It does not occur explicitly in the *Republic* which speaks, however, of pleasure as κίνησις (movement), 583E.

[136] "Already" in the *Gorgias*, 493E, 494C, and *Phaedrus*, 258E; *R.*, 584A–B. It has even been argued that the *Phaedrus* passage takes for

treat them as real, or to make them one's aim (except so far as our human estate requires), is to seek happiness in a process rather than a state,[137] in becoming rather than in being. It is to bind one's self to the wheel of Ixion and pour water into the bottomless jar of Danaids.[138] Far happier, far more pleasurable, is the life that consistently aims at few and calm pleasures, to which the sensualist would hardly give the name, a life which he would regard as torpor or death.[139]

Both the physiology and the psychology of this doctrine have been impugned. It has been argued that, up to the point of fatigue, the action of healthy nerves involves no pain, and must yield a surplus of positive sensuous pleasure. It is urged that the present uneasiness of appetite is normally more than counterbalanced by the anticipation of immediate satisfaction. Such arguments will carry no weight with those who accept Plato's main contention, that the satisfactions of sense and ambition, however inevitable, have no real worth, and that to seek our true life in them is to weave and unweave the futile web of Penelope. Whatever qualifications modern psychology may attach to the doctrine, it is the logical basis of Plato's ethics. The unfeigned recognition of the inherent worthlessness of the lower pleasures removes at once the motive and lures to evil.[140] It is the chief link in the proof that virtue is happiness. It insures the domination of reason over feeling and appetite. It molds man into that likeness to the divine pattern which is Plato's favorite expression for the ethical ideal,[141] for the divine life knows neither pleasure nor pain.[142] It is the serious argument that explains Plato's repudiation of the hedonistic formulas of the *Pro-*

---

granted the fuller discussion of the *Philebus* (W. H. Thompson, *Phaedrus, ad loc.*). And why not? Anything may be argued if the dialogues are supposed to grow out of one another and not out of Plato's mind.

[137] *Phlb.*, 53C ff.; 54E virtually = *Grg.*, 493E. The literal-minded objection of Aristotle, *EN*, X, 4, and some moderns, that pleasure is not strictly = motion is beside the point.

[138] *Grg.*, 493B; *Phaedo*, 84A; *Grg.*, 507E; *Phlb.*, 54E.

[139] *Phaedo*, 64B; *Grg.*, 492E; *Phlb.*, 54E. In *Laws*, 733, 734B, the hedonistic calculus of the *Protagoras* is retained, but is applied not-directly to the individual acts, but to types of life. The life of moderate pleasures is *a priori* the more pleasurable because it necessarily yields a more favorable balance than the life of intense pleasures.

[140] *Phaedo*, 66C; *R.*, 586A–B, 588.

[141] *Tht.*, 176B ff.; *Laws*, 716D, 728A–B; *R.*, 352B, 612E; *Phlb.*, 391E.

[142] *Phlb.*, 33B.

tagoras, and justifies the noble anti-hedonistic rhetoric of the *Gorgias,* the *Phaedo,* and the *Philebus.*[143]

4. Plato's insistence on the necessity of proving the coincidence of virtue and happiness marks another difference between him and modern writers. The question is rarely put in the forefront of modern ethical discussion, except for the polemical purpose of proving that an opponent's philosophy supplies no basis or sanction for morality. The majority of modern ethical writers relegate the problem to a digression or a footnote. They are content to establish a "general tendency" or "strong probability." Or they frankly admit that while everybody would be glad if the proposition could be proved, it is not susceptible of mathematical demonstration. But this was not enough for Plato. His own faith was adamantine.[144] He was as certain that happiness is inseparable from virtue as of the existence[145] of the Island of Crete. Even if it were only a probability, he would not permit it to be impugned in a well-ordered state.[146] Just how much positively immoral and cynical philosophy was current in Plato's day is, as we have seen, a disputed historical question. But Plato himself was haunted by the thought of the unscrupulous skeptic who sought to justify his own practice by appeals to the law of nature or theories of the origin of justice in a conspiracy of the weak against the strong.[147] His imagination was beset by the picture of some brilliant young Alcibiades standing at the crossways of life and debating in his mind whether his best chance of happiness lay in accepting the conventional moral law that serves to police the vulgar or in giving rein to the instincts and appetites of his own stronger nature.[148] To confute the one, to convince the other, became to him the main problem of moral philosophy. It is a chief duty of the rulers in the *Republic* and the *Laws,* and the Socrates of the dialogues is at all times ready and equipped to undertake it.

Plato is not always overnice in the arguments by which the skeptic is refuted. It is enough that the "wicked" should not have

---

[143] *Grg.,* 507, 512, 513; *Phaedo,* 69; *Phlb.,* 66A; *R.,* 580B.
[144] *Grg.,* 509A; *R.,* 360B, 618A.
[145] *Laws,* 662B.
[146] *R.,* 392A–B; *Laws,* 663B.
[147] *R.,* 358, 359, 365; *Grg.,* 483 ff. *Cf. R.,* 358C; *Prt.,* 333C; *Euthd.,* 279B; *Phlb.,* 66E; *Grg.,* 511B; *Laws,* 889D–E, with *Tht.,* 177C–D.
[148] *R.,* 365B; *Grg.,* 510D; *Laws,* 662E.

the best of the argument.[149] Socrates in the first instance puts forth just enough dialectical strength to baffle a Callicles or a Thrasymachus.[150] This, as we have seen, is the quality of much of the argument of the *Gorgias*,[151] though it is intermingled with hints of deeper things, and supplemented by noble eloquence. In the *Republic*, however, Plato undertakes not only to confute and silence, but to convince.[152] The real ground of conviction is the total underlying conception of the true nature, harmony, health, and consequent happiness of the soul.

But the formal proof is summed up in the ninth book in three arguments which, as Plato repeatedly tells us, constitute the framework of the whole design.[153] To these, in form at least, all other interests of the book are subordinate—the construction of the ideal state, the higher philosophical education, the idea of good, the character-sketches of degenerate types. The first argument is based on the comparison of the individual and the state which runs through the entire work from the second to the ninth book. It takes two forms: (1) That of a mere external analogy. As the happiness of the ideal state is to the misery of the ochlocracy or the tyranny, so is the happiness of the well-governed just soul to the wretchedness of the man whose soul is the prey of a mob of appetites, or the slave of a ruling passion.[154] (2) The force of this external analogy is derived wholly from the psychological truth that it embodies. Unity or factious division, the sovereignty of reason, or the usurpations of passions and appetite, harmony or discord, health or disease, as

[149] *Tht.*, 176C–D; 177B. The whole passage is a description of the *Gorgias. Cf.*, 527A, *Laws*, 907C.

[150] *E.g.*, the argument in *R.*, 349, 350, is a mere illustration of the game of question and answer. Thrasymachus sets up the thesis, οἱ ἄδικοι φρόνιμοι καὶ ἀγαθοί, and Socrates forces him to contradict himself. Zeller (p. 752) lists it among Plato's fallacies.

[151] Strictly speaking, Socrates's dialectic is employed merely to force from Callicles the admission that some pleasures are bad (449B–C; *cf. R.*, 505C). From this point the argument, abandoning ethical theory, discusses social and political ideals at Athens. "Good" is treated as distinct from "pleasure," as it is in *Phdr.*, 239C. But the question whether it may not ultimately prove to be the favorable balance of pleasure (*Prt.*) is not raised. The crude identification of the terms is rejected for reasons still held valid in the *Philebus. Cf. Phlb.*, 55B, with *Grg.*, 498C There is no contradiction. The three dialogues, differing in mood, are logically consistent and supplement one another.

[152] *R.*, 357A–B, 358B, 367A–B, 367E.

[153] 369A–B, 392A–B, 427D, 445A, 544A.

[154] 576C ff.

used of the soul, are more than mere figures of speech; they are the exact expression of inevitable alternatives resting on indisputable psychological facts. The dominance of the higher reason over disciplined emotion and controlled appetite is the sole and effective condition at once of the unity, harmony, and health of spiritual life which is happiness, and of the unswerving fulfilment of obligation which is the external manifestation of justice and virtue.[155] To ask whether happiness is compatible with a diseased soul is still more absurd than to expect it to dwell in a diseased body.[156]

The second argument is very brief, and Plato is probably aware that at the best it commands assent rather than inspires conviction.[157] The three faculties of the soul, taken abstractly, yield three types of pleasure—the pleasures of pure intelligence, of ambition, and of appetite. Plato assumes that the pleasures of intelligence belong to the man in whom the intellect directed toward the good controls the other faculties. In other words, he takes for granted the coincidence on the highest plane of intellect and virtue which he found in Socrates and which the education of the *Republic* secures in the guardians.[158] Now, the advocate of the intellectual and virtuous life has necessarily had some experience of the pleasures associated with gratified ambition and appetite. The ambitious man and the sensuous man know little or nothing of the higher order of pleasure. The preference of the "intellectual" for his own type of pleasure must be ratified as based on a completer experience. It would be a waste of time to cavil on minor fallacies or rhetorical exaggerations with which Plato burdens the argument in his eagerness to make a strong case.[159] The argument itself is familiar enough through its acceptance in substance by John Stuart Mill; who, however, seems to think Plato's use of it fallacious. It has been rejected as a fallacy on the ground that pleasure is not an objective measurable entity, but a relative individual feeling. Again at the limits of human thought we are confronted by an alternative the terms of which it is impossible to realize distinctly. Is it better to be a completely contented pig than a man? But if we waive the claim that the argument is an absolute proof, and turn from these unreal abstractions to the facts of life, what Plato affirms

---

[155] 442E.

[156] 445A, 591B, 589E; *Grg.*, 512A, 479B; "already" in *Crito*, 47D–E.

[157] *R.*, 580D ff. [158] *Cf. supra*, pp. 10–11.

[159] Grote and Mill object that this argument, even if conclusive, is addressed to the wrong point, because the life supposed is not that of

is simply that it is more pleasurable in the end to develop and foster the capacity for the "higher" pleasures than that for the lower, as is shown by the judgment of those who have experienced both. In this less absolute form the argument leans for support on that which precedes, and still more on that which follows it.

In the third place, the lower pleasures as compared with the higher are illusory, unreal, and impermanent, and they tend to destroy the healthy balance of faculties which is the condition of all true pleasure.[160] This is a repetition or anticipation[161] of the theory of the negativity of pleasure which we have already met in the polemic against hedonism.

This completes our sketch of the Platonic ethics. The rest is exhortation, inspiration, myth, delightful things, but not within the scope of the present study, nor indeed reproducible in any study. For the ethical and religious spirit that informs every page of Plato we must go to the master himself.

---

the simple, just man, but that of the philosopher. But the case of the simple just man is met by the main arguments drawn from the order, harmony, and health of the soul, and from the analysis of pleasure. Here Plato is renewing the debate between the "philosopher," the sensualist, and the politician begun in the *Gorgias*. He is indulging his feelings in a demonstration that in the Athens of his day the "philosophic" life is a higher and happier type than the life of the politician or the sensualist; and he holds that no real reform is possible until men can be found who approach political life as a necessary, not a desirable, thing, condescending to it from a life which they feel to be higher and more pleasurable (*cf. R.*, 521 B). The form of the arguments of the *Republic* is determined by the purpose of contrasting the extreme types of the virtuous philosopher and the finished tyrant. But it applies to other men in proportion as they approximate to these types. And the statement of the argument in the *Laws* applies to the simple just man, 663C, τὰ ἄδικα .... ἐκ μὲν ἀδίκου καὶ κακοῦ ἑαυτοῦ θεωρούμενα ἡδέα, etc., ... τὴν δ᾽ ἀλήθειαν τῆς κρίσεως ποτέραν κυριωτέραν εἶναι φῶμεν; πότερα τὴν τῆς χείρονος ψυχῆς ἢ τὴν τῆς βελτίονος.

[160] *R.*, 583B–586C.

[161] Zeller thinks it a résumé of the fuller treatment of the *Philebus*. Those who put the *Philebus* late regard it as a preliminary sketch. The *Philebus* is probably late, as Mill affirmed before *Sprachstatistik* was conceived. But the psychology of pleasure in the two dialogues supplies no evidence. *Cf. infra*, "Plato's Psychology," and Part II.

Chapter I of *The Unity of Plato's Thought* by Paul Shorey (The University of Chicago Press, Chicago, 1903). [The editor has abbreviated a few of the notes, omitted some untranslated Greek phrases, and added English translations of others.]

2

A FALLACY IN PLATO'S *REPUBLIC*

DAVID SACHS

Recent writers on the *Republic* tend to refrain from detailed discussion of the argument about justice and happiness, the main argument of the work.[1] In the last decades there have been few assessments of Plato's conclusions about the relationship of justice and happiness, namely that just men are happier than any men who are unjust, and that the more unjust a man is, the more wretched he will be. Equally rare have been attempts to examine critically the argument by which Plato reached those conclusions.[2] In this paper I make such an attempt. My aim is to show that Plato's conclusions are irrelevant to what he sets out—and purports —to establish. The fallacy of irrelevance that, in my judgment, wrecks the *Republic's* main argument is due to the lack of connection between two conceptions of justice that Plato employs. I begin with an account of the two conceptions. While discussing them, I try to correct some errors and possible confusions about Plato's argument and his understanding of it. In particular, I try to show that Plato consistently viewed his defense of justice as one made solely in terms of justice's effects. I then examine the fallacy in detail. At the end, I briefly speculate about why Plato proceeded as he did.

THE TWO CONCEPTIONS OF JUSTICE

Like other dialogues that have been called "aporetic" or "dialogues of refutation," *Republic* I ends with an avowal of ig-

[1] "Justice," "injustice," etc. are notoriously unsatisfactory translations of many occurrences in Plato's dialogues of δικαιοσύνη, ἀδικία, and their relevant cognates. My use of the conventional translations does not, however, affect the claims of this paper. I am indebted to Prof. Gerald Barnes and Prof. Marshall Cohen for helpful discussion of some of the points I have tried to make.

[2] To my knowledge, the last detailed criticism of both Plato's procedure and conclusions is to be found in H. A. Prichard's inaugural lecture, *Duty and Interest* (Oxford, 1928), and in the title essay of the same author's posthumously published collection, *Moral Obligation* (Oxford, 1949).

norance by Socrates. Plato has him say that, not knowing what justice is, he can hardly know whether it is a virtue and whether its possessor is happy or not. An impression likely to be made by Socrates' last words in Book I is, as Richard Robinson remarked of the early dialogues as a whole, "that Socrates thinks that there is no truth whatever about *x* that can be known before we know what *x* is."[3] Robinson observes that though Socrates never actually says this, Socrates also never places any limits on the priority of answering questions of the form "What is *x*?" As a result, there is a general problem about the dialogues of refutation; do they include any assertions of doctrine by Plato?[4] Thus, in *Republic* I, Socrates makes various statements about justice; is his avowal of ignorance intended to question all of them? Certainly no doubt is cast upon one repeatedly implied claim, a claim taken for granted in the later books and presupposed by the over-all structure of the *Republic*: namely, that whether one should lead a just or unjust life is to be decided by determining which life is the happier.[5] It is, however, indispensable for evaluating the main argument of the *Republic* to realize that this claim cannot be understood in the same way throughout; it cannot, because of the two conceptions of justice in the *Republic*. I will call the first the vulgar conception of justice, the second the Platonic conception.

The Vulgar Conception

Toward the end of *Republic* IV, immediately after the first exposition of the Platonic conception of justice, there is an important text for what I am terming the vulgar conception of justice. Socrates, speaking to Glaucon, says:

"We might . . . completely confirm . . . our own conviction . . . by applying . . . vulgar tests to it." "What are these?" "For ex-

[3] Richard Robinson, *Plato's Earlier Dialectic* (2nd ed.; Oxford, 1953), p. 51.

[4] It is widely held that Socrates' professions of ignorance have to be discounted to some extent. For instance, Plato often—if not always— must have thought that the "absurdities" he had Socrates elicit really were absurdities. For an example, in *R.* I, see 333E1–2 *et supra*.

[5] See, e.g., 344E1–3; 345A2–7; 352D5–6; 347E2ff.; as these lines, together with the contexts in which they occur, show, the formulations in terms of an advantageous or profitable or better life are intended as equivalent to the formulation in terms of happiness. See also 392A–C; 420B–C; 427D; 472C–D; 484A–B; 544A; 545A–B; 578C; 580 *ad fin.*

ample, if an answer were demanded to the question concerning that city and the man whose birth and breeding was in
harmony with it, whether we believe that such a man, entrusted with a deposit of gold or silver, would withhold it and
embezzle it, who do you suppose would think that he would be
more likely so to act than men of a different kind?" "No one
would." "And would not he be far removed from sacrilege
and theft and betrayal of comrades in private life or of the
state in public? . . . And, moreover, he would not be in any
way faithless either in the keeping of his oaths or in other
agreements. . . . Adultery, surely, and neglect of parents and
of the due service of the gods would pertain to anyone rather
than to such a man. . . . And is not the cause of this to be
found in the fact that each of the principles within him does
its own work in the matter of ruling and being ruled?"[6]

As Plato states them in this passage, the vulgar criteria for justice
consist in the nonperformance of acts of certain kinds; and, of
course, injustice, according to the vulgar conception, consists in
performing such acts. The passage shows that Plato supposes that
the just man—as he conceives him—is less likely than anyone else
to perform those acts, to embezzle, thieve, betray, behave sacrile-
giously, fail to keep oaths or agreements, commit adultery, neglect
his parents or the service he owes to the gods. Plato thinks the
conduct of his just man, far from being at variance with the vulgar
conception of justice, will exemplify it.

The vulgar conception is shared at the start of the *Republic* by all
of Socrates' interlocutors: Cephalus, Polemarchus, Thrasymachus,
Glaucon, and Adeimantus. (This is not to say that the vulgar conception exhausts the notions of justice they hold, or that they all
believe in behaving in accord with it.)

Thrasymachus, at 344A3–B5, describes consummate ($\tau\epsilon\lambda\epsilon\omega$-
$\tau\acute{a}\tau\eta s$) injustice and several kinds or "parts" ($\mu\acute{\epsilon}\rho\eta$) of injustice;
his list of kinds of injustice emphasizes gross types of immorality
and evil-doing: temple-robbing, kidnaping, swindling, and so
forth (see 348D5–8). On Thrasymachus' view, to perpetrate such
acts is to do injustice; not to commit them is essential to being just.

---

[6] 442D10–443B2; I have excerpted the passage from Shorey's translation in the Loeb Classical Library (Cambridge, Mass., Vol. I, 1937;
Vol. II, 1942). Except where otherwise indicated, I use Shorey's
translation.

Similarly, when Glaucon, for the sake of the argument, extols injustice, he finds it apt to relate the story of Gyges' ancestor, a man who seduced his king's wife, murdered the king, and usurped the kingdom; Glaucon then alleges that no one who enjoyed the impunity of Gyges' progenitor would "persevere in justice and endure to refrain his hands from the possessions of others and not touch them . . . [but would] take what he wished even from the market place and enter into houses and lie with whom he pleased, and slay and loose from bonds whomsoever he would" (360B5–360C2). Here, again, is a list of acts set forth as incompatible with justice and as constituting injustice. It should be stressed that the examples of unjust acts are presented by Socrates' interlocutors in such a way that it is plain they conceive the commission of any of them as injustice, and not committing any of them justice.[7]

The Platonic Conception

Although the speeches of Glaucon and Adeimantus at the beginning of Book II give expression to the vulgar conception of justice, elements of the Platonic conception are also prominent in them. Commentators have often recognized that the speeches are vital for an understanding of how Plato conceives justice and for grasping what he tries to establish concerning it.

Glaucon, before his speech, asks Socrates if he really wishes to persuade them that it is in every way better to be just than unjust. The phrase "in every way" ($\pi\alpha\nu\tau\grave{\iota}\ \tau\rho\acute{o}\pi\wp$, 357B1) is then glossed by Glaucon's classification of goods and his and Socrates' discussion of it. The classification appears to be roughly the following: goods valued for their own sake, goods valued for their own sake and their effects, and goods valued only for their effects. The second type of goods is the one better in every way and Socrates says that, if a man is to be happy, he should thus regard justice; that is, value it both for its own sake and for its effects.

[7] This statement of conditions for injustice and justice exhausts the notion of justice of Socrates' host, the scrupulous and fearful Cephalus; that Polemarchus shares much of the ordinary understanding of morality (and, unlike Thrasymachus, remains largely committed to it) is shown by the manner in which he reacts when Socrates reduces one of his positions to the absurd consequence that being just requires a "kind" of stealing ($\kappa\lambda\epsilon\pi\tau\iota\kappa\acute{\eta}\ \tau\iota s$). See 334B3–7. The few examples of injustice that Adeimantus gives are among those mentioned by Thrasymachus and Glaucon.

Plato's use of the expressions which I have conventionally rendered by the phrase "valued for their own sake" has perplexed readers about the main argument and aroused controversy.[8] The difficulty to which it has given rise is this: on the one hand, Socrates states to Glaucon that justice is to be valued for its own sake as well as for its effects, and Glaucon and Adeimantus stress in their speeches that they want Socrates to praise justice in itself (358D1–2; 363A1–2; cf. 367C5–D5); on the other hand, throughout the *Republic*, Socrates confines himself to an attempt to show that being just eventuates in happiness and pleasure for the just man; that is he praises justice solely for what he alleges are its effects. Consequently, it has been charged that Plato, at the start of Book II, misconceived the task he thereafter tried to carry out; that he promised to prove that justice is good both for its own sake and for its effects, but addressed himself only to what he presumed were its effects.[9]

The expressions Plato uses are indeed likely to perplex contemporary readers, but an examination of the contexts in which they occur can help to remove the perplexity. When characterizing the first of the three types of goods, Glaucon says, "Are there not some which we should wish to have, not for their consequences, but just for their own sake, such as harmless pleasures and enjoyments that have no further result beyond the satisfaction of the moment?" The sentence just quoted is Cornford's very free translation of the

---

[8] E.g., αὐτὸ αὑτοῦ ἕνεκα ἀσπαζόμενοι (357B6); αὐτό τε αὑτοῦ χάριν ἀσπαζόμενοι (357C1); αὐτὰ . . . ἑαυτῶν ἕνεκα . . . ἂν δεξαίμεθα (357C8). For a compilation of the troubling expressions, see J. D. Mabbott, "Is Plato's Republic Utilitarian?," *Mind*, N.S. XLVI (1937), 469–470 [reprinted in revised form below, selection four].

[9] A quarter of a century ago, M. B. Foster criticized Plato on this score (M. B. Foster, "A Mistake of Plato's in the Republic," *Mind*, N.S. XLVI [1937], 386–393). J. D. Mabbott replied, claiming that Plato does try to prove justice good for its own sake, or a good in itself (*op. cit.*). Foster, in answer to Mabbott, modified his criticism of Plato, saying that the vexing expressions made merely for a verbal ambiguity, "two different (and mutually inconsistent) ways of expressing what he [Plato] nevertheless conceived always as the same thing." According to Foster, Plato always meant to be claiming that justice is valuable because of its effects. Foster continued to maintain, in my belief rightly, that Plato did not try to prove justice a good in itself, or good for its own sake—in the sense which those qualifying phrases usually bear at present. See M. B. Foster, "A Mistake of Plato's in the Republic: A Rejoinder to Mr. Mabbott," *Mind*, N.S. XLVII (1938), 226–232. See n. 14 *infra*.

problematic lines 357B4–8; it has the merit, in comparison to other translations, of forcibly suggesting that αἱ ἡδοναί signifies activities or objects which produce pleasure, and not the pleasure produced.[10] The clause beginning "that have no *further* result" should suggest that "for their own sake" is not being contrasted with "for (all and) any effects whatsoever" and that, instead, a distinction *among* effects is implicit. This is also suggested by the mention of enjoyment (χαίρειν ἔχοντα 357B8), which one would naturally take to be an effect; indeed, if the sole effect of something is pleasure or enjoyment, it would appear to be an instance of the first type of goods in Glaucon's classification.[11]

When Socrates is asked where he places justice in the classification, he replies, "In the fairest class . . . amongst those which he who would be blessed, must love both for their own sake and their consequences."[12] Again, a present-day reader may wonder: how does Socrates conceive the relation of justice, which he places among the second type of goods, to blessedness or happiness? Socrates' remark is difficult, but Glaucon's comment on it is helpful: "That is not the opinion of most people. . . . They place it in the *troublesome* class of good things, which must be pursued for the sake of the reward and the high place in public opinion which they bring but which *in themselves are irksome* and to be avoided."[13] Glaucon's words are clear; according to the many, he is saying, justice in itself, since it is harsh or painful, should be avoided. The troublesomeness and harshness of it, then, are included under the heading "in itself." By analogy, the blessedness or happiness which Socrates thinks being just produces may be placed under the same heading. The need for discriminating the kind of effect intended by

[10] F. M. Cornford (trans.), *The Republic of Plato* (New York, 1945), p. 42. If, contrary to Cornford and following most translators, αἱ ἡδοναί at 357B7 is taken to mean pleasure(s) rather than what produces it, the conclusion of Plato's sentence presents a considerable obstacle: since ταύτας in καὶ μηδὲν εἰς τὸν ἔπειτα χρόνον διὰ ταύτας γίγνεται ἄλλο ἢ χαίρειν ἔχοντα refers to αἱ ἡδοναί, it will have to be understood as pleasure which produces enjoyment, i.e. pleasure. Plato would then implausibly have to be understood as thinking that pleasure produces pleasure.

[11] For a surprising yet likely example, cf. 584B.

[12] A. D. Lindsay (trans.), *The Republic of Plato* (New York, 1957), p. 44, 358A1–3.

[13] *Ibid.*, 358A4–6; my italics.

the phrases "in itself" and "for their own sake," from those intended by "effects" or "consequences" said *simpliciter*, is plain.

The distinction among effects is clarified by the repeated and virtually identical demands made of Socrates in Glaucon's and Adeimantus' speeches. Glaucon's request at 358B4–7 is typical (see 366E5–9; 367B3–5; 367E1–5; also 367A1–8; 367C5–D5). He asks to be told the powers (δύναμεις) that justice and injustice, being present in the soul, exert *by themselves*—leaving aside the rewards and effects of both. From these passages it can be seen that Plato conceived of justice as good in itself, a good for its own sake, in terms of the effect which he supposed it exerted within the soul of its possessor. In the same way, he thought injustice an evil in itself. (The expressions literally translated by "for its own sake" and "in itself" might be paraphrased in a less confusing way for present-day readers by the locutions "on its own" and "by itself.") For Plato, *no other* effects of justice and injustice were grounds for characterizing them as good or evil in themselves—and notably not those effects due to the knowledge or opinion others have of one's justice or injustice.

Glaucon's classification of goods, then, proves quite complex: first, items which by themselves (or on their own) are productive of good and of nothing else; second, those which by themselves are productive of good and, in conjunction with other things, have additional good effects; third, those which by themselves have bad effects but also have good ones which outweigh them.

Obviously, the classification is neither exhaustive nor neat, but if my account of the vexing phrases that occur in it and in Glaucon's and Adeimantus' speeches is correct, then Plato is not open to the charge of having promised to undertake what he never attempts.[14]

Plato's notion of the effects of the powers of justice and injustice in the souls of men is fundamental to the Platonic conception of

[14] Even Foster's charge of verbal ambiguity (cf. n. 9 *supra*) should be dismissed. It imports into Glaucon's and Adeimantus' speeches a possibly anachronistic interpretation of "good for its own sake" and "good in itself," one in which those phrases mark a contrast with things that are good because of their effects, even when the good they produce is happiness or pleasure. As I have argued, Glaucon's and Socrates' remarks show that Plato did not intend this contrast. See 367C5–D2, where Adeimantus places justice among ἀγαθὰ γόνιμα τῇ αὐτῶν φύσει; cf. Adam's conjecture *ad loc.*, and Foster, in *Mind*, N.S. XLVI (1937), 392–393.

justice (see 366E5–6 ff.; 367B2–5). When Adeimantus complains
that no one has adequately stated how justice and injustice, because
of their powers, constitute respectively the greatest good and the
greatest evil in the soul, he is anticipating theses Socrates will expound in Books IV, VIII, and IX. Adeimantus' speech is especially
important because it repeatedly expresses Plato's aim of delineating
the powers of justice and injustice as powers exerted solely by their
existence or presence in the soul (see 366E5–9). In this connection
the word "power," though it correctly translates δύναμις, can
prove misleading. For if it is conceived after the model of other uses
of "power"—indeed on the model of other uses of δύναμις in
Adeimantus' speech (e.g., 366C2; 366E4)—it will not be thought a
power which *must* be exercised. What Adeimantus asks to be shown,
however, is the good which justice inevitably works by its mere
existence in the soul. Injustice, likewise, is to be proven an inescapable evil for the soul in which it is present. And these, of course,
are the very demands Socrates attempts to meet in Books IV,
VIII, and IX.

The most familiar evidence that Plato is intent on characterizing
justice and injustice as things which cannot but work good and evil
is, of course, contained in the famous similes of Book IV, where the
just soul is compared to the healthy body, the unjust to diseased
bodies, and the entire ἀρετή, or virtue, of the soul is called a kind of
health and beauty and good condition, its contrary, κακία, being
termed the soul's disease, ugliness, and enfeeblement (see 444C–E
et circa).

If Socrates were to succeed in proving that justice by itself cannot
but be good for the soul of its possessor, and injustice evil, he still
would not be meeting Glaucon's and Adeimantus' challenge; for
they ask him to show that justice is the greatest good of the soul, injustice its greatest evil. Further, showing this will not be sufficient
unless Socrates thereby shows that the life of the man whose soul
possesses justice is happier than the life of anyone whose soul is unjust. The latter is required of Socrates when Glaucon asks him to
compare certain lives in terms of happiness. Glaucon envisages a
just man's life "bare of everything but justice. . . . Though doing no
injustice he must have the repute of the greatest injustice . . . let
him on to his course unchangeable even unto death . . . the just
man will have to endure the lash, the rack, chains, the branding-
iron in his eyes, and finally, after every extremity of suffering, he

will be [impaled]."[15] On the other hand, the unjust man pictured by Glaucon enjoys a position of "rule in the city, a wife from any family he chooses, and the giving of his children in marriage to whomsoever he pleases, dealings and partnerships with whom he will, and in all these transactions advantage and profit for himself," and so forth, including a not unreasonable expectation of divine favor.[16] Socrates has to prove that a just man whose condition is that described by Glaucon will still lead a happier life than anyone who is unjust if he is to show that, in terms of happiness, which is the Platonic criterion for the choice among lives,[17] one ought to choose the just life. Again, if Socrates is able to show that an unjust man who enjoys the existence depicted by Glaucon is more wretched than any just man, that will suffice for choosing to reject any unjust life. As Prichard remarked, "Plato certainly did not underrate his task. Indeed, in reading his statement of it, we wonder how he ever came to think that he could execute it."

Some questions present themselves here. Assuming that the reader is acquainted with Plato's characterization of justice as a particular ordering of the parts of the soul, I will discuss these questions very briefly. Could Plato have thought it possible to lead a life which was neither just nor unjust? In Books VIII and IX he ranks kinds of souls according to degrees of injustice in them; might he have held that some souls lack both justice and injustice? On the Platonic conception of justice, the answer has to be no because, first, Plato is obliged to affirm, concerning numerous actions which may involve no one besides the agent, that they are done either justly or unjustly; for they, too, can alter the ordering, the polity or constitution, of the soul's parts. Secondly and decisively, even if one could avoid all actions that, on Plato's encompassing view, are just or unjust, the soul's parts would nevertheless be ordered one way or another; that is, either justice or injustice would be present (cf. 449A1–5).

Another question, one often touched upon by H. W. B. Joseph

[15] Excerpted from 361C3–362A 2; cf. the entire passage, 360E1–362C8.

[16] Compare 613C8–614A3.

[17] See the passages cited in n. 5 *supra*. Cf. also Foster, in *Mind* (1937), 387, and (1938), 229, 231–232; A. W. H. Adkins, *Merit and Responsibility, A Study in Greek Values* (Oxford, 1960), pp. 264, 283 ff., especially 290–291.

in his *Essays in Ancient and Modern Philosophy*,[18] can be posed as
follows. Few persons, if any, are perfectly just or consummately
unjust; does Plato really try to maintain that all such intermediate
lives are less happy than any perfectly just man's life would be?
Since Socrates agrees that there are a variety of good things besides
justice,[19] this question might be put by asking whether Plato
thinks that a life which includes an abundance of goods other than
justice—but involves some injustice—must be less happy than,
for example, the existence of Glaucon's beleaguered though just
man. Anyone familiar with the *Republic* will know that this question
has to be answered in the affirmative. Plato's consideration of the
matter, it should be observed, is developed in terms of his own conception of justice. Thus in Book IV, Socrates states that there is one
form of ἀρετή, or excellence, of the soul but limitless ones of κακία,
or defect (cf. 445C5–D1; also 449A1–5), four of which are worth
special notice; they are the defects responsible for the timocratic,
oligarchical, democratic, and tyrannical polities of the soul, the
famous discussion of which occupies Books VIII and IX. There,
while contending that the man whose soul possesses its ἀρετή is
happier than any man whose soul lacks it, Plato tries to determine
which of the four forms of κακία produces the least unhappiness
and which the greatest wretchedness. Clearly, what Plato attempts
to establish—but again in terms of his own conception of justice—is
that any intermediate life, any soul characterized by some degree
of injustice, is inferior in point of happiness to the perfectly just,
despite any other good things an intermediate life might include;
and that the extent to which a soul is unjust is paralleled, *pari passu*,
by the misery of the man whose soul it is (cf. 576B–E; 580A–C).

   To summarize thus far: I began with the familiar observation
that Plato held that the choice between the just life and an unjust
life is to be decided by determining which is the happier. I then
claimed that this position of Plato's is complicated by the presence
in the *Republic* of two conceptions of justice, Socrates maintaining a
distinctively Platonic one and Thrasymachus a vulgar one, while
Glaucon and Adeimantus give expression to both. After stating the
vulgar conception, I discussed some aspects of the Platonic one. In
my discussion of the latter I tried to clarify what was meant when
Socrates affirmed—and when Glaucon and Adeimantus insisted

[18] Pp. 76, 80–81, 140–141, 153–154.
[19] See, however, *R.*, 491C–495A, 505A ff., 521A.

that he establish—that justice is good for its own sake or good in itself, and injustice evil in itself. Plato, I contended, characterized justice and injustice in these ways because he thought that on their own—or by themselves—they effect the soul's greatest good and greatest evil; this being due, Plato believed, to the powers which they inevitably exert upon the souls in which they are present. I further claimed that, on Plato's view, justice or injustice—one or the other but not both—must exist in every soul, and that the man in whose soul justice exists will be happier than a man whose soul includes any degree of injustice, happiness varying inversely with injustice.

In what follows, I argue that Plato failed to relate the two conceptions of justice adequately and that it is implausible to suppose that the omission, a complex one, can be repaired. Consequently, Plato's conclusions about happiness and justice—as he conceives the latter—prove irrelevant to the dispute between Socrates and Thrasymachus (and Glaucon and Adeimantus, in so far as they, too, are concerned with the happiness of vulgarly just and unjust men).

THE FALLACY

Toward the end of Book IV, Socrates formulates the Platonic conception of the just man: a man, each part of whose soul attends to its business or function, performing no tasks but its own. Further, Socrates says that if an action preserves or helps to produce the condition of the soul in which each of its parts does its own task, one ought to believe the action just and name it so, and believe an action unjust and name it so if it has a contrary effect (see 443E4–444A2). In accord with this, Socrates suggests that acting justly is to be understood as acting in a way which will produce the condition of justice in the soul, and that acting unjustly is to be understood as behavior which produces a contrary condition. Glaucon, I take it, is sounding a like note when he affirms that just acts are necessarily productive of justice, unjust ones of injustice (444C1–3; 444C10–D2).

It will be recalled that Thrasymachus, in stating his position, mentioned among unjust acts temple-robbing, kidnaping, swindling, thieving, and so forth. This list, again, was enlarged by Glaucon's mention of sexual relations with whom one pleases, killing, freeing from bonds anyone one wishes, and so forth; that is, acts commonly judged immoral or criminal. The man of whom it was to be proven that his life will be happier than other lives is the man who does not commit such acts.

What Plato tries to establish, however, is that a man each of the parts of whose soul performs its own task, and who conducts himself throughout his days in such a way that this condition will remain unaltered, leads a happier life than any men whose souls are not thus ordered. Regardless of Plato's success or failure in this endeavor, for it to be at all relevant he has to prove that his conception of the just man precludes behavior commonly judged immoral or criminal; that is, he must prove that the conduct of his just man also conforms to the ordinary or vulgar canons of justice. Second, he has to prove that his conception of the just man applies to—is exemplified by—every man who is just according to the vulgar conception. For, short of this last, he will not have shown it impossible for men to conform to vulgar justice and still be less happy than men who do not. Plato had to meet both of these requirements if his conclusions about happiness and justice are to bear successfully against Thrasymachus' contentions and satisfy Glaucon's and Adeimantus' demands of Socrates. There are passages in the *Republic* which show that Plato thought there was no problem about the first requirement; there are, however, no passages which indicate that he was aware of the second. In any event, the fact is that he met neither requirement; nor is it plausible to suppose that he could have met either of them. Before I argue that this is the position as regards the main argument of the *Republic*, some objections which may be raised here should be faced.

For the purposes of this paper, which are the internal criticism and incidental clarification of the main argument of the *Republic*, I am not questioning—what have often been questioned—Plato's conclusions to the effect that men who are Platonically just are happier than men who are not, and that the farther a man's soul is from Platonic justice the more wretched he will be. My object is to show that these conclusions of Plato's are irrelevant to the dispute between Socrates and Thrasymachus and Thrasymachus' sometime advocates, Glaucon and Adeimantus. However, to press both of the requirements that I have stated may seem too stringent. It may be felt that, if Plato's conclusions are granted, he then need fulfill only the first requirement; that is, provide a demonstration that the Platonically just man cannot perpetrate vulgar injustice.

For Plato's conclusions, together with such a demonstration, would have the consequence that the happiest men are among those who conform to vulgar justice; thereby, Thrasymachus' position would be refuted. But even granting Plato's conclusions, had he met the first requirement and not the second, he would have left open the possibility of Platonically unjust men who were vulgarly just and yet no happier, perhaps less so, than vulgarly unjust men. Alternatively, it may be thought that the satisfaction of the second requirement—namely, a demonstration that the vulgarly just man is Platonically just—would, together with Plato's conclusions, have sufficed. For it would then follow that no one was happier than vulgarly just individuals; and this, too, would refute Thrasymachus' position. It would, however, leave open the possibility of there being men who were Platonically just, and consequently as happy as anyone else, yet capable of vulgar injustices and crimes. Because of these considerations, both requirements had to be satisfied.

Both explicitly and by implication, Plato distinguished his special conception of justice from the ordinary understanding of morality.[20] Moreover, he repeatedly alleged connections between the two. In Book IV, after Socrates defines the virtues (441C–442D), he and Glaucon agree that the Platonically just man is least likely of all men to commit what would ordinarily be thought immoral acts; and in Book VI, Socrates attributes the vulgar moral virtues to men of a philosophical nature—to men, that is, whose souls are pre-eminently ordered by Platonic justice (484A–487A). Doubtless, then, Plato thought that men who were just according to his conception of justice would pass the tests of ordinary morality. But although Plato more than once has Socrates say things to this effect, he nowhere tries to prove it. Attempts to show that Platonic justice entails ordinary morality are strikingly missing from the *Republic;* Plato merely assumes that having the one involves having the other. The assumption, moreover, is implausible. On Plato's view, the fulfillment of the functions of the soul's parts constitutes wisdom or intelligence,[21] courage, and self-control; and if these

[20]In addition to the passage cited on page 37 *supra*, see 517D–E and 538C–539D.

[21] Because "wisdom," the orthodox translation of σοφία, is the name of something intimately connected with justice and morality as they are ordinarily understood, I suggest, as an alternative, "intelligence"; whatever Plato intended by his employment of σοφία toward the end of

obtain, justice, according to Plato, also obtains. Intelligence, courage, and self-control are, however, *prima facie* compatible with a variety of vulgar injustices and evil-doing. Neither as usually understood nor as Plato characterizes them are those virtues inconsistent with performing any of the acts Thrasymachus and Glaucon mention as examples of injustice. In this regard it is tempting to assert that the most that can be said on behalf of Plato's argument is that crimes and evils could not be done by a Platonically just man in a foolish, unintelligent, cowardly, or uncontrolled way.

In Books VIII and IX, where Plato sketches the degeneration of the polities of city and soul, the motives he uses to characterize the timocratic, oligarchical, and democratic types of soul are motives which, especially when strong, may lead to vulgar immorality and crime. But Plato, it should be noted, does not state or even suggest that it is inevitable for them to do so. By contrast, his account of the tyrannical soul, the opposite extreme from the Platonically just, is replete with the description of crimes that men who have tyrannical souls commit (573E–576A); their immorality and wickedness, aggravated if they become actual tyrants, is said to pertain necessarily to them (580A1–7). However, the suggestion that men with souls of a timocratic or oligarchical or democratic kind are prone to perform immoral acts of course fails to satisfy the first requirement for Plato's conclusions to be relevant. And if it were granted that men whose souls are tyrannical are somehow necessarily evil-doers, this still would not meet the requirement. That is, neither separately nor conjointly do the theses of Books VIII and IX about other types of soul exclude the possibility of men whose souls are Platonically just committing what would ordinarily be judged immoral acts. Any supposition to the effect that the theses of Books VIII and IX were meant by Plato to establish the claim that vulgarly unjust acts can be performed only by men whose souls lack Platonic justice is unconfirmed by the text of those books;[22] in any case,

---

Book IV, one is not entitled to assume without argument that a man who possesses it will be ordinarily just or moral. There is some warrant for using "intelligence" because, in at least one relevant passage, Plato employs φρόνησις interchangeably with σοφία. See 433B8 *et circa*.

[22] As I have stated, at other places in the *Republic* Plato makes unsupported claims tantamount to the assertion that if one's soul is Platonically just, one will be vulgarly just, and this of course implies that, if vulgar injustice is done, it is done by men whose souls lack Platonic justice.

Books VIII and IX contain neither proof nor intimation of a proof for that further thesis.

The first requirement, then, is left unfulfilled. Plato merely has Socrates reiterate the implausible assumption a demonstration of which was needed. The second requirement, it will be recalled, is a proof that the vulgarly just man is Platonically just. While there are passages in the *Republic* which indicate that Plato thought there were no difficulties about the first requirement, the position is not even this favorable in regard to the second: he nowhere so much as assumes that men who are just according to the ordinary conception are also Platonically just. Indeed, there is no reason to suppose that this was his belief; but the omission of a claim to that effect within the framework of his argument cannot but seem surprising. Plato abundantly represents Thrasymachus, Glaucon, and Adeimantus as questioning the happiness of ordinarily just, moral men. It seems incontrovertible that when they ask to be shown how justice, because of its power, constitutes the greatest good of the soul, Glaucon and Adeimantus are taking for granted that the souls of vulgarly just men will enjoy the effects of justice. Nonetheless, an examination of Socrates' reply to Glaucon and Adeimantus (an examination, that is, of Book II, 367E to Book X, 612B) fails to uncover any claim whose import is that vulgar justice entails Platonic justice.

A remark I quoted earlier may seem capable of being drafted into Plato's service here. After Socrates and Glaucon agree that the Platonically just man is the least likely of all men to commit vulgar injustices, Socrates says, "And is not the cause of this to be found in the fact that each of the principles within him does it own work in the matter of ruling and being ruled?" (443B1–2). Socrates is here stating that the cause of the Platonically just man's vulgar justice is precisely that he is Platonically just. Perhaps someone might be tempted, on the basis of the remark, to think that Plato was suggesting that Platonic justice is a necessary condition for vulgar justice. There is, however, no warrant for extending the remark in this way. Although Plato sometimes speaks of an item as the cause ($\alpha\iota\tau\iota\alpha$) of something where it seems that he thinks of it as a necessary condition of it (for example, when he speaks of the "forms" as causes at *Phaedo* 100C–D *et circa*), his uses of $\alpha\iota\tau\iota\alpha$ are by no means always of this kind. Nor do I see any reasons for thinking he is so using it at 443B1–2. A more likely construction of those lines would take them as equivalent to the claim that Platonic justice is sufficient to insure vulgar justice; that is, as equivalent to the implausible assumption, a proof of which is my first requirement.

Apart from the fact that Plato never states that being vulgarly just entails being Platonically just, one may wonder if such a claim is at all plausible. It does not seem to be; for instance, scrupulous, rule-bound men of the very type evoked by Plato's portrait of Cephalus at the beginning of the *Republic* provide examples of men who are vulgarly just but whose souls lack Platonic justice, and men with timocratic souls might provide additional Platonic counterexamples to the claim that vulgar justice entails Platonic justice.

My criticism of Plato's argument, it is worth observing, is unaffected by considerations of how he understood happiness (εὐδαιμονία) or blessedness (μακαριότης); and, again, my criticism is independent of the success or failure of his attempts to establish the happiness of *his* just man. Had Plato succeeded in showing that the happiest or most blessed of men are those who are just according to his conception of justice, and that the farther a man is from exemplifying Platonic justice the more unhappy he will be, Plato still would not have shown either that Platonic justice entails vulgar justice or the converse. That is, he would still have to relate his conclusions to the controversy which, plainly, they are intended to settle.

In conclusion, a speculation: it concerns one of the possible philosophical motives for Plato's conception of justice. In the first interchanges of the *Republic*, the existence of exceptions to moral rules of conduct is emphasized. Plato has Socrates more than once assert—both of telling the truth and paying back or restoring what one owes—that it is sometimes just to do these things, sometimes unjust (331C4–5; cf. 331C1–332A5 entire). Partly on this basis, partly because of similar passages in other dialogues, I believe it likely that Plato held that there are allowable exceptions to every moral rule, or virtually every moral rule, of conduct.[23] What is

---

[23] Cf., e.g., the vexed passage, *Phaedo* 62A1–7 *et circa, Symposium* 180E4–181A6; 183D3–6. The remarks in Pausanias' speech in the *Symposium* are, of course, of dubious value as evidence for Plato's own views. For further discussion of the point and additional references, see G. Santas, *The Socratic Paradoxes and Virtue and Happiness in Plato's Earlier Dialogues* (unpublished Ph.D. dissertation, Cornell University, 1961), p. 68 *et passim*.

more, I believe that Plato was so impressed by what he took to be permissible exceptions to moral rules of conduct that his certainty of the existence of those exceptions, together with his certainty that no defining logos could have any exceptions, led him to—or confirmed him in—the view that rules of conduct do not constitute anything essential to morality or justice. This, I believe, was one of the principal motives for his characterization of justice, a characterization not in terms of conduct and the relations of persons, but in terms of the relations of parts of the soul.

Originally published in *Philosophical Review* 72 (1963), 141–58. Reprinted by permission of the journal and the author.

3

A FALLACY IN PLATO'S *REPUBLIC?*

RAPHAEL DEMOS

An article published by Professor David Sachs in the *Philosophical Review*[1] offers a scholarly and penetrating interpretation of some of Plato's views. Indeed, on some matters I believe that it makes a contribution to our understanding of Plato. In this discussion, however, I will be mainly concerned with Sach's attribution of a fallacy to Plato, as stated in the title of his article. I agree that there is a gap in the argument, but a gap is a lacuna and a lacuna is not a fallacy. Mathematicians often skip steps in an inference, thinking them obvious. I take it that a fallacy is invalid inference: it exists when a proposition is inferred from a premise when, in fact, it is not entailed by it. I hope to prove that Sachs has not made his point; more particularly, that he has failed to prove that Plato's conclusion could not logically follow from his premise.

Sachs makes a vital distinction which helps clear up a confusion in Plato's argument. Sachs insists that we must keep apart two questions: (a) Does justice entail happiness? (b) Does justice entail vulgar or conventional morality (*Republic*, 444E3)? He rightly insists that an answer to the first question has no bearing on the answer to the second. In other words, were we to succeed in proving that a just man will be happy, we should still not know that he will be conventionally moral.

A very important use of "justice" by Plato is the rendering to every man his due. This is the refrain running throughout *Republic* I; it is the ordinary, the conventional meaning of justice; it is the conception of justice as a social virtue. But in Book IV, Plato comes up with a different and unconventional definition of justice; it is, so far as I know, unique with Plato among Greek philosophers, and indeed Sachs calls it Platonic justice. This is the view of justice as (a) the state of the soul in which no part of the soul interferes with

[1] "A Fallacy in Plato's *Republic*," *Philosophical Review* LXXII (1963), 141–58 [reprinted above, selection 2 in this volume; page references will be to this selection only].

the functioning of the other parts—call it the principle of nonintervention—and (b) the state of the soul in which the various parts are working in mutual harmony and friendship (351D3; 433E2–4). Should anyone wonder whether there is any significant difference between the two notions, let him reflect on this pair: desegregation and integration.

What is odd about Plato's "Platonic" justice is its seemingly striking departure from ordinary usage. Customarily, justice indicates the relation of a given person to other persons; it is a virtue which operates in social contexts. But Platonic justice is a personal virtue, defined purely in terms of the agent. One wonders why Plato should have introduced this unusual meaning; is it possible that he regarded it as the same meaning? Plato likens the soul to the city. In contrast to the outer city, the soul is an inner city; it is a community of parts—of reason, *thymos*, and innumerable appetites. Can he then be charged with changing, or even stretching, the meaning of the word, if by Platonic justice he means giving every part of the soul its due? The change, if change there be, would seem to be in the conception of the soul as a community, not in the conception of justice. And if my suggestion is correct, it should throw light on the lacuna, or what Sachs calls the fallacy of irrelevance.

Sachs finds two missing links in Plato's argument. Plato, he says, has to show not only (a) that Platonic justice entails vulgar morality but (b) that the latter entails the former as well. In this paper I will discuss the trouble caused by (a) only; I am not really sure that (b) is necessary to Plato's argument. Sachs refers to Cephalus; now, Cephalus certainly was just in the vulgar sense, yet he lacked philosophical intelligence. But what of it? Cephalus surely possessed right opinion; in this way a man may achieve the level of demotic (vulgar?) and political (social) virtue (*Phaedo*, 82A10–B1; also *Republic*, 500D8). Therefore I will limit myself to Sachs' (a), and there will be trouble enough in making sense out of Plato, even so.

Sachs is surely quite right in criticizing Plato's way of dealing with (a). Plato blandly assumes that a man who is Platonically just will conform to the canons of vulgar morality. ("Plato merely assumes that having the one involves having the other" (p. 47).] How could inner harmony entail that a man will not steal, will not betray his friends, will not commit adultery, and so forth? It seems entirely obvious to Plato, and it is entirely unobvious to us. Since I had been acutely aware of this problem long before I came across

Sachs's article, I hope I may be allowed to put it in my own way, without, I trust, doing injustice to Sachs's argument. Platonic justice is an individual virtue—how a person behaves toward himself; in fact, it is the harmonious realization of the soul in all its parts. But so defined, justice is self-regarding. How then can it possibly imply a concern for other people (rendering to everyone his due)? In short, there seems to be a leap from the conception of justice as caring for one's own good to caring for other people's good. Plato asserts that justice is to the human soul what health is to the human body; but surely no living body aims at anything but its *own* health. Platonic justice is the proper ordering of one's own life; why then should a just man in this sense of justice care to bring about a proper ordering of *other* people's lives?

There certainly is a gap; is there a fallacy? Sachs's reasoning to show that there is a fallacy (of irrelevance) seems to consist of two steps. First he says—what I have already agreed to—that Plato fails to show that Platonic justice entails vulgar morality. This is only a lacuna; what is needed, in order to demonstrate a fallacy, is a proof that Platonic justice could not (logically) lead to vulgar morality. So let us proceed to Sachs's second point. Sachs goes on to say that the assumption is implausible ("The assumption, *moreover*, is implausible" [p. 47], italics mine.). What is characterized as implausible is the supposition that there exists a logical connection (entailment) between premise and conclusion. To say, however, that it is implausible is not to say that the logical link does not in *fact* exist. How much force does the word "implausible" carry? To me it suggests a first look, a first impression, to be followed by detailed exploration: I find no such exploration in Sachs's article. Sachs does not prove (does not even try to prove) that the conclusion is not entailed by the premise. All his reasoning shows is that we do not *know* whether there is a fallacy or not; at best it shows that there *may* be a fallacy.[2]

In the comments that follow I will suggest that a logical connection can be found, and I will indicate what this may be. But first,

[2] Referring to the second requirement which Sachs lays down in order that Plato's argument be complete—namely, that vulgar justice entails being Platonically just—Sachs writes: "Apart from the fact that Plato never states that being vulgarly just entails being Platonically just, one may wonder if such a claim is at all plausible. It does not seem to be" [p. 50]. Notice the weakness of "it does not *seem* to be."

two reservations. I claim only that the intervening links which I will supply are consistent with Plato's general theory; I do not claim that they are links he actually had in mind. Also, nothing that I have said in the preceding paragraph is undermined, even if my arguments fails. Should the latter be the case, we remain agnostics.

Plato says that one is Platonically just in the sense that each part of his soul does its own work in the matter of ruling and being ruled (443B1–3). Of course the ruling principle is reason, and (a) reason is the apprehension of the truth and of the good. (b) Reason is also a form of desire (ἐπιθυμία, 580D6–8). Thus reason is both an apprehension and an aspiration to the ideal. (c) The good which is the target of reason includes or entails justice; in order to understand the nature of the various virtues (including justice) we must travel along a longer way, so Plato tells us, and this is the path leading to the good (504C10; see also 506A6–10). (d) Reason grasps forms—that is, universals: the good, or wisdom, or justice as such, not my good in a sense which would exclude the good of others. (e) Finally, we know from the *Symposium* that the *eros* of the good and of beauty leads to accomplishment; that is, to instantiations of the forms (*Symposium*, 205C–206E). To aim at the good is also to aim at the *production* of good things; thus for an individual to aim at justice means that he cares not only for justice in the abstract, but also that justice should be embodied in human beings in general.

Earlier I said that each soul cares for its own health just as the body does. But now this statement, though true, is seen to be open to a different interpretation. The health of the soul includes, above all, the fulfillment of its reason: and the concern of reason is that the good should be exemplified everywhere. The concern for my self-fulfillment is analyzable into a concern that everyone should attain psychical fulfillment; that I am inwardly just means that I want everyone to have his due.

Such, then, I suggest is the bridge which links Platonic justice with justice in the sense of rendering to everyone what is his due. I have not, to be sure, literally shown that Platonic justice inevitably leads to vulgar morality (Sachs's formulation of the problem). But is there really any difference between the vulgar and the "noble" senses of morality? To embezzle money, to steal, to betray friends, to be faithless in one's promises, to commit adultery, to neglect parents and to exploit orphans, and all the rest of it—is not all this a case of failing to give others what is their due? Surely these various kinds of vulgarly bad actions are no more than specific violations of the principle that one should avoid acts of injustice to others.

Originally published in *Philosophical Review* 73 (1964), 395–95. Reprinted by permission of the *Philosophical Review* and Mrs. Raphael Demos.

4

IS PLATO'S *REPUBLIC* UTILITARIAN?

J. D. MABBOTT

I. INTRODUCTION

In this Inaugural Lecture as Professor of Moral Philosophy in Oxford in 1928, entitled 'Duty and Interest', Professor H. A. Prichard made out a case for the view that Plato in the *Republic* maintains a utilitarian theory of the relation between right acts and their consequences. He held that Plato accepts the sophistic principle 'that it is impossible for any action to be really just, i.e., a duty, unless it is for the advantage of the agent', and that he differs from the Sophists only in the type of consequences which he adduces as the justification of justice. They said that no one would be just except for the sake of honour or reputation or gain or some other external reward. Plato looks to the effect of justice on the soul of the man who acts justly and finds there its defence. The effect to which he refers is *happiness;* his whole argument then is an attempt to show that 'it is by doing what is right that, at any rate in the long run, we shall become happy'.

I had long thought that the most striking piece of evidence against this view was the classification of 'goods' made by Glaucon at the beginning of *Republic* II. Some things are good in themselves, some are good both in themselves and for their consequences, and some are unwelcome in themselves but acceptable for their consequences. The second class is the best and there justice must be found. Justice is good in itself, as well as good for its consequences.

I was therefore more in sympathy with Mr. M. B. Foster, who recognized that the three-fold classification of goods is inconsistent with a utilitarian interpretation of the whole work. But, as he believed this interpretation to be correct, he regarded the classification as a mistake of Plato's. If we eliminate this passage and some later phrases which recall it, the position is again clear. Glaucon and Adeimantus ask Socrates to prove that justice pays and

Socrates does so.[1] Prichard's case had already been answered on
general lines by Professor C. R. Morris.[2] So, in an article in *Mind*,
'Is Plato's *Republic* Utilitarian?', I concerned myself with Mr.
Foster's argument.[3] Mr. Foster replied to this with a 'Rejoinder'.[4]
Subsequently Mr. D. Sachs in a paper entitled 'A Fallacy in Plato's
Republic'[5] has given some support to Mr. Foster's view.

The present paper is in the main a reprint of my *Mind* article,
amended to meet some of Mr. Foster's criticisms. In rewriting it, I
admit that I have become more aware of the ambiguities and
possible confusions to be found in Plato's language on this issue.
But I remain convinced that the main lines of my argument still
stand firm.

The first point to be made clear is what Plato means by justice.
Prichard's argument is made more plausible by his concentration
on just *actions*. Justice is the common character of particular acts.
Plato, says Prichard, looks to the effect of just actions on the soul of
the man who acts justly and finds in it their justification. But, for
Plato, justice *is* a condition of the soul and not a characteristic of
actions; and the only references he makes to the good effect of
just actions are that they make the soul just (444E, 588A,
591A–C).

It is true, as Sachs says, that he does nothing to show that a soul
which is just (in his sense) will be likely to do actions which are
just in the ordinary sense—actions such as refraining from cheating,
etc. But we must take Plato on his own ground. The question therefore is *not* whether he argues that the only reason for refraining
from cheating etc. is that this will bring me happiness in the long
run. The question is whether he maintains that the only reason for
having a just soul is that having a just soul will make me happy in
the long run.

The two crucial passages here are the speeches of Glaucon and
Adeimantus in Book II and the closing section of Book IV. I shall
consider them first. I shall then discuss some 'utilitarian' phrases
scattered throughout the book, and finally the argument of
Book IX.

---

[1] 'A Mistake in Plato's *Republic*', *Mind*, NS 46, pp. 386 ff.
[2] *Proceedings of the Aristotelian Society* (1933–34).
[3] *Mind*, NS 46, pp. 468 ff.   [4] *Mind*, NS 47, pp. 226 ff.
[5] *Philosophical Review* (1963) [reprinted above, pp. 35–51].

II. GLAUCON AND ADEIMANTUS

After Glaucon has explained his three-fold classification of 'goods' and Socrates has placed justice in the best class, Glaucon develops his attack.

(a) Ordinary men regard justice as 'something burdensome to be pursued for the sake of the rewards and the reputation from public opinion which it brings but in itself to be avoided as irksome' (358A).

(b) He therefore wishes 'to hear what each of them (justice and injustice) is and what power each has of itself when it exists in the soul, leaving out of consideration rewards and consequences' (358B).

(c) and 'to hear justice praised for its own sake' (358D).

(d) In order to compare just with unjust we must strip justice of its rewards and reputation and give them to injustice 'so that when the two of them come to these extremes we can decide which of them is better off' ('more *eudaemon*'—see below, section IV, for the arguments against translating this as 'happier') (361D).

Adeimantus follows up this attack. Parents commend justice to their children on the grounds that it brings repute among men and rewards from the gods. But they (like the ordinary man in 358A) err because the rewards they cite can be equally acquired by the unjust man if he takes care to appear just to others and if he offers propitiatory sacrifices to the gods. Their error lay in attacking injustice and praising justice not for themselves but for their repute.

(e) 'What each does by its own power, dwelling in the soul of its possessor, undetected by gods and men, no one has ever thoroughly argued either in poetry or in common talk, that injustice is the greatest evil a soul can contain within itself and justice the greatest good' (366E).

(f) If this had been clear 'no dissuasion from injustice would have been needed, for each man would be his own best warder, fearing lest if he were unjust he would harbour the greatest of evils' (367A).

(g) 'Do not therefore content yourself with proving justice is stronger than injustice, but show us by doing what to its possessor the one is bad in and for itself and the other good' (367B).

(h) 'You have agreed that justice is in the best class of things, those worth having for their consequences, but much more so for themselves, such as sight, hearing, thought, health and other such things which are genuinely good in their own nature and not for their reputation only. So now praise justice for this, that in its own nature it benefits its possessor and injustice harms him, and leave to others the praise of its rewards and reputation' (367C). Adeimantus concludes with a repetition of 367B, the demand to be shown that justice and injustice are good in themselves.

(i) Then all unite in begging Socrates 'to investigate what they are and how things stand concerning their advantages' (368C).

Mr. Foster argues that all these passages (with the exception of a few phrases which recall the mistaken and unfortunate classification of goods in 357) exhort Socrates to show that justice benefits the just man, by an appeal to its natural and inevitable consequences as contrasted with its 'rewards' conventionally attached to it, such as honour and reputation. It must be admitted that the evidence is far from clear. But it seems to me that the passages (b), (c), (e), (f), and (g) ask to be shown that justice is good in itself and (d) and (i) that it is good for its consequences. On closer inspection (c) and (f) remain quite unequivocal and it is surely a strain of meaning for Mr. Foster to have to translate *auto kath' hauto* in (c) as 'for its natural consequences and apart from those procured by its reputation' (p. 389). But in (b), (e), and (g) there are the phrases 'what power each has' and 'what each does'. There is certainly ambiguity here. But I think that, if Plato had been asked whether he meant that a man who had justice in his soul had also as its natural consequence, happiness, for the sake of which alone it was worthwhile to be just, he would have rejected this interpretation. What does justice 'do to a soul'? What does beauty do to a poem? By its presence it renders the poem beautiful. So justice has the power to render the soul harmonious. But its harmony *is* justice and not a consequence of justice. (See further on this in Section III below.)

While Foster and Sachs have to regard all passages which suggest that justice is good in itself as mistakes or inconsistencies, I do not have to explain away passages which claim that justice has good consequences. For, in my view, Socrates has to show that justice is good both in itself and for its consequences.

Sachs differs from Foster in his method of dealing with Glaucon's three-fold classification of goods in 357. He takes 'good in itself' to mean 'productive of happiness, irrespective of other rewards, reputation, etc.'. Here he follows Prichard who also takes 'good' to mean 'productive of happiness'. But Sachs is in difficulties with the examples Plato gives of things which are good in themselves, namely, 'enjoyment and those harmless pleasures which produce in the future nothing other than enjoyment'. Sachs argues that 'pleasures' here must mean 'acts or objects that produce pleasure' (p. 146); but 'enjoyment' at the end of this sentence cannot *also* mean acts or objects which produce enjoyment. Therefore 'enjoyment' (*chaerein*) as the first example (at the beginning of the quotation) cannot mean this either. Thus 'enjoyment' *is* good in itself, and this cannot mean that it is productive of happiness.

III. JUSTICE GOOD IN ITSELF

It is my contention that in *Republic* IV Plato shows that justice is good in itself. The vital passage must be quoted in full:

> To produce justice is to put the parts of the soul in their natural relations of authority or subordination to each other; injustice is to bring about relations of this kind contrary to nature.
>
> Certainly.
>
> Then virtue will be a health and beauty and good condition of the soul, vice a disease, ugliness and weakness.
>
> That is so.
>
> Do not fair practices lead to the acquirement of virtue and base practices to the acquirement of vice?
>
> This must be the case.
>
> It now remains for us to enquire whether it is profitable to act justly and to follow fair dealings and to be just, whether or not the just man is known to be so; or whether acting unjustly and being unjust is profitable, even if the unjust man escapes punishment and is not reformed by correction.
>
> But, Socrates, it would seem to me that we have reached a ridiculous question here. It seems clear that when the constitution of the body is ruined life is not worth living, not with all the food and drink and money and power in the world. So can we ask, when the constitution of the very principle by which we live is overthrown and destroyed, whether life is still worth living even if a man may do whatever he pleases except to cease from vice and injustice and to acquire justice and virtue now we know what justice and injustice are. (444D ff.)

There would seem to be a logical difficulty in proving that anything is good *in itself*. The proof would be a reason why it is good
and therefore an admission that it is not good in itself. Plato, I
think, realized this. When we know what justice is, it is absurd (as
he says) to ask whether it is good. The analogy with health helps us
to see this evident truth.

Justice *is* the correct relationship between the parts of the soul. It
is the good condition of the soul. The analogy with health not only
makes the point clear, but it also seems to me evidence that
Socrates had not forgotten his promise in 357 to show that justice is
in the best class, the class of things both good in themselves and
good for their consequences. For health is one of the examples of
this class given in 357.

On my view Plato shows in Book IV that justice is good in itself
and in Book IX that it is good for its consequences. In his 'rejoinder'
to my article, Mr. Foster said he had originally thought that Book
IV showed what justice was and Book IX that its consequences
were good. He had changed his mind as a result of my argument.
He had come to hold that Book IV proves that the just man is
happy; but this is not enough, for it must be shown that the unjust
man is unhappy and this is done in Book IX. I find this difficult
because there is no mention of happiness in the Book IV passage,
and Book IX, as I shall argue below, does attempt to prove that the
just man is happy.

IV. SOME UTILITARIAN PHRASES

Scattered throughout the *Republic* are many phrases linking
eudaemonia with justice (352D, 354A, 419–420, 427D, 472C, 544A,
545A). There are other passages asking whether it pays to be just
(344E, 347E, 353E, 392C) or is more gainful (345A).

Now, if *eudaemonia* is translated 'happiness', all these passages
would swell the evidence that Plato is recommending justice for its
consequences. But there can be serious doubts about this. The best
evidence for an alternative meaning is in Aristotle's *Ethics*.

Aristotle asks what is the supreme good attainable by human
action and answers that most people agree in naming it *eudaemonia;*
they identify it with living well and doing well. Some identify it
with health or wealth or honour, some with pleasure. Aristotle himself defines *eudaemonia* as virtuous activity of the soul (*EN* I, 4, 7).

He repeatedly *identifies eudaemonia* with some activity or other (political or theoretical) (cf. 1153B11, 1169B29, 1176A30, 1177A12 etc.). His question is not 'what causes *eudaemonia?*' but 'what is *eudaemonia?*'. It is *identified* with living a good life, with political activity, with the activity of contemplation. It is agreed that these activities cause pleasure or are accompanied by pleasure.

Even the word 'happiness' in English is not consistently used to describe the feeling of well-being which accompanies or is caused by successful activity. It often indicates that unimpeded successful activity itself. If one is asked to 'go and see if the children are happy' and one finds them intently painting or building a Meccano crane, the answer is 'Yes' and it is *not* an ascription of glows or thrills or feelings.

At the end of Book I, Plato argues that the virtue (*aretē*) of anything is the effective performance of its specific function. Justice is the virtue of the soul. The soul's function is to live. Justice is therefore to live well. Therefore the just man has *eudaemonia*. Most readers (translating *eudaemonia* as 'happiness') think that this is simply a fallacious transition in the meaning of 'live well'—from 'live a good life' to 'have a good time'. But it seems to me that Plato is here agreeing with Aristotle. A man who has *eudaemonia* is to be congratulated. He lives under divine protection. He is *makarios* (354A, 419A), blessed or fortunate. And even the use of the phrase 'justice pays' is not conclusive. It is naturally taken to mean that justice has good consequences (namely *eudaemonia*). But, again at the end of Book I, Plato says 'It does not pay to be miserable but to be *eudaemon*' (354A). But this cannot mean that the *consequences* of *eudaemonia* are worth having. It must mean that a man is blessed, well off, to be congratulated, if he is *eudaemon*. To say *eudaemonia* pays is to say it is good in itself. So too for living a just life or having a just soul.

V. JUSTICE AND ITS CONSEQUENCES

In Book IX (576 onwards) the best and worst cities and men are compared. It is said that there is no doubt that the Kingly City is the best and the Tyranny the worst. And the question is then what about their happiness and misery. It is to be noted that Plato regards these two judgments as separate; and if so 'best' cannot simply *mean* 'happiest'. As with the city, so with the soul; the tyrannical soul is miserable; most miserable of all if it is the soul of a tyrannical ruler. For it will be enslaved, unsatisfied, impotent and haunted by fear.

The final judgment is stated in 580A–C and is followed by a demonstration that the life of philosophy (which, in a manner typical of this stage of the argument, has been substituted for the life of justice) is vastly more pleasurable than that of the tyrannical man. While this is the most fully demonstrated part of the argument, I was mistaken (as Foster pointed out in his 'rejoinder') in saying it is the *only* result of justice cited in Book IX. At least by implication the Kingly soul is held to be free, satisfied, competent and devoid of fear (since these are the opposites of the failings attributed to the tyrannical soul). And, after the pleasure arguments, other rewards of justice are cited. 'If the good and just man so much outdoes the evil and unjust man in pleasure, is it not incalculable how greatly he will surpass him in grace, nobility and virtue?'[6] But are these consequences? Clearly *aretē* (virtue) is not a consequence of justice, nor are the other two; they are general features of justice.

Then again,
On what terms and for what reasons can we say there is profit in injustice or incontinence or base conduct, if by them a man gets money or power but with it becomes a worse man?
On no terms.
Then how can it profit a man to act unjustly and avoid detection and penalty? If he is not found out does he not become more wicked, while if he is caught the beast in him is made to lie down and is tamed, while the gentle part is freed and the whole soul is set in the direction of the best nature and by becoming temperate and just achieves a condition more valuable than the condition of the body, which with health acquires strength and beauty, in proportion as the soul is more precious than the body?
That is surely the case.
Then will not the man of good sense live with all his capacities extended to this end honouring those studies which will fashion such a soul and despising all others? (591A–C)

---

[6] εὐσχημοσύνῃ τε βίου καὶ κάλλει καὶ ἀρετῇ (588A).

Again the *result* appealed to is a well-organised soul. The goal is that the soul should be in a good condition. But that condition *is* justice.

The main reason for Prichard's attack on Plato was his conviction that Kant was right in thinking that duty must be done for its own sake and that anyone who does what is right because he believes it will make him happier if he does so can claim no moral worth for his action. No doubt, as Kant admitted, actions may be done from mixed motives and it is never easy to be sure about the purity or even the presence of the best motive. Nevertheless the moral issue is clear. 'Honesty is the best policy' and 'Crime doesn't pay' are persuasions addressed to people who would otherwise be likely to be dishonest or criminal. If they live honest lives solely for this reason their lives have no moral worth.

We have noticed above that Plato's 'justice' is a state of the soul and not a characteristic of particular acts. But the same question arises. Why should Plato consider consequences at all, and particularly why should he devote the main argument to the pleasure consequences of justice? There are two possible answers to this, both of which avoid the Kantian objection that the pleasure or happiness of the agent is not a moral justification for any state or action.

First, he may be meeting the Sophists on their own ground. Thrasymachus has said that injustice pays, and this is the answer to him.

Second, Plato's aim may be to establish the status of justice in the whole picture of the world. If it is the case that injustice pays then the world is a very unjust world and the gods are unjust to men.

This paper, published originally in *Mind* NS (1937), 386–93, has been substantially revised by the author for the present volume. Reprinted by permission of the journal and the author.

5

JUSTICE AND HAPPINESS IN THE *REPUBLIC*[1]

GREGORY VLASTOS

I shall use "justice" and "just" merely as counters for *dikaiosynē* and *dikaios*, whose sense is so much broader: they could be used to cover all social conduct which is morally right. I shall use "justice pays" as a handy capsule for what Socrates undertakes to prove in response to Glaucon's challenge (358B ff.): justice is good in and of itself, not merely for its consequences; and it is so great a good that no good securable by injustice could be greater. Here "good" is an

[1] A draft of this paper appeared under the title "The Argument in the *Republic* that 'Justice Pays,'" in the *Journal of Philosophy* 65 (1968), 665–74, along with the other principal papers presented at the annual meeting of the Eastern Division of the American Philosophical Association in 1968. That draft was discussed both in my Princeton Plato seminar in the fall of 1968 and at the symposium of the meeting of the A.P.A. at which it was read. For valuable criticisms, which have led me to correct some mistakes in that draft and to improve on it in other ways in a subsequent paper, "Justice and Psychic Harmony in the *Republic*," in the *Journal of Philosophy* 66 (1969), 505–21 (substantially identical with Sections III to VI.1 of the present version), I am particularly indebted to Mr. Richard Kraut and Mr. Andrew Robison, graduate students at Princeton; to Professors Stanley Rosen and John Cooper, fellow symposiasts at the meeting, particularly to the latter, who made a number of cogent criticisms; and to Professor A. D. Woozley, who followed up with written comments an objection he made at the meeting. Though the paper has been drastically revised in the light of their criticisms and of other corrections I was led to make on further reflection, it still retains the form of presentation forced on me by the stringent space-limit imposed on the original draft: it is still abrupt in argument, short on exposition, and sparing in its references to the secondary literature (which I allow myself only when I find it strictly necessary in order to explain or justify a variant interpretation). I particularly regret that, because of these restrictions, I have been unable to discuss in detail my differences with positions taken on the same topic in the following recent papers:

R. Demos, "A Fallacy in Plato's *Republic?*" *Philos. Rev.* 73 (1964), 395–98 (reprinted as selection 3 in this volume, pp. 52–56 above).

R. Weingartner, "Vulgar Justice and Platonic Justice," *Philos. and Phenomenological Research* 25 (1964/65), 248–52.

ellipsis for "good for the just man himself,"[2] i.e. contributes to his well-being or happiness (*eudaimonia*).[3] So the thesis that justice pays is that one has more to gain in happiness from being a just man than from any good he could obtain at the price of becoming unjust. Now performing a single just act, or some odd assortment of just acts, is by no means equivalent to being a just man or, in Plato's phrase, "having justice in the soul."[4] So in "justice pays" *justice* is a property not of actions as such, but of agents;[5] it stands

---

J. Schiller, "Just Man and Just Acts in Plato's *Republic*," *Jrnl. of Hist. of Philos.* 6 (2968), 1–14.

I am indebted to each of these (cf. notes 36 and 47 below), and to each of the following: Mr. Jerry Neu, who read a paper on this topic to my Plato seminar in 1966; Mr. Richard Kraut, who did the same (and more thereafter in his thesis); Professor David Wiggins, with whom I had a most helpful discussion while still writing this paper.

[2] *Not* for "morally good" (morally praiseworthy). For Plato "justice is (morally) good in and of itself because it makes the just man happy" would be *false*, while "justice is good in and of itself (for the just man) because it makes the just man happy" would be true, and analytically so: to say that X makes me happy would be for Plato part of what it means to say that X is good for me in and of itself.

[3] Following the general practice I shall use "happiness" for *eudaimonia*, but with the caveat that the strongly hedonistic connotations of the English term (under the influence of nineteenth-century utilitarianism) should not be read into *eudaimonia*. For a Greek moralist the question "Is *eudaimonia* pleasure, or is it something else?" is always a significant one (cf. the *Philebus;* and Aristotle, *EN* 1098B22 ff.; and the contrast between the "happier" and "more pleasurable life" in n. 7 below).

[4] Or "present" (*enon*) in the soul (358B5–6; 441C7). Same implication in "having" (*echein*) justice (367B4 and E3; 435C1) or "possessing" (*ktasthai*) it (455B3; 591B5–6). So too in the use of *hexis* of 435B7, 443E6, and 591B4. For the moral virtues as dispositional properties see also 518D–E, where they are said to be like the virtues of the body in that "they can be produced by habituation and exercise." That Plato is not thinking of just acts as such, but of a condition of soul which expresses itself in such acts, is rightly stressed in J. D. Mabbott, "Is Plato's *Republic* Utilitarian?" *Mind* 46 (1937), 468–74, at 474 (reprinted as selection 4 in this volume, pp. 57–65, and in Schiller, *op. cit.*, 6 ff.)

[5] That Plato should at times state the thesis in terms of "acting justly (*dikaia prattein*) pays" (so e.g., in 588B7 and E4) instead of "being a just man pays" is no objection, since "acting justly" can be used to refer to the form of action characteristic of the just man and is so used when articulating the thesis: clearly so in 588B–E; and cf. 445A1–2, where "acting justly" is used in apposition to "being a just man."

for the active disposition to behave justly towards one's fellows.[6]

I

The argument to be examined here is the one in Book IV, supplemented by the studies in moral psychopathology in VIII and IX
(to 580D) and by the terminal reflections in IX (588B ff.)[7] Correctly
analyzed, this argument will be seen to consist of two sub-
arguments whose theses are logically distinct:

> THESIS I. There is a condition of soul—"psychic harmony,"
> I shall call it—which is in and of itself a greater good to one
> who has it than would be any he could secure at the cost of the
> contrary condition of soul.
> THESIS II. One has psychic harmony iff[8] one has a firm and
> stable disposition to act justly towards others.[9]

[6] That *any* just act, or arbitrarily selected set of just acts, must "pay"
would be patently false (except perhaps for an egoistic utilitarian who
might so define "just act" as to make it true); and that Plato would
think it false is distinctly implied in the *Republic*, e.g., in the portrait of
the "oligarchic" man (553E ff.): though unjust (he defrauds orphans),
this man has a fine reputation for justice in his business; so there would
be sᴛᴇtches of his life during which he performs only just acts, and if
just acts *per se* made one happy he would have stretches of happiness;
but as Plato pictures him he is never happy: he is "torn in two by
internal conflict," harbors "drone-like" and "criminal" desires only
"held down under stress of fear, which makes him tremble for the
safety of his whole fortune" (554C–D, following F. M. Cornford's
translation [Oxford, 1945]).

[7] Ignoring the further argument (580–588E) that the just life is not
only happier, but more pleasurable as well (note the terms in which the
conclusion is formulated: "the good and just man" has been proved
superior "*in point of pleasure*," though he is also superior "in grace and
beauty of life and in other excellence," 588A7–10), and this because
his pleasures are preferable and "more real," while four other types of
life, increasingly unjust, yield increasingly inferior and unreal pleasures.
Additional, and puzzling, questions arise here, which I cannot tackle
in this paper. The argument I shall discuss is a self-contained one, and
is presented as such in Book IV: it is supposed to demonstrate that
"justice pays" (and does so to Glaucon's satisfaction [445A–B] without
making even anticipatory reference to 580D–588E].

[8] The customary abbreviation of "if, and only if."

[9] Plato unfortunately does not distinguish these two theses as clearly
and does not present them in the proper order: instead of first telling us
what a precious thing psychic harmony is and *then* going on to demonstrate its connection with the disposition to act justly, he does the
opposite, reserving the praise of psychic harmony for the conclusion of
his argument in Book IV (444C–E).

Plato's argument for Thesis I is that this is the condition of the human soul when it is healthy,[10] beautiful,[11] and in the ontologically correct, hierarchic,[12] internal order. This part of his story I shall not discuss; there is no need to do so, since my interpretation here would differ little from that generally held. I proceed at once to Thesis II, for here my interpretation breaks with accepted opinion and has to be expounded and defended in detail.

II

1. Late in Book IV we come across the following definition:

> . . . in the case of each one of us, whosoever is such that each of the three [psychic elements] in him *does its own*, he is a just man . . . (441E12–442A1).

The italicized phrase, translated in this baldly literal way, makes awkward English.[13] But this is not an unmixed evil. It will serve as a

[10] 444C–D; 591B–C (by implication: justice is the condition in which the soul "returns to its nature at its best" [Paul Shorey's translation (*Plato: the Republic*, 2 volumes, London, 1930 and 1935) of *eis tēn beltistēn hexin kathistamenē*], which is for it what "health and strength" are to the body); 609B–610E (injustice destroys the soul as disease the body; justice makes one "alive" [*zōtikon*], 610E). And cf. *Grg.* 504B–D, 512A–B.

[11] *Kallos* (444E1); *euschēmosynē* (588A9). The same implications in the very notion of psychic *harmony* and its description in terms of musical consonance and concord (443D–E). Cf. *Grg.* 503D ff., where the notion that the morally good (just and *sōphrōn*) soul is the one that has the beautiful order (*kosmos*) of a work of art, where all the parts are fitted together in a harmonious composition, first comes into Plato's work (this being its first recorded expression in Greek thought: cf. Helen North, *Sōphrosynē* [Ithaca, N.Y., 1966], 162–63, and W. Jaeger, *Paideia*, II [English translation, Oxford, 1947], 146).

[12] The "natural" and "fitting" order in which the part which is rational, "divine," and "superior by nature" rules the parts which are irrational, corporeal, and "inferior by nature": 444B1–5, 444D3–11; 590C3–D6 (with which cf. 577D3–5 and 589C5–D3) 591B1–7; cf. *Phaedo* 79E–80A and *Laws* 726–728B). Cf. M. B. Foster, "On Plato's Conception of Justice in the *Republic*," *Philos. Quart.* 1 (1950–51), 206–17; and Vlastos, "Slavery in Plato's Thought," *Philos. Rev.* 50 (1941), 289–304, at 294 ff.

[13] It goes over well enough into German as "*das Seinige tun*" (so in O. Apelt's translation [Leipzig, 1916]). So far as I know L. Versenyi (*Socratic Humanism* [New Haven , 1963], 94 ff.) is the only writer to

constant reminder that what we get in the original is an idiomatic, formulaic expression which is expected to suggest, rather than state in full, what is in Plato's mind.[14] If he wanted to be more explicit he would have filled out "its own" with *ergon* ("work" or "function"), a term introduced in Book I, and explained as follows: the *ergon* of anything (of a tool, like a pruning-knife, or of a bodily organ, like an eye or an ear) is that activity which can be "performed either exclusively by that thing or else more excellently (*kallista*) by it than by anything else" (353A)—i.e. the activity in which that thing gets its best chance to realize the excellence (*aretē*) proper to its own specific nature[15] and to contribute to the excellence of other things associated with it.[16] The things the definition has in view are the components of the soul disclosed in the tripartite analysis of the soul: *logistikon, thymos, epithymia*—the reasoning, spirited, and appetitive parts of the soul (cf. VI.2.i below). One is a *just* man, the definition tells us, if each of these three parts functions optimally, and there results that state of inner peace, amity, and concord which I have called "psychic harmony" (I above; cf. VI.2.ii below).

2. Two things about this definition are most perplexing:

(i) It presents no discernible link with ordinary usage. What people commonly understood by *dikaiosynē* we know from a wide variety of sources, including Aristotle's splendid analysis in the opening paragraphs of Book V of the *Nicomachean Ethics*. The word

---

conserve the unaugmented Greek phrase in English. The usual practice is to render it by "doing one's own business" (Shorey) or "minding one's own business" (Cornford, following A. D. Lindsay, *The Republic of Plato*, [London, 1935]). L. Robin, *Platon: Oeuvres Complètes*, Vol. I (Paris, 1950), translates it as *"faire la tâche qui est la nôtre."*

[14] The Greek phrase, *ta hautou prattein*, is elliptical, and could mean different things in different contexts. In *Chrm.* 161B it is cited as a definition of *sōphrosynē*, it is again associated with *sōphrosynē* in the *Timaeus* (72A). Only in the *Republic* is it cited as a definiens of *dikaiosynē*, and here only with grave qualifications (cf. III.1 below).

[15] Cf. H. S. Thayer, "Plato: The Theory and Language of Function," *Philos. Quart.* 14 (1964), 303–18, Section 1.

[16] It is a standing assumption in Plato that if *x* and *y* are associated, *y* is bound to benefit if *x* does its own *ergon* and realizes its own goodness: "To injure is not the *ergon* of the good, but of his opposite. . . . Then neither is to injure the *ergon* of the just man, but of his opposite . . ." (335D).

could carry a sense broad enough to cover all virtuous conduct towards others, though for the most part it was used in a more specific sense to mean refraining from *pleonexia*,[17] i.e. from gaining some advantage for oneself by grabbing what belongs to another—his property, his wife, his office, and the like—or by denying him what is (morally or legally) due him—fulfillment of promises made to him, repayment of monies owed to him, respect for his good name and reputation, and so forth. What holds these two senses together is that *dikaiosynē* is the pre-eminently *social* virtue:[18] it stands for right dealings between persons. And this is precisely what is missing in the Platonic definition, which purports to define a man's justice in terms of the order which prevails within his psyche.[19] This is odd, and altogether without parallel in the

[17] I despair of an adequate English translation. Its occurrence in 359C5 is rendered by "self-advantage" in Shorey, by "*la convoitise*" in Robin, by "*Habgier*" in Apelt; Cornford's "self-interest" is intolerably loose: only when self-interest is sought at the expense of others and in contravention of *isotēs* (equity, fairness) would the Greeks speak of *pleonexia*. W. D. Ross and M. Ostwald translate *pleonektēs* in *EN* V. 1 and 2 by "grasping," J. A. K. Thompson by "covetous." In Glaucon's great speech *pleonexia* is illustrated by the Gyges story and by "going to the market-place to take whatever he pleases, entering houses and sleeping with anyone he pleases, killing [any person] or freeing from bonds [any criminal] he pleases . . ." (360B–C). Aristotle explains it (*loc. cit.*) as immoral action from "gain"; though the gain of which he speaks is mainly pecuniary, it is clear from this and other contexts that any advantage gained at the expense of *isotēs* would count: *pleonexia* "is concerned with honour or money or safety, or that which includes all these, if we had a single name for it" (1120B2–3); he speaks of *pleonektein* "glory or good *simpliciter*" (1136B22) and even "gratitude or revenge" (1137A1): "greed" or "covetousness" would seem to fit best in most of these contexts, though neither of these would be exactly right.

[18] As Aristotle insists (*EN* 1129B26–1130B5) it is "virtue in relation to another" (*aretē pros heteron*). (But cf. n. 54 below.)

[19] Cf. E. Barker's complaint that Plato's "representation of justice in the individual (as a relation of the parts of the soul which issues in harmony . . .) . . . hardly accords with the *social* quality inherent in the term" (*Greek Political Theory*, 3rd Edition [London, 1947], 212, n. 1), and R. Demos: "What is odd about Plato's Platonic justice is its seemingly striking departure from ordinary usage. Customarily, justice indicates the relation of a given person to other persons; it is a virtue which operates in social contexts. But Platonic justice is a personal virtue, defined purely in terms of the agent" (396 in the paper cited in n. 1 above [p. 53, this volume]).

Platonic corpus. Though Plato sometimes redefines Greek words, his formulae manage to keep good contact with the usual meaning —contact enough to enable one to tell instantly from the formula what is the word it purports to define. Not so here. If a contemporary had been told that there is an enviable state of soul, characterized by proper functioning of every one of its parts, only by accident could he have guessed that this is supposed to be the moral attribute of *justice*.

(ii) Stranger still it is that Plato should want to offer such a definition in just this context. For what is his mouthpiece, Socrates, trying to accomplish? To convince Glaucon that "justice pays." And by "justice" Glaucon, like everyone else, understands observance of the constraints of morality and law in one's social conduct.[20] How could Socrates have expected to prove to Glaucon that it pays "to keep hands off from what belongs to others" (360B6) by proving to him that it pays to have a well-ordered, harmonious soul, choosing to call *this* "justice"? Unless we are to suppose that on this occasion Plato lapsed into flagrantly illogical and thoroughly uncharacteristic conduct, we must assume that he will be undertaking to *prove* that, appearances to the contrary notwithstanding, having that kind of soul is what "being a just man" means. I submit that Plato has an explicit argument to prove this.[21] But before proceeding to it we must consider his account of the "justice" of the polis.

III

1. Long before that definition of the "just" soul had been presented, another definition of "justice" had been stated which did not make the remotest allusion to the inner structure of the soul:

[20] If there were any doubt of this, another look at his speech would resolve it. Cf. the citation from 360B–C in n. 17 above.

[21] 441C ff., to be analyzed and criticized below (V. 2 and 3). It is almost incredible, but true, that those very commentators who saw quite clearly the discrepancy between Plato's redefinition of justice in psychological terms and the common signification of the word failed to take notice of the argument by which Plato undertakes to *demonstrate* his definition. Neither Barker nor Demos pays the slightest attention to what happens in 441C ff. From their comments one would get the impression that Plato just *assumed* that this is what a person's "justice" means.

What we laid down at the start as a general requirement when we were founding the polis,[22] this, or some form of it, is justice. We did lay down, and often stated, if you recall,[23] that every single person ought to engage in that social function [literally: that function which concerns the polis] for which his own nature is best fitted. —We did say this. —And indeed that to do one's own and not to be meddlesome is justice, this we have often heard from many others and have often said ourselves. —We have said it. —This then, my friend, if taken in a certain way, appears to be justice: to do one's own. (433A–B).

The defining formula is imprecise, and is meant to be: that is the force of the qualifying phrases, "this, or some form of it, is justice"; "this . . . if taken in a certain way, is justice."[24] Plato refers to the very start of the investigation of the nature of justice in Book II (368D ff.), where he had presented the division of labor and production for the market as the generative principle of a polis (369A ff.). He understands this principle to mean that a polis arises when, and only when, men come to direct their individual energies with a view to the needs of others no less than their own,[25] each of them

[22] Here and hereafter I shall use "polis" instead of "state" or "city" since neither answers precisely to the sense which *polis* carries in many of its uses. That the ideal polis which is described in the *Republic* is meant to have all the attributes of a state (including supreme control over the use of physical coercion in a given territorial area and maintenance of a legal order in that area) is clear. But though these are sufficient conditions for the existence of a polis they are apparently not necessary for Plato, else he would not have called the primitive community in 369 ff. which clearly antecedes the existence of a state (no provision for governmental functions) a "polis."

[23] The back reference is to such passages as 370A–C; 374A–D; 395B–C; 397E.

[24] It cannot be emphasized too strongly that if "doing one's own" meant only the "one man, one trade" principle, Plato would never have thought of using it as a definiens of "justice"; hence the qualification "this, or some form of it" at the start of the citation, warning the reader that the principle of functional specialization in the division of labor has to be further qualified before it can be taken in all seriousness as the essence of justice. When endorsed without this qualification (*Laws* 846D–847A) the principle is *not* taken as a defining formula of justice.

[25] The basis of the polis is human interdependence (369B5–C4); if each man were self-sufficient, each able to meet his individual needs by "himself doing his own for himself" (*auton di' hauton ta hautou prattein*), there would be no polis.

pursuing a line of work which will best mesh with that of others to their joint benefit. Plato then proceeds to generalize this principle, so that it will apply not only to economic activity but to all of the forms of associated living which go on within the polis.[26] And he gives it a normative twist, making of it an imperative addressed to every person in a polis: keep to that line of social conduct by which, given your natural endowments and acquired skills, you can contribute maximally to the happiness and excellence of your polis.[27] He seizes on the catch-phrase "to do one's own" as a convenient stand-in for this maxim.

2. Though not many of Plato's contemporaries would have agreed with this definition of *dikaiosynē*, I submit that none would have failed to see that it has good links with common usage, since on this definition, as on any other, justice would involve refraining from *pleonexia*. That Plato is counting on instant agreement on this point shows up best in the second of the three arguments by which Socrates seeks to persuade Glaucon that this is a good definition of "justice." Pointing to judicial justice as bearing out his definition, he asks:

> Will they [the guardians] not aim at this above all when judg-
> ing law-suits: that *no one shall have what belongs to others or be*
> *deprived of one's own?* —At nothing but this. —Because that is
> just? —Yes. —So in this way too it would have to be admitted

[26] The first generalization is at 374B ff.: the principle is invoked to justify a professional soldiery at this point; a sub-class of these "guardians" is then selected (412C ff.) for the still higher task of government. In a broader sense the principle is expected to hold even of the activities of children and slaves (433D).

[27] I get this by putting together the following: 374B9–C2 (we assigned to each person that one *ergon* for which "he is fitted by nature," done best only when practiced on a full-time basis); 412D9–E2 (for guardians select those who "will be most eager to do whatever they think is for the best interest of the polis"); 420D4–5 (as in a work of art, what we do for a part will depend on whether or not we can thereby maximize the excellence of the whole); 421B3–C6 (greatest possible happiness not for any one class, but for the whole polis; hence "the auxiliaries and the guardians are to be compelled and persuaded to do what will make them the most excellent craftsmen of their own *ergon*, and similarly all others"); 465E4–466A6 (back reference to 420B–421C, reaffirming its principle); 519E1–520A4 (another back reference to the same, adding that "the law" requires of the citizens "to contribute to one another that by which each is able to benefit the community . . .").

that the having and the doing (*hexis te kai praxis*) of what belongs to one and is one's own is justice? (433E6–434A1)

The phrase I have italicized strikes at the very core of *dikaiosynē* in
its most specific sense (cf. II.1 above).[28] For since *pleonexia* is
"having more," i.e. more than what is rightfully one's own ("what
belongs to one"), to "have what belongs to others" would be to
perpetrate *pleonexia*, and to "be deprived of one's own" would be to
suffer it.[29] In this argument Plato proceeds on the assumption that
having all, and only, what "belongs to one" is biconditionally re-

[28] Cf. the definition in Aristotle, *Rht.* 1366B9–11: "justice is the
virtue because of which all have their own (*ta hautōn . . . echousi*) and in
conformity with the law; injustice that by which they have what belongs to others (*ta allotria*) and contrary to the law." Aristotle adds the
reference to the law to make explicit the special ethico-juridical sense
(cf. n. 29 below) in which the expressions "one's own" and "another's"
are used in contexts in which they are associated with justice. Ulpian
adds "*jus*" to "*suum*" to make the same point in his famous definition,
"justice is the constant and unremitting will to render to everyone his
own right (*jus suum cuique tribuere*)." As the Aristotelian definition
shows, the scope of *ta hautou* and *ta allotria* in such contexts is broad
enough to cover everything to which persons would be morally or
legally entitled. Professor H. L. A. Hart ("Are There Natural Rights?",
Philos. Rev. 64, 1955, 175–91 at 176, n. 4) gives no evidence for his
opinion that these and the roughly equivalent expression "what is due
to one" (*ta opheilomena*, cf. the popular definition of justice ascribed to
Simonides in 331E, 335E) "are confined to property or debts": why
so, if a man could claim so much more as "his own" and his "due"?
[29] One could hardly overstress the normative load carried in the
above argument, as in the Aristotelian definition cited in the preceding
note and in innumerable other contexts in Greek prose, by expressions
like "one's own" (*ta hautou*) and "that of others" (*ta allotria*, which I
translated "what belongs to others" in its occurrence in 433E7 and in
the Aristotelian definition). Cf. also the use of the latter in 360B6,
apechesthai tōn allotriōn kai mē haptesthai (which I translated "to keep
hands off from what belongs to others" in II.2.ii above), and the import of the fact that *spheterizō* (literally, "to make mine what is theirs")
comes to mean commonly "to *mis*appropriate, to usurp." If one misses
this special accent that is put on the "one's own" in the "doing one's
own" and "having one's own" formulae in the above argument, it will
seem, as it does to Sir Karl Popper, "nothing but a crude juggle with
the meaning of the term 'one's own,'" and "about as sound as the
argument: 'It is just to keep and practice what is one's own. This plan
of stealing your money is my own. Thus it is just for me to keep my
plan, and to put it into practice, i.e. steal your money'" (*The Open
Society and Its Enemies*, Vol. 1 of 4th Edition [Princeton, 1963], 97).

lated to "doing one's own." If this is not obvious at first sight, let me rephrase the argument, abbreviating to make the essential point more perspicuous:

> That each shall have one's own is what judges should aim for.
> What judges should aim for is justice.
> *Therefore,* that each shall have one's own and that each shall do one's own is justice.

The premise speaks only of each "having one's own" and says nothing of each "doing one's own." How then did the latter get into the conclusion? And get there it must, since the whole point of this argument is to defend that phrase as a definiens of "justice." So unless we are to suppose that Plato's powers of reasoning have failed completely at this juncture, we must assume that the above argument is elliptical, carrying a suppressed premise:

Each shall have one's own iff each does his own. . . . (S) Intercalating the missing steps—(S), and a further, obviously implied step, (T), below—to get the complete argument, this is what Plato is maintaining:

> That each shall have one's own is what judges should aim for.
> What judges should aim for is justice.
> [*Therefore,* that each shall have one's own is justice. . . . (T)
> But each shall have one's own iff each does one's own. . . . (S)]
> *Therefore,* that each shall have one's own and that each shall do one's own is justice.

That Plato should thus rely on (S) as an unstated premise in this argument shows how confident he feels that the link between "doing one's own" and the common conception of justice would be fully apparent to his readers: he is counting on them to understand his definition to imply that in any community in which everyone lived up to the maxim "do your own" there would be no *pleonexia.*

3. But what is rightfully "mine" and "another's"? For the answer the ordinary Greek (i.e. any contemporary Greek who did not have a special *theory* of justice) would refer to (i) the standard precepts of morality—do not steal or betray your comrades or forswear your oaths or default on agreements; care for your parents, honor the

gods, and the like (cf. 442E–443A)—and (ii) the laws of the state.[30] For Plato (ii) would be no final point of reference: law counts for nothing in the *Republic* unless it is just. As for (i), the trouble with all these precepts is that they are full of gaps.[31] Plato's definiens for "justice" would fill these gaps. Thus consider how he tackles the question of whether or not the rulers of his state should have private property. Common morality supplies no answer. It does say depriving unlawfully another of his property ("stealing") is unjust. Who, if anyone, should own property it does not say. Plato here applies his own criterion of "doing one's own": his guardians would be "more excellent craftsmen of their own work" (421C1–2) without, than with, private property. This settles the matter: real estate and chattels are not to be "theirs."[32] In the last analysis all questions of what does, or does not, "belong to one" would be adjudicated in this manner.

4. Two more things which call for special mention:

(i) The "doing" in the "doing one's own" formula involves not only on-the-job conduct, but the whole of one's life, *including one's private life*. Platonic morality leaves no room for a conception of private life in which one has the right to do what one pleases without thought to social service. For Plato all conduct is subject to

[30] For (ii) cf. the Aristotelian definition of *dikaiosynē* in n. 28 above.

[31] A point made with great emphasis in the argument with Polemarchus in Book I, 331C, and alluded to again in Book V, 479D ("the many conventional notions [*nomima*] of the many concerning the beautiful and the rest [i.e. the just, the pious, 479A]" are said to "tumble about between being [*sc.* just, pious] and not being [*sc.* just, pious]," presumably because there are so many cases in which a thing reckoned "just" or "pious" by one of the traditional precepts will have to be reckoned "unjust" or "impious" by another).

[32] There is no explicit appeal to the definition of "justice" at this point (as indeed there could not, since the definition is still to come). But see how the justification of another practice which would entail a sacrifice of the happiness for the philosophers as a class is handled in 519D–520A: "we shall be doing no injustice to the philosophers who arise among us, when we compel them to concern themselves with the other citizens and to guard them [i.e. to take part in the day-to-day administration of the state]"; it is just, because required by the duty of maximizing one's service to the polis inherent in the "doing one's own" principle.

regulation by the rulers of the state,[33] whose task it is to embody the vision of the Good "into the dispositions of men, *both private* and public" (500D). By the same token, everyone, philosopher, soldier, or tradesman, must consider in each of his actions: will this make of me a better craftsman at my work? (More on this in IV.2 below.)

(ii) The definition is meant to absorb, not invalidate, common morality. When the ordinary duties prescribed by the latter are condescendingly called *phortika* ("common" or "vulgar"),[34] this is done only with an eye to more onerous obligations,[35] more flexible in form only because they are so much more stringent in their substance. Thus Plato's philosopher-rulers must avoid "the lie in the soul" (382A–C; 485C). This is a more exacting demand than just to refrain from telling lies and will require them to tell some lies (414B ff.) in the course of "doing their own."

[33] In this respect Plato's point of view would be much closer to that of the average Greek of his time than to ours. Though the distinction between the private and the public *within* the conduct regulated by law was all too familiar to the Greeks (see e.g., J. Walter Jones, *The Law and Legal Theory of the Greeks* [Oxford, 1956], 116 ff.), the recognition of an area of private life which ought to be exempt from regulation by law is a late and precarious achievement, and it is hard to find a clear-cut affirmation of it in Greek literature in the classical period: the closest approximation to it known to me is in Thucydides, whose Pericles celebrates the ethos of civilized tolerance for what individuals choose to do for pleasure (2.37.2) and whose Nicias reads into the claim that Athens was "the freest fatherland in the world" the notion that there "everyone was free to live his daily life without orders from anyone" (7.69.2). How little the Athenian conservatives would have been willing to stomach that freedom of private tastes and pursuits for which J. S. Mill pleads in his *Essay on Liberty* is clear from the pleas of people like Isocrates for the restoration of the (real or fancied) ancient powers of the Areopagus to exercise censorious supervision over the private morals of the citizens (see e.g., *Areop.* 37–49).

[34] 442E–443A. The things itemized here would be included among the *kala nomima*, 589C7 (clearly equivalent to the *dikaia*, 589B8), whose purpose is said to be to subjugate the "beastly" to the "divine" parts of man's nature, i.e. to serve the very highest ends of Platonic justice: cf. n. 12 above.

[35] Cf. 538C–D: men "with even a particle of decency" (Cornford for *mēth' hotioun metrious*) would resist the flattering solicitations of pleasure which tempt them to act contrary to those "convictions about what is just and honourable in which we have been nurtured from our childhood years." Much more could be expected from men conforming to the highest standards of justice.

IV

1. The two definitions of "justice" in Book IV I shall call respectively the "psychological" (section II above) and the "social" (III above) definitions. They occur in separate passages: the psychological one in 441C–443B, where the virtues of the individual are defined, the social one in the preceding (427E–434C) discussion of the virtues of the polis. At the end of that discussion it had been made clear that "doing one's own" was not meant to constitute a definition of the justice of an individual person:[36] Socrates tells Glaucon (434D–E) they must now look beyond the polis to the individual and find out if "there too" (i.e. in the case of the individual as well as in the case of the polis) the same "character" (i.e. the disposition to do one's own) is justice. He would not have said this if he had understood "doing one's own" as a definiens of the justice of the individual.

However, though this formula is not meant to serve as a *definition* of the justice of the individual, it is still meant to be a true *description* of it: it is not hard to show that for Plato every just man must have the disposition named by the "doing one's own" formula. For he declares that "the same [moral] characters and dispositions (*eidē te kai ēthē*) which exist in the polis exist in each one of us: they could not, surely, have come to it from any other source" (435E; cf. 544D–E). So he holds as a fundamental principle (one which "it is most necessary to admit," *loc. cit.*) that

P(I) *A moral attribute is predicable of a given polis only when, and exactly because,[37] it is predicable of the persons who compose that polis.*

[36] As I had erroneously maintained in the first of the two papers cited in n. 1 above, against strong objections from A. Robison and R. Kraut and subsequently from Professors Cooper and Woozley as well as others at the A.P.A. meeting; their criticisms helped me to see that I had been misled by the deceptively elliptical form in which the definition is stated in 433A–B. On the face of it, the definiendum is "justice" and the definiens "doing one's own." In fact, the definiendum is "(the) justice (of a polis)" and the definiens "(the) doing of their own (by individuals and classes in a polis)" (only individuals in 433A–D, only classes in 434C and 435B; but see n. 38 below).

[37] To say no more than "only when" would not do justice to Plato's insistence that a given character "comes to" (*aphiktai*) and "arises in" (*engegonenai*) the polis "from the individuals" (*ek tōn idiotōn*) (*loc. cit.*). It is the fact that the (appropriate set of) individuals who make up a polis are *F* that makes the polis *F*, not the other way round.

It follows directly from P(I) that if a polis is just, it is such only in so far as its people are just persons: only *their* justice could make it just. And it follows tautologously from the social definition of justice that what makes the polis just is the disposition of these same persons "to do their own."[38] Thus from the social definition and Plato's adherence to P(I) we get unavoidably a specification of the justice of the individual persons who compose a polis: each of them is just iff each "does his own."[39]

2. How much of a person's conduct would this specification cover? Clearly, all of it which affects the justice of the polis, hence, to begin with, everything persons are called upon to do in the line of public duty. Since their vocational activities *are* construed as public duties in this ultraprofessional society, all on-the-job conduct would obviously count. What then of their private life? Would this be exempt? I have already implied (III.4.i) that it would not: for Plato vocational excellence is unthinkable without personal virtue. Thus his rulers, who "are to be consummate craftsmen of the liberty of the polis, must practice nothing which does not conduce to this."[40] To attain perfection in their work they must have morally exemplary dispositions. Their manifold technical qualifications—that they are to be clever legislators, shrewd economic planners, efficient bureaucrats, expert eugenic breeders—are taken for granted. All of the emphasis falls on their philosophic wisdom, on the one hand, and on their virtue, on the other. The latter is under constant surveillance: up to the age of fifty they are being

---

[38] The declaration in 434C7–10 and 435B4–7 (still operative in 441D8–10) that it is the "doing one's own" by each of the three classes that constitutes the justice of each class and makes the polis just is no objection. By P(I), as by ordinary common sense, the "doing one's own" disposition and the character "justice" could be ascribed to social classes only if, and because, they were ascribable to their members in the first place.

[39] To my knowledge, this simple deduction has never been drawn in the scholarly literature. Had it been drawn, it would surely have been noticed that this description of the individual's justice, so patently different from that provided by the psychological definition, is in urgent need of being tied by logical argument to the latter; then the significance of the argument in 441C ff. (V.2 below), as providing just this tie, could hardly have been missed.

[40] Whence it is inferred that, from childhood up, they must never "imitate" characters of low moral quality in dramatic productions, 395B–C.

"tested to see if they will stand firm against all seductions" (540A): moral perfection is built directly into their job. And there are further indications in the text that the justice specified in the "do your own" formula extends over the whole of a person's conduct, public and private, in the polis:

(i) The formula is applied even to slaves,[41] who, not being citizens, could hardly be thought of as having civic duties; also to children, who as yet have no civic duties (433D2–3).

(ii) Things people do in private contexts—the play of children, the respect shown the old by the young, the clothes and shoes people wear, even haircuts—have the gravest consequences for the whole of society (424A ff.); thus if children play "lawless" games, the "laws and the constitution" will be eventually overturned (424D–E).

(iii) If the scope of the "doing one's own" formula were not broad enough to cover refraining from all kinds of *pleonexia*, public or private, the biconditional "each shall have his own iff each does his own"[42] would fail. So I can see no escape from the conclusion that everything in one's social conduct within the polis—all of one's dealings with other persons in the context of the only form of social life considered in the *Republic*—would come directly or indirectly within the scope of justice as specified by the "doing one's own" formula.

3. Why is it then that Plato does not accept the formula as an alternative definition of the justice of the individual, co-ordinate with, and complementary to, the psychological definition? The answer can only be guessed at. I, for one, would find the clue in the terms in which Plato contrasts the "doing of one's own" by a person with the "doing of their own" by the parts of his soul in 443C: he calls the first "a kind of image" of justice, and goes on to add:

> The truth of the matter was, it seems, that justice was that sort of thing (*toiouton ti*), but not in regard to one's external action,[43]

---

[41] Some scholars have sought to explain away this reference, suggesting that at this point Plato may be no longer thinking of the ideal state but of the contemporary world. I have argued against this suggestion in "Does Slavery Exist in Plato's *Republic?*" (*Class. Philology* 63 [1968], 291–95, at 294–95). However, the force of the above remark would not be blunted even if that suggestion were correct.

[42] Proposition (S) in III.2 above.

[43] *peri tēn exō praxin tōn hautou.*

but in regard to the internal action which concerns truly one's own self and what is one's very own.

What a man does is for Plato only an "image" of what he is; his "external" conduct is only a manifestation of his "inner" life, which is the life of the "real" man, the soul.[44] Hence when he asks himself in what it is that a man's justice "truly" consists he feels constrained to look to what goes on inside a man, in a man's soul; and since he thinks of a definition of F as a statement of what F "really is," he could only count the psychological formula as the true definition of an individual's justice.

V

1. However, after fully conceding this privileged status of the psychological formula for the definition of the individual's justice, we are left with the undeniable fact that each of Plato's definitions of "justice" lays down conditions which every person in a polis will meet iff he is just. From the social definition we learn what a just person's "external" activity will be like: he will obey the "do your own" maxim in his dealings with others in the polis. From the psychological definition we learn what a just person's "inner" life will be like: each of the elements of his soul will be "doing its own" and psychic harmony will result. These two specifications are entirely distinct—so much so that if both were correct and we[45] knew only the former, we would be able to determine that a man satisfies it without our knowing, or even suspecting, that he satisfies the latter also, and vice versa. How then do we know that the two must always be satisfied together? This is what Plato has to show us, else the whole of Socrates' argument against Glaucon would come to naught (cf. 11.2.ii above): to show Glaucon that it pays to have the "justice" of a harmonious psyche would do nothing to show him that "justice pays" unless it were proved that whoever has this "inner" disposition *will* have too the "outer" disposition

---

[44] In Plato's metaphysics this is the "really real" man (*ton onta hēmōn hekaston ontōs*); the body is only a "similitude" or "image" of the soul (*Laws* 959B).

[45] I.e. those of us who are not Platonists. On Plato's assumptions to know either specification one would have to know the Form of justice, and this would disclose both specifications.

to deal justly with his fellows. Plato is not blind to this. The demonstrand of his argument in 441 C–E reads:

> ... in the case of each one of us, whosoever is such that the three kinds [of elements] in him does its own, he is a just man *and a man who does his own.* (441 D–E)[46]

I have italicized the terminal phrase: this is what makes it clear that the new definition which is advanced here is meant to connect with the earlier definition of "justice" in 433A ff., and so connect with it that anyone who instantiates the new one *will* meet the specification of the individual's justice which is implied by the social definition. This is what Plato thinks his argument in 441 C–E has established. Has it? Let us run through it.[47]

2. First the isomorphic structure of state and soul, a carry-over from the preceding discussion, is acknowledged:

> (A) We have agreed with good reason that the same three kinds [of elements] exist in the polis, on the one hand, in the soul of each of us, on the other. (441 C5–7)

Socrates then asks,

> (B) Must it not follow at once that the individual will be wise in the way (*hōs*) and through that element (*hōi*) by which the polis is wise? (C9–10)

From what is this supposed to follow? From a premise laid down back in 435A5–7: "If two things, one greater, the other smaller, are called the same, will they be similar or dissimilar in the respect

[46] Cited, without the terminal phrase, in II.1 above. Cited in full as (G) below.

[47] The account of the argument in 441C ff. I give in the following paragraph is meant to supersede completely the one in the earlier of the papers cited in n. 1 above, 668–69). This employed unforgivably strong-armed methods in restructuring Plato's argument and moreover failed to take explicit account of the role of the premise laid down earlier (435A5–7), on which, as I have since come to see, the reasoning directly depends, as was emphasized by Professor Cooper in his contribution to the symposium.

in which they are called the same?" This is a fundamental Platonic principle.[48] Let me restate it a little more formally:

P(II)   *If the same predicate is predicable of any two things, then, however they may differ in other ways, they must be exactly alike[49] in the respect in which it is predicable of each.*

Given P(II) and (A), (B) would indeed follow: If "wise" is predicated of a polis[50] in virtue of the fact that one of its elements has a certain character, then it must be predicated of a person in virtue of the fact that an analogous element in him has the *identical* character: were this not so, polis and person would not be "exactly alike" in the respect in which "wise" is predicable of each. Socrates proceeds:

(C)   And must it not also follow that after the same manner in which the individual was brave, and in virtue of that [element], after that manner and in virtue of that [element], the polis will be brave . . . ? (D1–2)

Here from the same premises the same inference (*mutatis mutandis*)[51] is drawn for "brave" as for "wise" at (B). Thereupon Socrates generalizes:[52]

[48] Taken over uncritically from Socrates, whose search for definitions is guided by the explicit assumption that all of the things correctly called "*F*" have an identical character, *F*, and that each of them is so called only because each has this self-identical character: *Euthyphro* 5D1–5, 6D9–E6; *Meno* 72A ff.

[49] That "exactly alike" is what Plato does mean is clear from the inference he draws from the cited statement: "Hence the just man *will not differ in any way* (*ouden dioisei*) from the just polis in respect of the very character of justice, but will be like it" (435B1–2). Cf. Socrates' insistence that any two things which are called "*F*" "will not differ" in respect of being *F*: *Meno* 72B5, C2–3; E6–73A3.

[50] I am putting (B) into the formal mode to bring it into line with P(II); the difference between the formal and the material mode is systematically ignored in Plato and would, in any case, make no difference to the reasoning in this argument.

[51] Except for the fact that while in (B) the reasoning moved from polis to person, in (C) it reverses, moving from person to polis; but this difference is irrelevant to the reasoning, for the similarity relation is symmetrical.

[52] That Socrates should not deal with the case of temperance, after that of wisdom and courage, before drawing the generalization may cause surprise. But this is easily explicable from expository considera-

(D) . . . and must it not follow that polis and person will possess in the same way anything which pertains to virtue [i.e. any moral quality whatsoever]? (D2–3)[52a]

He applies this at once to the case of justice:

(E) And we shall say, O Glaucon, that a man is just in the same way[53] in which the polis is just. (D5–6)

Confident that all has gone well so far, Socrates proceeds to get the conclusion he wants in two more steps:

(F) And surely we have not forgotten that it [the polis] was just in virtue of each of the three kinds [of elements] in it doing its own? (D8–10)

(G) Therefore, let us bear in mind that also in the case of each one of us, whosoever is such that each of the three kinds

---

tions: in the present argument Socrates draws out the implications of P(II) for wisdom and courage, without taking the time to state the definiens of either and to identify the elements in polis and person that have each of these virtues. These omissions are repaired in the sequel (441E–442D), which parallels the present argument, adding information omitted in this one. In that sequel the case of temperance is treated as fully as that of wisdom and courage. Moreover, the essential identity of temperance in polis and person had been anticipated (430D–432A) in the earlier section on the virtues of the state, where the nature of temperance had been explained at considerable length. To have reaffirmed that identity in 441C–E would have involved more repetition than Plato cares to allow himself in an argument whose premises are kept as trim as possible so that the weight of the composition may fall on its concluding portion, (E), (F), and (G) below.

[52a] This is a proposition of such extreme plausibility that even Aristotle subscribes to it, asserting it as a self-evident truth: "the courage, justice, and wisdom of a polis have the same meaning and form as those [virtues] by whose possession each individual man is called 'just' and 'wise' and 'temperate'" (*Pol.* 1323B33–36). This is in Book VII of the *Politics*, one of his earlier political writings, possibly composed before he had developed his doctrine of "focal meaning" (cf. n. 59 below). But there is no indication that Aristotle ever rejected or modified the proposition he asserts here in the light of his new semantic doctrine.

[53] *Tōi autōi tropōi.* For the use of the same locution to express the same thought—that when "*F*" is correctly predicated of *a* and *b*, *a* is *F* "in the same way" as *b*, i.e. has the identical character—see *Meno* 73C1–2: "Hence all men are good in the same way. . . ."

[of elements] in him does its own, he is a just man and
a man who does his own. (D12–E2)

3. The simplest way to diagnose the error in this argument is to call
attention to an equivocation whose precise role in it does not seem
to have ever been spotted in the literature: In its primary signification "just" is a relational predicate; to speak of a person as having
this property is to think of the way in which he habitually relates
himself to persons[54] or groups in his conduct. This is all too plainly
true on the popular notion of justice (II.2.i above), both in its
generalized sense of "virtuous conduct towards another" and the
narrower one of refraining from *pleonexia*. It would be no less true
on the conception of the individual's justice which is implied by
Plato's social definition: "to do one's own" is an obligation one has
to one's polis and *to* the other persons with whom one has to deal.
But it so happens that among the derivative uses of "just" there is
one in which it functions as a one-place group-predicate, predicable of groups as such, on condition that their members, or sub-
groups composed of their members, are just in the primary sense,
i.e. behave justly to one another. Using "just$_1$" for the primary,
"just$_2$" for this secondary sense, let us apply the distinction to
Plato's argument, starting with (E), where "just" makes its appearance: ". . . a man is just in the same way in which the polis is
just." In its first occurrence, we would expect "just" to carry its
natural sense when applied to an individual. So it would have to
mean "just$_1$" here, unless some warning to the contrary had been
given, as none is. What of its second occurrence? Here "just$_2$"
would be the natural sense, since it is applied to a polis; and this is
quite clearly the sense Plato had in mind when defining the justice
of the polis in 433A ff., since he explained it by the "doing of one's
own" in the mutual relations of the persons who compose it
(433D1–5) or of its classes (434C7–10), *not* by "the doing of *its*
own" in its relations to other poleis.[55] Hence in its second occur-

[54] Not necessarily to persons other than himself: the relation may be
reflexive. Aristotle's formula for justice in its most general sense,
"virtue towards another," misses this point, but only because of the
(purely technical) failure to notice that a relation need not be alio-
relative.

[55] The use of the "doing one's own" formula to elucidate the notion
of a polis which is just in its external relations would have been only an
embarrassment to Plato: the central notion in this formula—making

rence "just" must indeed mean "just$_2$". Let us rewrite (E) with this notation to resolve the ambiguity:

And we shall say, O Glaucon, that a man is just$_1$ in the same way in which the polis is just$_2$.

And when we do this it becomes evident that (E) is quite false: person and polis are not just "in the same way," but in the very different ways represented by just$_1$ and just$_2$.[56] And with (E) false, the deduction of (G)[57] is worthless: the demonstration has collapsed.

VI

If my diagnosis of Plato's error in the argument in 441C–E is correct, his mistake is neither inexplicable nor irreparable:

1. Not inexplicable.

He is misled by two things: *first*, by his P(II). Like Socrates, he takes this for an axiomatic truth. Seeing that this holds in the standard cases—if we are to call two specimens "bees" (Socrates' example in the *Meno*)[58] they must indeed be "exactly alike" in respect of being bees, though they may differ in a hundred other

---

the best contribution one's nature allows one to make to and in one's community (III.1 above)—is inapplicable to a state in its foreign relations; the notion of a community of poleis is not mooted in the *Republic*.

[56] If anyone is made uncomfortable by the fact that "in the same way" could mean any number of different things in this context, he might be reminded that as Plato uses that slippery expression, to find a man who is "exactly like" a just$_2$ polis we would have to find a just$_2$ man, i.e. one whose psychic components "do their own" inside him as the social components of the state "do their own" inside it; a just$_1$ man would be "exactly like" (in the relevant respect) a just$_1$, not a just$_2$, polis.

[57] Where the equivocation which vitiates (E) recurs to mislead Plato in another way: having failed to sort out the difference between "just$_1$" and "just$_2$", he fails to realize that the definiens laid out here could *only* be the definiens of "just$_2$" and cannot be assumed to be also the definiens of "just$_1$", as it would have to be if the addendum, "and a man who does his own," were to be warranted by the reasoning.

[58] 72B–C: the example which he thinks shows that any two persons are exactly alike in respect of being virtuous.

ways—he infers that it is true in all cases, making no provision for those in which the predicate applies to some things in a primary sense, and to others in derivative senses, materially different from the primary one, though formally so related to it as to be definable in terms of it. Had Plato seen (to turn now to an example in Aristotle)[59] how absurd it would be to expect that a man, a complexion, a habitat, and a diet must be "exactly alike" in the respect in which the predicate "healthy" applies to each,[60] he could scarcely have failed to see how little his P(II) would cover the case of a predicate like "just." *Secondly,* he is misled by the false analogy on which he relies in generalizing from the cases of "wise" in (B) and "brave" in (C) to *all* moral predicates in (D), including "just." Not that (C) is true without qualification even in the case of the former: "wise" and "brave" hardly apply to polis and person in the same way in all respects. However, each does apply to both alike in the way which is vital for Plato's argument: when predicated of persons or of poleis, they function as *one-place predicates* in both cases. And this is precisely what is false in the case of "just," which, as we have seen, is a one-place predicate only in its secondary sense, while in its primary sense it must be a relational predicate, since justice is the social virtue par excellence. Plato has often been criticized for his use of the polis-soul analogy. I trust it will now be clear that this is not, of itself, the source of his error. The

---

[59] *Metaph.* 1002A34–B1 and 1060B36–1061A7; *Top.* 106B33–37. The linguistic phenomenon Aristotle illustrates by "healthy" and by "medical" in these contexts is not precisely the same as that exemplified in the difference between "just$_1$" and "just$_2$": the derivative senses of "healthy" and "medical" to which he refers do not differ from the primary one as would a one-place term predicable of groups from a two-place term predicable of individuals (this specific difference is not noticed by Aristotle, to my knowledge). But the two phenomena are so closely related—in both cases we have a logically primary sense, and one or more derivative senses definable in terms of the primary one —that if Plato had anticipated Aristotle's investigations of "focal meaning" (G. E. L. Owen's felicitous rubric for what Aristotle calls *pros hen kai mian tina physin legomena:* "Logic and Metaphysics in Some Earlier Works of Aristotle," in *Aristotle and Plato in the Mid-Fourth Century,* ed. by I. Düring and G. E. L. Owen [Göteborg, 1960], 163–90, at 169), he would have seen that his P(II) cries out for qualification and then he could scarcely have made the error in (E).

[60] If they were "exactly alike" a healthy complexion would have, like a healthy man, a well-functioning heart and liver, and so would a healthy climate and healthy food.

analogy is, of course, loose; but it is not the less illuminating on that account. By representing that deceptively simple thing, the soul, as the analogue of the polis, the simile makes us see the soul as the complex of forces which it is—forces which may war among themselves in ways as destructive of its own well-being as was the class-war of that of the city-state. That a man, no less than a polis, can, and should be, just$_2$ is a memorable insight, which need not have caused logical error, and would not, if the difference between this new sense in which a man might be called "just" and the usual one had been kept straight.[61]

2. And the mistake is *not irreparable.*

Plato has all the materials required to construct an alternative argument to do the job which his present one failed to do: to prove that *a man is just$_2$ iff he is just$_1$.* This thesis has the full support of (a) his moral epistemology and (b) his moral psychology: to reject it one would have to fault basic Platonic doctrines in the area of (a) or of (b) or of both. I submit that this is how Plato would have argued had he realized the utter inadequacy of the argument in V.2 above. Part (a) of this argument would seek to convince us that if reason is "doing its own" it will be making correct moral judgments. This I shall not try to report. Part (b) would proceed as follows:

(i) The ultimate sources of wrong-doing—of injustice—are sensuality, cupidity, and vanity, the first two being by far the most prolific: they make up that monstrous beast of physical appetite[62] which is ever ready to grow new heads in every direction, absorbing a commensurate quantum of psychic energy with each new head it

---

[61] One could still object to the form in which Plato casts the new insight, taking upon himself to say that the word "just" should now be used in a drastically different way (we are to "deem and name 'just' that action which preserves and promotes this disposition," *sc.* the psychic harmony which results when all three components of the soul are "doing their own work," 443E6–7). Such linguistic innovations are dubious business, and I have no wish to defend Plato on this score. But I would still insist that even so no logical error would have been incurred if the linguistic legislation had been grounded on a clear understanding of the just$_1$-just$_2$ distinction.

[62] "Physical" (which I add here for emphasis only) should always be understood as preceding "appetite" when used to name the "third" part of the soul (rather than as a general term for "desire": cf. 580D–E).

is allowed to grow.[63] The practical reason would be impotent to induce us to act justly at any given moment if all it did was to declare what justice requires of us. Long before that moment it must have shaped the development of the beast and also that of the leonine *thymos*, with its insatiable hunger for prestige; it must have prevented from starting, or decapitated at their start, all appetites but a handful of "necessary" ones; and it must have so tamed the *thymos* as to make of it a faithful ally against the beast.

(ii) Where there is justice$_2$, and therewith psychic harmony, control over the lion and the beast (or what is left of it) has been secured at so deep a level that reason's dominance no longer calls for the exercise of repressive force. All three are reconciled to their respective roles and so to one another. The subordinates concur willingly, even affectionately, in reason's hegemony;[64] they are slaves so attached to their master that they feel servitude as friendship.[65] In such a state of soul how could reason's orders fail to be carried out? And since reason orders only what is just, how could a soul so integrated within itself engage in unjust conduct?

(iii) Suppose, conversely, that one's state of soul has been that of injustice$_2$. If one's reason has not been doing its job, concupiscence would have waxed unchecked and would now be making its huge, insistent demands, and the lion too would be roaring after prey of its own, each of them asking for more than one could procure for them by just means; what could there be then to stop one from resorting to unjust ones? Nothing, ever, in the case of the "tyrannical" man, with blood-curdling consequences. The not-quite-so-bad, "democratic" man achieves a *modus vivendi* among his motley appetites, good and bad, so that all get their turn; when the bad ones are on top moral scruples would be of no avail.[66] As for the "oligarchic" man, all that restrains him from injustice is his obsessive greed; so he is just when justice is good business, but when he

[63] For this and what follows see especially 588B ff.

[64] Note the emphases on *philia* within the psychic elements (442C10; 589B), and of the man becoming "*philos* to himself" (443D5); also the singling out of the repressive control of desire (554D1) as a sign of inner division and conflict.

[65] Take 444B1–5 with 590C8–D6.

[66] This is not said in 559D ff., but it is implied by the general theory taken in conjunction with the fact that the "democratic" ɪnan must be more unjust than the "oligarchic" one, being further down the slope of moral decline.

can grab with impunity (e.g., from orphans), he grabs. None of these men, nor any others who lack psychic harmony, could have that active disposition to abstain scrupulously from *pleonexia* which is entailed by justice₁ (III.1 and 2 above).[67]

VII

In a most valuable paper[68] Professor David Sachs has pressed two questions: Has Plato shown (a) that anyone whose justice meets Platonic standards will also meet the common ones? Has he shown (b) that if the latter standards are met, so will the former be? Sachs has argued that Plato merely assumes (a), failing to argue for it; and that he does not even assume (b). The foregoing analysis prompts different replies to Sachs's questions: if by the "Platonically just" man we are to mean with Sachs the man who satisfies the psychological definition (cf. IV.1 above), then Plato *has* argued for (a). He has an explicit argument (V.2 above), and also an implicit one (VI.2 above), to prove that one who satisfies the psychological definition will satisfy the social specification of individual justice too, i.e. that he will be a man who "does his own," and hence (III.2 above) will so govern his conduct that those whom it affects will "have their own," which will certainly involve compliance with the precepts of common morality (cf. III.4.ii above) so far as they give unambiguous determinations (cf. III.3.i. above) and are not over-ridden by the sovereign "do your own" impera-

---

[67] The above argument for the thesis that a man is just₂ iff he is just₁ may be summarized as a *reductio ad absurdum* of the denial of this thesis:

(i) Assume that someone is just₂, but not just₁. If he is not just₁, then he either (a) is or (b) is not cognizant of what he ought to be doing in order to be just₁. If (b), his reason is not doing its job, contrary to the assumption that he is just₂ (which entails that all three parts of his soul are "doing their own"). If (a), the dictates of his reason are failing of execution because of insubordination in the lower parts, hence they are not "doing their own," contrary to the assumption.

(ii) Assume that someone is just₁, but not just₂. If not just₂, one or more parts of his soul are failing to do their job: if the failure is in reason, he will not be making correct moral judgments, and hence he cannot be just₁, contrary to the assumption; if the failure is in one or both of the lower parts, their insubordination will frustrate the execution of the judgments of his reason, and he will not be just₁, contrary to the assumption.

[68] "A Fallacy in Plato's *Republic*," *Philos. Review* 72 (1963), 141–58 (reprinted above).

tive. In the case of (b) everything turns on what we are to mean by
the correlative to "Platonically just"—"commonly just," I shall
call it. Who is to count as the "commonly just" man? Not, surely,
the sort of man who follows common justice only when material
advantage so requires (like the "oligarchic" man above). Such
equivocal virtue Plato denounces in the *Phaedo* (68E–69C) as a
"delusive facade" (*skiagraphia*), a "slavish" thing, "with no health
or truth in it" (69B7–8); he who has it masters appetite only so far
as appetite masters him.[69] Since the last thing in the world Plato
would want to prove is that such pseudo-virtue brings happiness, it
is no blemish in his argument that he should not make the gro-
tesque assumption that the man who is commonly just in *this*
sense is Platonically just. So by the "commonly just man" we
could only mean one whose devotion to the precepts of common
morality is so sincere and deep that he would stand by them under
severe temptation, when fancy prizes can be had by dexterous
grabbing. To qualify for this sort of common justice, Plato would
argue, you must have psychic harmony, for if you don't, how
could you be counted on for more than fair-weather virtue? How
could anyone with Gyges' ring act differently from Gyges if the
condition of his soul is the usual mess?

VIII

1. It might be objected that Plato could not have used the argument I have laid out for him in VI.2 above, for it would expose him
to an awkward question: justice is mandatory for *everyone;* how
then could it be conditioned on so rare and difficult[70] an attainment
as psychic harmony? I agree that the question is pertinent and that
its implications are disturbing. I deny that Plato would have
thought them so. He would, if he had believed that only philosophers could achieve psychic harmony. For in that case, on the
argument I have given him, the lower classes in his utopia could
not have been just men, with fatal consequences for the justice of
his ideally just state. But it is false that Plato thought psychic

---

[69] This is a variant of a phrase used about *sōphrosynē* in 69A2; but
sōphrosynē and justice are often used quasi-synonymously by Plato: see
C. W. R. Larson, "The Platonic Synonyms, *dikaiosynē* and *sōphrosynē*,"
American Journal of Philology 72 (1951), 395–414—an excellent study, in
spite of the over-statement in its thesis.

[70] If one balks at "rare and difficult" one might re-read 443D–E.

harmony was only for philosophers.[71] To be sure, only they could have that vision of the Ideas whose moral effect was so energizing.[72] But the special love for justice, temperance, etc., kindled in the philosopher by his unique intellectual experience, is anticipated at the level of sense, emotion, imagination, and right belief by the effect of a massive psychological conditioning which begins in earliest infancy. That this is directed at all the citizens, not only at the philosophers-to-be, is certain: it is explicitly designed to inculcate *sōphrosynē*,[73] a virtue required of all three classes.[74] So all are subjected to what Plato calls "musical" *paideia:*[75] a process which not only employs music itself and the other arts, but manipulates everything in the social environment (down to games and haircuts) to stock the growing mind with the right beliefs and, what is more, the right emotive charges,[76] so that what he calls "just" he will feel

[71] For reason to "do its own work" it does not, of course, need to be *philosophical* reason. The special term Plato uses in the tripartite analysis (and only there) as a name for the intellectual part of the soul, *to logistikon* ("calculative"), should of itself make it clear that he is not making the absurd assumption that only theoretical, reflective intelligence (*dianoia, nous*) is involved. One does not need to be a philosopher to run through practical syllogisms whose major premises are true beliefs. True belief is quite sufficient for virtue in the *Republic:* cf. the definition of courage here (429B–430B) in terms of *doxa*, with the one in the Socratic dialogues in terms of *epistēmē* (*Laches* 194E–195), *sophia* (*Prt.* 360D). Cf. R . G. Hoerber, "More on Justice in the *Republic*," *Phronesis* 5 (1960), 32–34, at 33; R. W. Hall, "Plato's Just Man," *New Scholasticism* 43 (1968), 202–25, at 217 ff. And cf. n. 76 and 77 below.

[72] Cf. my paper "A Metaphysical Paradox," *Proc. and Addresses of the Amer. Philos. Assn.* 39 (1966), 5–19, at 14.

[73] 389D ff.; 399B–C; 402C; 410A.

[74] Cf. J. B. Skemp, "Comment on Communal and Individual Justice in the *Republic*," *Phronesis* 5 (1960), 35–38, at 36.

[75] Which would be quite consistent with differential education for other purposes (as is clearly implied in 466E ff., and probably also in 415C2 as well).

[76] Right belief lacking the requisite support from "musical" *paideia* will not do: it is denounced as "slavish and brutish" (430B); cf. *Laws* 698A–B: the "divergence of pain and pleasure from rational belief is the greatest ignorance." Conversely, right belief with *paideia* is sufficient for moral virtue even without philosophic wisdom: clearly so in the case of the courage of the auxiliaries in 429C–430B (their courage is *not* "slavish and brutish"), and also, by implication, in the case of the *sōphrosynē* of the producers in 431D–432B: neither would their virtue be "slavish and brutish," since it is produced by musical *paideia*. And cf. the next note.

irresistibly attractive and its contrary disgustingly ugly.[77] Thus the internal controls will be secured and a condition of soul induced which is emphatically called "harmony" in anticipation of the later use of this metaphor in the definition of temperance and justice$_2$.[78]

2. So this is what is left of the above objection: if Plato thought psychic harmony a necessary condition of a morally just disposition, he must have thought the latter attainable only by the people of his ideal state and, in the present world, by Platonic philosophers and their moral dependents (and, on a lower plane, by some of the citizens of the best timocracies);[79] and this would cut out the vast

[77] This marks a radical difference between (a) the virtue denounced so scathingly in *Phd.* 68–69 and *R.* 430B, and (b) that of the non-philosophers of the ideal state. The people in (a) act bravely, temperately, or justly only when, and because, they believe that some ulterior non-moral end of theirs can be the better advanced in this way; that is why Plato speaks of them in wilful paradox as "brave because of cowardice" and "temperate because of intemperance" (*Phd.* 68D–69A): they have no independent love of courage or temperance, they do not find these qualities of character desirable and admirable in and of themselves. In (b), on the contrary, we have people whose emotional and imaginative natures have been so moulded from earliest childhood by "musical" *paideia* that they have come to love virtue and hate vice regardless of other considerations: to engage in an action they felt to be cowardly or intemperate would be in itself a direct source of unhappiness to them. Hence there can be no warrant for conflating (a) with (b) as is done by Helen North, who says that (a) is in fact "the level of virtue with which all but the philosophers" must be content in the *Republic* (*op. cit.* 166, n. 3), and had been done earlier (though in more guarded fashion) by R. D. Archer-Hind (*Plato's Phaedo* [Cambridge, 1896], Appendix on "*Dēmotikē kai Politikē Aretē*," 149–55), who represents (a) as a form of (inferior) *dēmotikē aretē* (civic virtue): Plato could hardly have reckoned (a) *civic* virtue, since he brands it as "slavish" both in the *Republic* (430B) and the *Phaedo* (69B7); moreover the *Phaedo* passage shows clearly that he thought of (a) as *bogus* virtue ("delusive facade . . . no truth in it," 69B), while there is nothing bogus about the civic virtues of the lower classes in the *Republic*.

[78] 400D–401D; and, retrospectively, 522A.

[79] A conspicuous feature of Sparta and Crete was their *agogē*, a process which from birth onward subjected the individual to authoritarian institutional controls designed to inculcate virtue. Though Plato shudders at the neglect of "music" in these cultures, and at the mindlessness of the result, he thinks that the firmly controlled environment does provide, what was so sadly lacking elsewhere, that discipline over appetite which is the *sine qua non* of justice$_2$. For this reason his dis-

majority of our fellow-men, all of whom are expected to act justly. But why should this consequence bother Plato? He thinks the masses, if they lack the requisite *paideia*, capable of nothing better than a degenerate morality, that "delusive facade" of virtue:[80] they cannot be expected to do the just thing because they find justice beautiful, but only because they see in it the safest path to gratification. "But if that is what Plato thinks," it may be retorted, "is he not conceding that for the majority justice must be good only for its consequences, not in and of itself—the very thing Glaucon challenged Socrates to refute?" The answer is clearly, "Yes," and Plato could say so without inconsistency. Before getting to the proof that justice *is* good in and of itself, his Socrates embarked on a long search to find out what justice is.[81] His proof is clearly meant to hold for *this*—not for the fake the masses now call "justice": this, Plato would himself insist, *is* good only for its consequences.[82]

---

cussion of timocracy in 544C ff. is vastly more favorable to it than to the next three states, and allows that some of its citizens (non-philosophers, of course) may be good men; so e.g., the timocratic father of the oligarchic man (549C).

[80] VII above; notes 76 and 77 above.

[81] With which Glaucon and Adeimantus concur; indeed the very form in which the question came to be formulated by Adeimantus (366E5–6, 367A4–5, 367E3) distinctly implies that the "praise" of justice will have to be predicated on the disclosure of its "power" (and, therefore, of its "essence").

[82] This paper was a by-product of research on Plato's ethics undertaken in the course of my fellowship at the Center for Advanced Study in Behavioral Sciences, to which I acknowledge my grateful thanks.

6

THOUGHT AND DESIRE IN PLATO[1]

TERRY PENNER

"And appetite is opposed to reasoned choice (*prohairesis*); appetite is not opposed to appetite."

Aristotle, *EN* 1111B15

In this paper I try to make plausible the following views:

(i) An original, if bizarre, defence of Socrates' position on the impossibility of *akrasia* can be constructed from the view that in supposed cases of *akrasia*, though the person knows his course of action is not the best available, *his desire* does not; i.e. his desire is deceived.

(ii) This view involves the claim that one part of oneself thinks one thing while another part (vulgarly called "the person", "oneself", and by Plato called "reason") thinks another. Plato did not think this claim bizarre; indeed he was anxious to endorse it.

(iii) The notion of "part" involved is not "metaphorical" in the sense that no ontological conclusions are to be drawn from its use; nor is the doctrine of parts of the soul an incredibly loose doctrine which would justify an indefinitely large number of parts of the soul—rather, Plato's true view is the view in *R*. X, that there are only two parts of the soul, a rational part and an irrational part, and he allows himself *thumos* (spirit) for irrelevant political or moral reasons only.

(iv) In spite of (i) and (ii), the parts-of-the-soul doctrine is intended as a refutation of Socrates' view of *akrasia*.

(v) The premiss "All thirst is for drink and not for good drink or F-drink or etc." is directed (all but explicitly) against Socrates.

[1] "Socrates" I shall here use for the Socrates of the *Protagoras;* "Plato" refers to the Socrates of the *Republic*. In this paper I more or less confine myself to these two dialogues.

(vi) It is the use of this premiss which enables Plato to accept the claim in (ii) but still reject Socrates' view on *akrasia*. For it is this premiss which stops Socrates from going from "desire has a mistaken conception of its object" to "desire makes a mistake about *the good, all things considered*". It is this premiss which ensures that desire has *some* conception of its object, but not enough that we can say desire has a rival conception of the good.

One may note also that some parts of the paper are relatively independent of others. For example, there may be some who would accept my arguments for (iii)–(v) while not accepting the arguments for other theses. I deal with (i) in section I, (ii) in section II, and (iii)–(vi) in sections III–IV. Section V is devoted to objections described at the end of section IV.

I

In considering Socrates' views on *akrasia*, I begin with the analysis of the argument given by Santas (*Phil. Rev.*, 1966). Santas there points out that the statement of the impossibility of *akrasia*

> that many who know what are the best things [for them to do in the situation] do not wish to do them, but do other things instead . . . [because] overcome by pleasure. *Prt.* 352D–E

has two readings, depending upon whether one reads "overcome" in the language of psychological strength or in the language of choice; and hence that there are two formulations of the impossibility of *akrasia*. I offer the following:

(a) the desire A for a state of affairs α known [thought] to be better [more pleasant] is always stronger than the desire B for a state of affairs β known [thought] to be less good [less pleasant];

(b) no one could be so irrational as, other things being equal, to choose a state of affairs β known [thought] to be less good [less pleasant] over a state of affairs α known [thought] to be better [more pleasant].

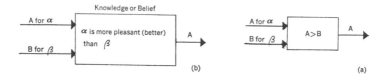

(b)

(a)

a, β are not actual states of affairs but possible states of affairs; and they are, of course, desired only under certain descriptions of them.[2] Santas points out that there is a gap in Socrates' argument, since he sets out to show (a)—down to 355D–E—and then, by explicating "overcome by pleasures" as "taking lesser pleasures in place of greater", switches to demonstrating (b) (from 355E on). So the defender of Socrates has to show that if one shows (b) one can then show (a). Santas takes it that Socrates has shown (b); for he interprets "choice" as Aristotle takes *prohairesis*—one chooses X only if one thinks X the best alternative open to one. If we follow him in this, the gap that remains to be closed is this: why shouldn't we have the situation where A is stronger than B though β is thought better than a? In that case, though the person wouldn't (in this sense) "choose" a, still he would act so as to obtain a; and isn't that enough for *akrasia*? Santas' reply on behalf of Socrates is to the following effect:

> In that case, if the person acts against what he would have "chosen", because of the strength of his desires, he acts out of psychological compulsion; he couldn't help himself.

Vlastos has convinced me that this way of closing the gap is just too convenient: there is no reason to decide antecedently that every case of weakness will turn out to be a case of compulsion. So the gap remains.[3]

I now offer the following defence to Socrates. If (a) can be false —if A for a (thought less good than β) can be stronger than B for β— what are we to say in general about the relations between the

---

[2] I am well aware that I have said an insufficient minimum here, and that difficulties lurk in every corner. In my fledgling understanding of these problems I was much helped by R. C. Jeffrey, *The Logic of Decision*, esp. pp. 57–59.

[3] Nothing in this analysis turns upon our going along with Santas' Aristotelian convention about "choice". With the ordinary sense of "choice" (b) as well as (a) would be attacked; but (a) would remain equally unpersuasive, as would the compulsion argument.

strength of a desire, the object of the desire and the person's idea of the object's worth to him? All we know is that (a) is false, though it would have provided a tidy, rational scheme for these relations. Are we then to suppose that just any relation is possible? Presumably some restrictions are necessary. For can one have an enormous desire for what one regards as bringing a merely trifling good or pleasure? Any theory of action, it seems to me, must give some restrictions if it is not to generate absurd cases (like Hume's example of the destruction of the universe being preferred to the scratching of one's finger). More specifically, if (a) is to be false in certain cases where a brings present good and β future or long-term good, any theory of the relation will have to account for this. But Socrates can make the simplest of amendments to (a) and deal with both the more general and the more specific question. It is this. The desire A overestimates the good to be gained in a, *even though the person who has A does not. I* know β is better than a, but *my desire* has the wrong conception of a, and this is what explains my desire for a being stronger than my desire for β. And the reason *why* this happens is given by *Prt.* 356A ff.—the deception is by perspective, the nearer looks bigger.

But this explanation shows that, after all, all supposed cases of *akrasia* are cases of deception or ignorance! To this it may be objected that this is not deception or ignorance in the ordinary sense. Presumably it would be a sufficient reply to this to show that this ignorance really did belong to the agent, that this ignorance did justify our saying of him that he acted in accordance with what seemed to him at the time the best course of action. This we might try to do by thinking of the case in the following way: suppose one part of you calculates thus (result: "β is better than a") and one part of you calculates thus (result: "a is better than β"), each side arguing its side of the question. Then one side wins the argument and you act accordingly. If your desire wins the argument, then you act in accordance with "a is better than β", and this shows your real opinion—in spite of what you say and in spite of our finding it natural to say that you know (think) that β is better than a. "But who is to say that the winning advocate won by persuasion rather than by force (surrounding the courthouse)?" This objection certainly shows that this Socratist move can be challenged. But all I wished to show was that a move to close the gap was open to Socrates.

In section III, I show how Plato heads off this Socratist move (or, more precisely: does not have to meet this move) and so avoids haggling over whether the winning advocate won by persuasion or by force. First, however, I show in section II that not only would Plato concede to Socrates the first part of what he needs for this move; he is himself anxious to insist that even when *you* are not deceived, sense can be made of a part of you being deceived.

II

In a quite precise sense of "part" (which I intend to make clear in the next section), Plato uses the existence of optical illusions to show that there are two parts of the soul. He says, having pointed to the existence of these illusions, that the arts of measuring etc. come to our aid. His point is not, however, that at first we are deceived about the size or shape of some visible object and then we correct this by measurement. His point is that *even when we have measured* and done some reasoning or calculation (*logismos* 603A4, *logizomai* 602D9) and so know the correct size or shape of the object, it *still* appears to us that the size or shape is what we wrongly took it to be before we measured. This situation Plato refers to as reason thinking one thing and the irrational part of the soul thinking (*doxazein*) the opposite. For he says,

> Often when reason *has measured* and is signifying to the soul that certain things are larger than (smaller than, equal to) certain other things, opposites appear *simultaneously* [see also 603D2, 604B4] about the same things. 602E4–6 (my italics)[4]

and then uses his principle—(3) below, in section III—to show that there are two parts of the soul, one of the parts being deceived about, having a false opinion about, the size or shape of the object.

There is every reason to believe that this irrational part is the same irrational part that at 436–439 opposes reason when reason

[4] The Greek may also be translated as follows:

> To this principle when it has measured and signifies that some given objects are greater or less than or equal to some others, the contrary appearances [to those deceptive ones which have already appeared] are often presented in connexion with the same objects at the same time. (Adam)

says what the good is in a particular situation and aims thereat.[5] If this is so, then we shall have established not just that Plato believed that even when (speaking with the vulgar) *you* are not deceived your desire may be deceived, but that, in the case of the desires of the irrational part winning over the desires of the rational part, Plato would have allowed Socrates the move of saying "In this case the irrational part is deceived". But on certain assumptions we can show that Plato would have found it plausible to make such a move himself—in particular the assumption that desire must have (at least some minimum) conception of its object. This corresponds to the belief which would nowadays be expressed by saying that the object of desire is intentional, where this does not mean simply "*The person who has* the desire has some conception of the object of his desire". If desires are indeed intentional and if there are desires of which the possessor is not conscious (they need not be unconscious in Freud's sense of resisting identification by the possessor), then this view is not a silly one, even though people might be as unhappy about the use of "conception" here as they are about the use of "thinking" for the irrational part of the soul. But this was apparently not a difficulty Plato felt; so I conclude that Plato would have conceded the Socratist move to say "Although (speaking with the vulgar) *I* was not deceived, my desire was deceived."

But in order to close off Socrates' move if he concedes this, Plato will have to deny that this bit of "deception" or "ignorance" justifies our saying of the *akratēs* that he did after all act in accordance with what seemed to him at the time the best course of action. There will have to be enough intellectual content to show that the words "deceived", "ignorant" and "thinks" (*doxazei*) can be used, but not enough to justify "act in accordance with what seemed to him at the time the best course of action, all things considered". In the next section I take myself to be showing how Plato does this. The demonstration might be both clearer and more persuasive, however, if I first show how this false opinion held by the irrational part is of minimal intellectual content.

[5] See esp. 603D5–7 with 439D6–8 and 580D11–E5, and also 606D1–2 where *thumos* is lumped together with *aphrodisia* and *all the other appetitive pleasures and pains* in the soul. Note also *alogiston* at 439D7, 604D9–10. (*Tōi alogistōs thumoumenōi* at 441C2 can only be explained after I have set forth the view suggested by the just-mentioned 606D1–2, that Plato doesn't really think *thumos* an extra part of the soul.)

In the kind of case Plato considers, it is essential that the irrational part's "false belief" is held *after* reason has been convinced that the "belief", formerly also its own belief, is false. But this does not mean that while reason has done its calculation which shows the belief false, the irrational part also has its own calculation. For there is no reason to think this. One does not have a *calculation* that insists the squash ball must move as in (c) rather than as in (d)—as one's reason, thanks to its knowledge of physics, tells us:

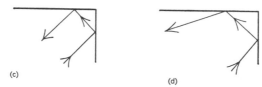

(c)   (d)

it's just that, in spite of oneself and in spite of one's knowledge, as one goes for the ball one still expects (or even half-expects) it to bounce as in (c). This is clearly the kind of case Plato is thinking of. Even when one knows, the "look" of the thing still partly takes one in. (The "look" can be literally visual, as with the Muller-Lyer lines, or not—as in the example just presented.)

It has been objected to me that these "beliefs" of the irrational part just do not qualify as beliefs in any acceptable sense, and that what Plato is doing in *R*. X is making the simple mistake of confusing "The stick looks bent" with "I think the stick is bent". This would certainly be a gross confusion. But as should be clear by now, I think Plato would not consider the case of the bent stick as relevant to his discussion just because no-one even *inclines* to believe that the stick is bent. But there is a vast difference between the bent stick case and the Muller-Lyer case—a difference which might be expressed by the difference between "looks F" and "appears to be F", though I am not here concerned with precisely which linguistic means is appropriate. The point about appearing to be F is that it is associated with some inclination to believe that the object is F—or, more strongly, a half-belief. (There are operational tests for such a notion—e.g. if though I believe p—which I believe to be incompatible with q—I still half-believe q, then when in haste or in relaxed circumstances I tend to make mistakes and assert or commit myself to something incompatible with p, I more often assert q than any other alternative, etc., etc. A full account would require qualification and elaboration, but I hope enough has been said to make plausible my claim. The half-belief so outlined could then plausibly be associated with these cases where the "look" takes one in, in some sense, even when one knows that what the look makes appear to be the case is in fact not the case.) Indeed, given that this is so, I do not see why there should not be cases where one's half-belief is so strong as to make one wonder in such cases which is the belief, which the half-belief. However, the main point is that Plato's use of *doxazein* is not the simple mistake one might think at first.

I conclude that Plato thought (with some justification) that besides what one believed oneself there could also be contrary beliefs that one also in some sense held; and that Plato put this by saying that reason believed one thing and another part of one, the irrational part, believed the contrary; and hence that he would have conceded the above Socratist reply—that one's desire might be deceived as to the worth of *a*.

III

I turn now to showing in more detail how Plato's argument for the parts of the soul goes, and why it requires the claim that thirst is for drink *simpliciter* and not for good drink. Plato holds that the position in the *Protagoras*—that knowledge cannot be dragged around (*perihelkomenēs:* 352C2) by pleasure, fear, anger, or whatever, that there is no such thing as being overpowered by pleasure into acting against what one thinks best at the time (352–353, ignoring the distinction between knowledge and belief, as at 358B7, C7, D1, since, as Aristotle saw, it is irrelevant to the argument)—is after all false. It is frequently the case that reason is overpowered by pleasure,[6] just as the lower classes frequently refuse to obey the ruling classes. Thus Plato is holding that

[6] The word *perihelkein* and the root *helk*- turn up often in later discussions related to *akrasia*. See *perihelkein* at Arist. *EN* 1145B24, 1147B16; *helkein* at Pl. *R.* 439D1, 604B1; *anthelkein* at 439B3; and (more distantly) *dihelkusas* at 440A1.

The wary reader will have noticed my shift from *knowledge* being overcome to *reason* being overcome. If for these purposes we ignore the distinction of knowledge and belief this transition will be justified.

Those who think Plato in the *Republic* could not have allowed the *logistikon* (reason) to be overcome by pleasure can be directed to the case of Leontius at 439E ff., esp. 440A1 generalized at 440A8–B1:

(1) In some cases, the desires which spring from a person's appetite are stronger than the desires which spring from his reason.

Once a position like this is taken up, however, one ought to feel a need to explain this use of "reason" and of "appetite". Is it that one is using these terms to refer to entities of some type, or do we have here just a metaphorical turn of speech? The latter has often been maintained, maintained by insisting that when Plato speaks of the "parts of the soul" he uses two words interchangeably—*meros* (part) and, more frequently, *eidos* (type of, form of)—and that the latter shows Plato is speaking metaphorically. I believe rather that the arguments Plato gives (to be expounded immediately) show that the commentators who have made it traditional to refer to "*parts* of the soul" were indeed correct in giving the point of Plato's doctrine. The parts of the soul are, like the Forms and like the soul it-

---

And don't we perceive this widely elsewhere—whenever desire forces [Cornford: would force] someone to act contrary to his reasoning, he abuses himself and becomes angry with that in him which does the forcing. . . .

It is clear from the Leontius case that *either* appetite *or* reason plus spirit may win out in the end. Cp. 431A–B (the worse element in the soul defeating a "smaller", better element), 444A–B, 444D10–11 (on the definition of injustice), 550B with 548C6–7, 581B12–C1, 587A3, 590C.

We can also see from 582A8–B6 that Plato felt confident that the money-lover (he in whom appetite reigns), *had* he experienced the pleasures of learning the truth itself, would instead have been a lover of wisdom. For he says that not only is it not necessarily the case that the money-lover never *will* experience the sweetness of this taste: even if he were keen to do so, *it would not be easy* for him to do so. (I take the *empeiros* at 582D4 to mean "really experienced"; and suppose that "not easy" here does not mean "impossible".) But the fudging of the language here and at 590C may well show (what Gregory Vlastos has suggested to me) that Plato shrank from saying that reason may be overcome by pleasure *even* when it has knowledge. Most important, though, the form of Plato's argument throughout is in the language of psychological strength; so he has no real grounds for denying that a soul with a weak *logistikon* may have knowledge.

In this connexion one should note that sometimes Plato uses *logos* and *logismos* for the highest part of the soul, and sometimes not (e.g. 549B3–7 when taken together with 550B1). Socrates allows Glaucon a gross equivocation at 441A9.

self, non-physical entities. If it then be said "But what is a non-physical part, even supposing we understand what a non-physical entity is? (Surely you are not going to hang *that* around Plato's neck?)", the reply is (a) Plato had quite a good idea of what it is to commit oneself to the existence of an entity (whether physical or non-physical), and (b) he gives an admirably clear criterion for parthood (whether physical or non-physical).[7] On, then, with Plato's argument.

First of all we shall want an account of "desires". Plato tries

(2) A desire for X is a positive impulse towards X, and a desire for non-X is a negative impulse towards X [i.e. an impulse away from X].

Plato now makes sure that the talk about impulses towards X is not construed metaphorically by finding separate authors for the two impulses towards X in question, by stating:

(3) It is impossible for one and the same thing simultaneously to have (a) a positive impulse towards X and (b) a negative impulse towards X, where "X" is construed in the same way in both (a) and (b).

Thus, where we are inclined to describe such a case as a single thing with opposite impulses, what we really have is two *parts* of the same thing doing opposite things (cp. a spinning top in a single place: the axis is stationary, but the rest of the top is moving—this, according to Plato, gives us a sufficient condition for ascription of parts to the top). Then given

(4) The soul is a thing ["soul" is a possible substitution for "thing" in (3)],

and

(5) The soul sometimes desires to drink [due to appetite having thirst] and to not drink [due to reason saying it is better not to],

[7] To think something an entity is to be ontologically committed to it. (see *Sph.* 250B7: *triton ara ti . . . en tēi psuchēi titheis;*). It seems to me no more difficult to see what kind of entities the parts of the soul are than to see what kind of entity the soul is. (You may think this is to say little enough.)

we can parallel the move made with the spinning top, according to the criterion in (3), and assert

(6) appetite and reason are two different parts of the soul.

Thus, from (2) (a quasi-definition, 437B–D), (3) (a principle justifying the attribution of parts to an entity, 436B8–9, E9 ff.), (5) (an empirical fact, 439A9 ff.) and (4) (a natural assumption to attribute to Plato, and one he would certainly have felt no need to state, it being required in all sorts of contexts where he deals with the soul[8]), we get (6); and since there is nothing about (6) which implies that the desires proceeding from reason *must* be greater than those proceeding from appetite, there seems no reason to doubt the support common sense gives to (1), to the possibility of *akrasia*. Plato has shown the possibility of *akrasia* by sticking to the language of strength.

We can now show how the Socratic counter-attack requires Plato to make use of the premiss he makes a great fuss over (to the puzzlement of many), that thirst is for drink and not for good drink. It might have been suspected in any case that Socrates is the opponent spoken of at 438A2, against whom this curious premiss is developed, for the reason the opponent gives is:

for all men desire goods [good things, the good]. 438A3–4

Murphy has correctly seen both that this shows Socrates is the opponent Plato is fending off (28–29), and that it shows that the position attributed—"all thirst is for good drink"—does not mean "all thirst is for drink which is good of its kind", but rather "all thirst, being desire, conforms to the principle: all desires are for what is thought to be the good in that situation" (45–47). If reason says "It is better not to drink", thirst does not just say "Drink!", according to Socrates, but "It is better to drink". With this understanding, we can now show that the premiss that thirst is for drink *simpliciter* is necessary against Socrates.

Let us examine a case of conflict of desires which is felt as a conflict of desires—one both wants to drink and wants to not drink. Then, according to Plato, there must be a plain desire for drink (thirst), and another desire, proceeding from reason, to not drink.

[8] For example, it is required in the proof of the immortality of the soul at 608E ff. See also the overtly ontological *Sph.* 246E–247E.

Since reason's injunction has the form "It is better to . . .", we see that this desire to not drink is an intellectualized desire for the good—a desire for the good accompanied by a calculation which says that, in this situation, the good is to be achieved by *not* drinking. It is reason that exercises the metric art of the *Protagoras* and it is quite impossible for it to choose what appears to it the less good course of action. Phrased in the language of choice, and applied solely to the highest part of the soul, Plato never gives up Socrates' belief about no-one erring willingly.

So we have two desires, one the plain desire for drink, the other of which incorporates some calculation of advantage. Why should the calculation be confined to one of the two desires, why shouldn't there be two intellectualized desires, one giving the reasons for drinking and one giving the reasons for not drinking (as in the penultimate paragraph of section I)? Suppose there are. Then is it clear how one distinguishes between the conflict being between the desires and the conflict being between the two separate calculations of what the best way to maximize good living is? Why should one not describe the case as one of a single general desire (for good living) caught in the situation where the person wavers between two answers to the question what the best thing is?[9]

Now the great merit of Plato's argument in *R.* IV is that it blocks the move to speak of the two intellectualized desires. Plato refuses to allow that thirst can be thirst for drink which is thought to be the good in that situation. For to grant that would be to grant that thirst, like desire to not drink, could be analysed as a desire for good which has associated with it a calculation of advantage, advocating drinking. Therefore, thirst must be for drink *simpliciter*. This stops Socrates from re-describing such cases of conflict as cases of a single desire for good wavering between two answers to the question what the good is in this situation. Thus the thirst-for-drink premiss blocks the Socratist attempt to defend the impossibility of *akrasia* by invoking the being deceived of desire.

Let us recapitulate. One wants to say that one can act not in accordance with one's reasoned estimate of the situation. The first

---

[9] Obviously it is desirable that this question, as well as the talk in terms of advocacy, be formulated in terms of a particular theory of practical reason, e.g. Aristotle's or the much more sophisticated one provided by Donald Davidson in "How is Weakness of Will Possible?" (in *Moral Concepts*, Oxford Readings in Philosophy, edited by Joel Feinberg [Oxford, forthcoming]).

attempt to say this was to speak of A being greater than B even
though a is thought (calculated) to be less good than β. To this it
was replied that *some* account has to be given of the relation between
A and a, so that the first attempt by itself is inadequate. But then
such an account was offered on behalf of Socrates even for the case
where one consciously works out that a is better than β, namely in
terms of the desire being deceived by perspective illusions. But
then—and we have now seen that this is the point at which Plato
challenges the argument—we face the move to the case of two
intellectualized desires just discussed. And in that case it appears to
be open to Socrates to claim that the situation is better viewed as a
case of one desire (the desire for what seems best) and two calculations; and while the person wavers between working out an answer
thus and working it out otherwise, so the desire for what seems best
manifests itself now as a desire for β which brings long-term pleasure or good, now as a desire for a which brings short-term pleasure
or good. Thus all supposed cases of *akrasia* may be re-described as
cases of failure of knowledge, ignorance, as cases of the person first
hesitating when faced with the hedonic perspective, and then
being deceived.

In his reply, Plato does not challenge talk about desire being deceived; but nor does he allow Socrates to speak of two intellectualized desires for good. He *might* have allowed this to Socrates and
still have insisted that it makes sense to speak of one having a
greater desire for the situation that, all things considered, one
thinks will bring one less pleasure—just because of the sheer bio-
logical force of the desire, because of the emotional or libidinal
charge it carries. But he does not. His reply to Socrates is his
blocking the move to two intellectualized desires for good: instead,
there is a plain desire to X and an intellectualized desire to not X
which has the form "It is better in this situation to not X", and the
size of these desires may vary independently. For the size of the
plain desire to X rests on no calculation of the advantage involved
in X-ing. Thus Plato to Socrates.

IV

Having established in section III that there are two parts of the
soul, reason and appetite, which have desires that can "conflict"
(in a sense of "conflict" given by (2) and (3) above), I now turn to

refuting attempts to get further "conflicts" among the myriads of psychological conflicts of everyday life, and so to generate more parts of the soul. If (i) we start with a case of *akrasia*, as we did in section III, we shall get reason and appetite as the first two parts of the soul (where appetite is the part of the soul which has the desire relevant to the occurrence of *akrasia:* in *R.* IV, the desire to drink), and if we further assume that (ii) if a soul has parts, every desire of the soul is a desire of one of those parts, then it follows that the only way to generate further parts of the soul will be to sub-divide either reason or appetite. Let us therefore begin at the most natural place, namely considering other standard desires of appetite, such as sexual desire, desire for food, desire for warmth, and see whether we can generate a "conflict" between one of them and the desire to drink. Clearly this might lead to a difficulty, for if my desire for warmth can "conflict" with my desire for drink as I lie, parched, in a warm bed on a cold English morning, why don't I have a warmth-desiring part of my soul as well as a drink-desiring part? And what about the golf-playing part and the television-watching part, etc., *ad inf.?* The argument for indefinitely many parts of the soul goes as follows (assuming that the desire for warmth is a desire of appetite: otherwise it must, by the above assumption, be a desire of reason, a case to be dealt with below):

(7) Appetite desires to drink.

(8) Appetite desires to be warm.

(9) In this situation, [to drink] = [to get this glass of water and then to drink it] = [to not stay warm in bed] = [to not be warm].

These identities are between possible states of affairs. Then by (7) and (9), we get

(10) Appetite desires to not be warm.

Hence, if we apply the arguments (2)–(5) above to (8) and (10), we get the result that there must be two parts of appetite. Let us call them the thirst-part and the warmth-part. This argument can be repeated indefinitely many times.

Many people have thought that something like the above argument commits Plato to indefinitely many parts of the soul; and there are places in the Platonic text where this might seem to be suggested (e.g. 443D, which is hardly conclusive, and similarly for the "that by means of which we . . ." formula: other passages are otherwise explained below, on *thumos*). Nevertheless, I believe that the conclusion is incorrect. For to make the move from (9) to (10) even plausible, one has to assume the substitutivity of equivalents in desire-contexts. However, it seems to me plausible to suppose that Plato would have regarded it as a necessary condition for substituting equivalents after "desires" that the *author* of the desire (be it a person, an embodied soul or a part of a soul) know or believe that the equivalents in question are equivalents.

Now the thrust of my earlier remarks (in section III about the thirst-for-drink premiss, in section II about the minimal intellectual content of the irrational part's belief) may become yet more clear. If we say that a desire, or the appetitive part of the soul (= the irrational part of the soul according to section II), is mistaken about its object, this entails that it has at least some conception of its object, that there is a cognitive element in the irrational part. But the question relevant to the present argument to sub-divide appetite is: is this cognitive element enough to ensure that it (the irrational part) perform the substitutions? I believe Plato's answer would have been a resounding "No"; such intellectual work as substitution of equivalents would be assigned only to reason. Thus arguments analogous to (2)–(6) may not be expected to sub-divide appetite.

Can we then succeed in dividing reason? No—for Socratic reasons. There is no reason to distinguish two opposite impulses of reason, since all such cases can be taken as reason wavering between two different calculations of the utility of different courses of action. (This reinforces our decision to represent Plato as not allowing Socrates to break a "conflict" of desires into two intellectualized desires; for in the light of the present remarks, he could not stop Socrates from representing these two desires as a single desire for the good associated with two calculations.)

I conclude that *if* our first conflict is that between reason and appetite and *if* we assume that desires of something must be desires of one of its parts (if it has parts) and *if* we deal in the characteristic desires that come up in a moral treatise like the *Republic*, then Plato has succeeded in stating a doctrine which, however bizarre-sounding, is not totally without interest or originality; and that this doctrine has its eye firmly fixed on a number of logical points and possible situations which, in my view, have been overlooked by many analytical philosophers, who have reacted too quickly and unsympathetically to the crude look of the doctrine. However, one might still ask: what happens to the theory if we don't make the first and third assumptions above? (The second assumption I am taking to be integral to the theory's understanding of "part", and so as not to be questioned independently of the theory itself.) Even more pressing, what about the third part of the soul, *thumos?* Haven't we been considering a doctrine of two parts of the soul, and don't I owe an account of how I can maintain a two-parts-of-the-soul doctrine, when Plato is so explicit about *thumos?* In the next section I consider the question of *thumos* and the question of the two assumptions mentioned.

v

I have two arguments for not being deterred by talk of this third part of the soul from accepting the above interpretation of Plato. The first is the extreme paucity and weakness of Plato's arguments for *thumos* as a separate part of the soul. In his first argument, at 439E ff., Socrates rejects the suggestion that *thumos* is of the same nature as appetite by citing the case of Leontius. This certainly establishes the distinctness of what we might call "moral indignation" from appetite: one part of the soul says "Look!" and the other says "Don't look!". However, the fact that *thumos always*[10] takes reason's part when there is a conflict with appetite suggests that Plato doesn't really have an argument for *thumos* and reason being different parts. Thus Socrates praises the second argument—Glaucon's—that children (who are so far without reason, *logismos*) have *thumos*, and himself adds that the same holds for animals. But (i) all of this is irrelevant to the criterion for parthood in terms of conflict, *even if "conflict" is understood in the ordinary way* (and not in the precise sense of conflict elucidated in section III). Moreover,

---

[10] "never in yourself . . . or in another" (440B4–7). There is a worry about 441A2–3 where the *thumoeides* is described as the helper of reason by nature *"unless* it is corrupted by an evil nurture". But, as Adam points out (Appendix IV to Book IV), with the tyrannical man, say, appetite subjugates *both thumos and* reason; so presumably in such a case reason too is corrupted.

(ii) the argument, even on its own terms, only looks plausible because Socrates allows Glaucon the equivocation on "participating in *logismos*" already mentioned (note 6: between having a reasoning part of the soul and being rational). And (iii) as Hardie rightly remarks (p. 141), even if the argument did establish the separateness of *thumos* in the sense of *high-spirited part*, it goes nowhere towards showing anything about the "moral indignation" involved in the case of Leontius. In fact, the closest Plato gets to suggesting a conflict of *thumos* and reason is at 441B–C (when he refers back to a case of *sōphrosunē*, self-control, he used at 390D)—the example of Odysseus rebuking his heart. The idea[11] is apparently that Odysseus' heart has got carried away in its defence of reason against appetite, so reason rebukes *tōi alogistōs thumoumenōi*. However, even this is not much of an argument. First of all, if *thumos* is in this case all that irrational, why wouldn't another desire of appetite, called forth by reason to oppose the original desire, do just as well? After all, grief at 603C–604D is represented as proceeding from the irrational part of the soul; what so distinguishes the emotion of Odysseus' heart that it cannot join sexual desire, hunger and grief within appetite?[12] Many eloquent words have been spoken about how *thumos* involves a conception of the self—one must have a belief that one is being wronged—but the same holds of grief: one must have a belief that one has been deprived of something to which one is closely related.[13] I conclude, therefore, that Plato's arguments for

[11] Here I am indebted to my undergraduate preceptees in the Plato course at Princeton.

[12] See *R*. IX, where Plato discusses the desires and pleasures of the three parts of the soul—though he rapidly forgets about the pleasures of *thumos*. At 580D11 and 590A7, Plato recognizes explicitly the *polueidia* of the appetitive part of the soul, its embracing within it a wide diversity of desires while remaining itself a single part. These passages, incidentally, are further evidence for the position that Plato was against the indefinite splitting-up of the appetitive part.

[13] The concern with being pained over one's own faring badly is pretty explicit at 603C. No doubt reason sometimes desires that one grieve or be angry (by whatever mechanism, e.g. whether as 604B suggests, by evoking to the right degree desires of appetite to weep or to rage, or, on the other hand, by simply signing a petition or wearing black, without evoking any particular emotions) but here *thumos* seems indistinguishable from reason; and there are also cases where anger or grief get carried away—as with Odysseus' heart and at 604D—but here *thumos* seems indistinguishable from appetite.

the existence of *thumos* as a third part of the soul are singularly few and weak.

My second, and equally important, argument is this: Plato in two crucial places in the *Republic* acts as if he really did think there were only two parts of the soul. The first is in the account of *sōphrosunē* at 431A ff., which is put entirely in terms of a better and a worse element in us (here we may also notice that Odysseus' heart at 390D was, along with Zeus's impatient sexuality, adduced as an example relevant to *sōphrosunē*). The second is *R.* X—which contains the only other uses of the parthood criterion (represented by (2)–(4) above) in the *Republic* besides 436–439, namely 602E, 603D. Here there is no hint of any part of the soul but an irrational part—one which includes all the appetitive desires, pleasures, grievings (pains), sexual pleasures *and thumos* (606D)—and a rational part. Or, as I should say, reason and appetite.

To summarize. (i) Plato had every reason to associate Leontius' anger and cases of moral indignation with reason, and every reason to associate children's and animals' high-spiritedness and Odysseus' irrational anger with appetite; (ii) Plato shrank from confronting *thumos* with his criterion for parthood; (iii) when he did elsewhere invoke the criterion he ignored *thumos;* and I now add to this (iv) Plato had compelling political reasons for making the *thumos* a part of the soul; and (v) he may (as various people have suggested to me) have felt it particularly important to show how there could be —what is in no way incompatible with the existence of just two parts of the soul—*a spirited man* (the guardians are, contrary to the doctrine of the *Protagoras*, brave but not wise).

I conclude that Plato had no logical or psychological arguments for going beyond two parts of the soul; and that he probably succeeded in partially blinding himself to this fact because of the political momentum he acquired from his creatures, the guardians.

I now turn to the consequences of not making the assumption that the first "conflict" is between reason and appetite. If in (7)–(10) we substitute "I" for "appetite", we immediately get a thirst-part and a warmth-part. (Although appetite can't make the substitutions in (9), I certainly can.) And thus to indefinitely many parts of the soul.[14] To this the following reply might be attempted

[14] I am grateful to Gregory Vlastos for pointing out this difficulty to me.

on Plato's behalf. Imagine the situation. You start up from bed for the glass of water—you desire to drink, and act straightway (is there here also a presumption that you *think it good* to get that glass of water since it is a means to drinking?). But as you start up, you feel a cold draught and lie down again quickly because of the cold (is there a presumption that you think it good to lie down as a means to staying warm?). Then you ponder: *it's surely best* to get the water while I stay warm, so is the situation such that I can have both? Thus Plato could argue that the substitutions are worked out because, other things being equal, the person desires to act both on his desire to drink and on his desire for warmth: he thinks the course of action which satisfies both desires, if there is one such, is the best alternative for him in the situation. Now for the situation to be relevant to (7)–(10), we must have (i) that the person discovers he can't both be warm and drink, and (ii) that the desire to be warm and the desire to not be warm persist together, that both these desires survive the reflection which produces (9).[15] Now, the positive desires—to drink and to be warm—must in general be supposed to persist. But does this guarantee that the desire to not be warm persists? It is open to Plato to claim that it does persist *only if* the person thinks it better to act upon the desire to drink (if upon reflection he had thought it better to be warm, he would have made the substitutions the other way, and could be said to desire to drink and to desire to not drink). For the making of substitutions in this way presupposes activation of a third desire, the desire for the good. Hence, although there may be situations with just two desires, desire to drink and desire to be warm, there is never a situation of "conflict" with just these two desires. All such supposed cases are re-described as cases of desire to be warm conflicting with a desire *of reason* to not be warm, a desire whose form is: choose to not be warm, since it is better in this situation to act on one's desire to drink (which, together with the facts of the situation, precludes one's acting on one's desire to be warm). Opposition to any standard positive desire of appetite will be from a desire of reason (see 439C9–D1: *to men kōluon . . . ek logismou*). Thus one may *either* offer the above as a justification of the assumption that the first "conflict" is a conflict of reason with some one desire of appetite, *or* so modify (9) that we include this presupposition: that substitution activates

[15] Just this point was made in section II, though in terms of beliefs rather than desires.

a desire for the good in the manner suggested above. This position seems to me both plausible in itself and of a kind that would commend itself to Plato.

Finally, I turn to the other assumption mentioned at the end of section IV. Let us suppose that all the obvious cases of desire are dealt with by (7)–(10) as now understood (e.g. desires Plato names in the *Republic*, desires on any list prepared by someone not aware of the existence of questions the present discussion raises). Still, perhaps there are implications of the introduction of the premiss "Thirst is not for good drink" which generate counter-examples? Or perhaps a really determined objector could construct a counter-example? For example, just because thirst is for drink rather than good drink, it doesn't follow that there can't, on Plato's view, be an *appetitive* desire *thirst*$_g$, which is for good drink.[16] If this is right, we can move anything of the form "desire for xyz" that got moved out of appetite (and from whose existence our attention was distracted by the insistence that thirst is for drink *simpliciter*) back into appetite —and in particular, desire for not-(xyz)! Again,[17] even apart from this line, one could simply claim that there is in appetite a desire which is a desire for non-drink (to not drink). But then on our assumptions we cannot block the argument to sub-divide appetite into a thirst part and a thirst$_n$ part.

How would Plato have dealt with such constructed counter-examples? These examples need not be wildly artificial[18]—an overworked tea-taster may develop desires to not drink which could plausibly be assigned to appetite (a gut-reaction) and yet on occasion be so parched as simultaneously to desire to drink; in the showers one may have a desire for warmth along with a desire for non-warmth. The shortest way for him to deal with them would probably be for him to fall back upon excluding these counterexamples by means of appeals to physiology. For example, is the appetitive desire to X a desire for what is in fact a replenishment biologically required by the body? (Cp. *Phlb.* 34E13 ff.) Plato might then pin his faith on the wisdom of the body to exclude from

[16] Just as, strictly speaking, there is not knowledge of health, but only *knowledge*$_h$ of health—not to be confused with healthy knowledge— knowledge itself being of the knowable *simpliciter*: see 438A–E.

[17] For this pleasingly direct counter-example I am indebted to Richard Kraut.

[18] Here I am indebted to David Glidden and Andy Robison.

appetite the desire to not drink: the body does not simultaneously have opposite replenishments, or if it does they cancel each other out and so cannot result in contrary desires of appetite. (I am inclined to think the argument to the impossibility of a simple desire for X occurring together with a simple aversion for X less difficult to make out from physiological premisses than from—the more usual—behavioural premisses. There is hope of getting along without the latter, since the case has to be made out only for desires of appetite.) More complex candidates (like desire for a warm drink) would then be analysed as being either sub-species of desires of appetite or combinations of other desires of appetite and desires of reason, or desires of appetite described in terms of their (e.g. intellectual) causes, etc. Thus it might be claimed that the tea-taster's aversion requires certain *recognitions* of causal properties, and hence is too cognitive for appetite. And the case of desire for non-warmth (where this is *not* a simple aversion to warmth) might be dealt with by arguing that "non-warmth" must be further specified (e.g. to exclude saltiness): and we must know *which* explicit contrary of warmth is in question, e.g. coolness, coldness, stinging heat, etc. But then, Plato might claim, substitution will be necessary in the argument to divide the soul.

I do not think this reliance on physiology is in itself a defect of Plato's view. And it is arguable that it offers hope of meeting constructed counter-examples as well as the more obvious ones.

VI

To conclude. I have now completed my attempts to make plausible[19] (i)–(vi) at the beginning of the paper. Because of the extremely wide-ranging and bizarre character of the theses and interpretations I have been putting forward, I have omitted much that could legitimately have found a place in this paper—either about Plato elsewhere than the *Republic* or about the implications for Aristotle's express Socratism. (Does the doctrine of false pleasure confirm or falsify this view? Does Aristotle's "ignorance of the minor premiss activated by desire" [as opposed to the ignorance

---

[19] I say "make plausible" rather than "argue for" because I realize I have given less a detailed interpretation of all the relevant Platonic texts than a programme for such an interpretation. I don't see how the former job can be done in less than a book.

of the involuntary or self-indulgent acts] support our readings of Socrates and Plato or not? Does Aristotle ever show awareness of the motivation of the parts-of-the soul doctrine?) Again, I have not tried to knock off the edges of what Plato says by de-mythologizing it. (Thus, consider the compatibility of "He wants to smoke" with "He wants to not smoke", or of "He believes that p" with "He believes that not-p". These compatibilities have been found difficult by philosophers. But by sheer genius, Plato manages to accommodate these possibilities—by the parts-of-the-soul doctrine. Similarly for "appearing to be F", thought-independent desires[20] etc.) To talk of "knocking off edges" may well suggest that Plato doesn't really get right something the average modern philosopher naturally sees. I have found it more a case of Plato often supplying insights that I at least had missed.

All of this may merely suggest my own deep confusion on these difficult matters. So let me present the paper as an invitation firstly to midwifery, and only then (if we have here a genuine child, however mangled) to further philosophical and exegetical investigations.[21]

[20] A discussion of thought-independent desires in Hampshire had to be cut from an earlier version of the paper for reasons of space. This much may be said, however. An incautious reader of *Freedom of the Individual* (pp. 46–47), noticing that a desire of Smith to buy the most expensive picture in the gallery is declared to be *thought-dependent* on the grounds that if Smith is persuaded the picture is not the most expensive, that desire disappears, may suppose the following:

A desires X thought-independently ≡ no persuasion of A about the nature of X would result in the vanishing of his desire for X.

But consider: even an addict can be drawn off from his desire for heroin if he can be persuaded that the fix comes from a special quality of the needle he's always had up till now for injecting the heroin, but which is now not filled with heroin, while the heroin fills another, ineffective, needle. (Alternatively, persuade him that that white powder is not heroin but a poison.) So on this criterion a number of desires one would want to say were paradigmatically thought-independent turn out to be thought-dependent. What this shows, I think, is that thought-independent desires should not be identified in terms of how the agent conceives of those desires in their particular situations, though *what he tries to get* as a result of that thought-independent desire must be so identified. If I desire a fix and think heroin gives me what I want and think this white powder is heroin, then I shall, as a result of that initial desire, try to get the white powder. But—and here I present a partial de-mythologization—Plato would not allow us to conclude "Therefore he desires the white powder" *simpliciter;* for him that would be an equivocation. For although there *is* a desire for the white powder, the situation is for him no longer one of a single (thought-independent) desire, but—as we can see from the substitutions—also includes a desire for what the agent takes to be the good for him in that situation. (For the line of thought that leads to this, see pp. 114–15, 115–16 above.) Thus when the addict desires heroin (or, in Plato's terms, desires what is in fact a satisfaction of this craving, what is in fact a bodily "replenishment"), and so desires this white powder, it is false that he thought-independently desires the white powder, but still true that he thought-independently desires the bodily satisfaction or replenishment in question—and true that he thought-dependently desires this white powder (as a good). (The agent may in addition have a rival conception of the good in that situation which leads to the command "*Don't* take the white powder"; then to get Plato's analysis we must reanalyse the situation into a thought-independent desire "seek the bodily replenishment" and the single thought-dependent desire "don't seek the bodily replenishment since it does not lead to your good". Then these two desires engage in a trial of strength.) Are there then no substitutions allowable for the object of a thought-independent desire? Plato would probably allow true general physiological equivalents (whether or not the agent knows or believes them to be equivalents). (Cp. Hampshire: "When I am starving, my desire to eat . . . depends solely on my stomach", p. 47.)

I am aware that much, much more needs to be said about the implications and consistency of this development of the Platonic view set forth in the text and in this note. I hope only that enough has been said to show that the Platonic view merits the consideration of those interested in articulating the thought-independent/thought-dependent distinction. At least, Plato must have had Hampshire's idea that there are two kinds of desire, and that physiological considerations enter very differently in the two cases.

[21] I owe two enormous debts as a result of this paper. The first is to the Oxford tradition of philosophical commentating on the *Republic*—in particular to Joseph, Hardie and Murphy, all of whom noticed important points about Plato's psychology, in particular the relevance of Aristotle's statement which appears as the motto of this essay, and is the key to it. The second is to my colleague Gregory Vlastos, who both first interested me in the account of *akrasia* in the *Protagoras* and also raised, in private discussions and in his own seminars on Plato, many powerful objections to accounts I have tried to give of it and of the parts-of-the-soul doctrine. It should not be assumed that he endorses any of the theses of this paper in their present, or any other, form. I also gratefully acknowledge objections and help from many other friends and colleagues.

This selection has not been previously published.

7

THE DOCTRINE OF EROS IN
PLATO'S *SYMPOSIUM*

F. M. CORNFORD

The *Symposium* is held to be near in date to the *Phaedo*, in which the deliverance of Socrates by a self-chosen death from the Athenian prison becomes the symbol of the deliverance of man's soul from the prison-house of the body by its own passion for wisdom. Whichever of the two dialogues was finished first—and I suspect it was the *Phaedo*—Plato felt the need to hang beside the picture it gave of Socrates another picture as different as possible.

Every genuine drama has a physical atmosphere. The storm is as necessary to *King Lear* as the stillness after storm is to *The Tempest*. The atmosphere of the *Phaedo* is the twilight that precedes the night: 'the sun is still upon the mountains; he has not yet gone down'. It ends at sunset, with Socrates' mythical discourse about an Earthly Paradise for purified souls. The atmosphere of the *Symposium* is steeped in the brilliant light of Agathon's banquet, celebrating the victory of his play in the theatre. Socrates on his arrival, replying to the poet's welcome, speaks of his own wisdom as 'a sorry thing, questionable, like a dream; but you are young, and your wisdom is bright and full of promise—that wisdom which, two days ago, shone out before the eyes of more than thirty thousand Greeks'. And the *Symposium* ends at daybreak, with Socrates arguing with the two drowsy poets till they fall asleep and he goes off to take a bath and to argue all the rest of the day at the Lyceum.

The *Phaedo* had brought out the ascetic strain in Socrates, the man of thought to whom the body with its senses and appetites is at best a nuisance. There was that strain in him. The Cynics were destined to fasten upon it and follow the track that leads from the denial of the flesh to a point where the sage will be found taking refuge in a dog-kennel—the tub of Diogenes ὁ κύων (the Dog)—and advertising his singular virtue by outraging not only the graces but the decencies of life. Plato's word for such men is ἄμουσος—uncultivated, ungracious, unmusical. Socrates was not such, but rather the chief and indispensable guest at the elegant young poet's table. If he was a man of superhuman self-restraint, that was not because there was nothing in his nature to restrain. He could drink more wine than anyone else, but no one had ever seen him drunk. He had not, as some later critics said, ignored or 'abolished' the passionate side of human nature; he had done something else with it. The man of thought was also the man of passion, constantly calling himself a 'lover', not in the vulgar sense—the speech of Alcibiades was to make that perfectly clear—but still a lover. The *Symposium* is to explain the significance of Eros to the lover of wisdom.

In the *Republic* Plato divides the soul into three parts: the reflective or rational, the spirited or passionate, and the concupiscent; and he defines the several virtues of wisdom, courage, temperance, and justice as they appear in the complex nature of man in his present state of imperfection. An essential point of this triple division is that each so-called 'part' of the soul is characterised by a peculiar form of desire. Moreover, these three forms of desire are themselves characterised by their peculiar objects. Thus, where Plato proves that the tyrannical man is of all men most miserable, he observes that each part of the soul has its own pleasure and its own characteristic desire and says one of the three may take control. The reflective part desires understanding and wisdom; the passionate aims at success, honour, and power; the concupiscent is so called because of the special intensity of the desires of nutrition and sex; it is acquisitive, loving money as a means to sensual gratification. There are, accordingly, three main types of human character determined by the dominance of one or another desire, three lives seeking respectively the pleasures of the contemplation of truth, of contentious ambition, and of material gain. The inferior pleasures are declared to be in some sense false and illusory. On the other hand, the two lower parts are not to be merely crushed and repressed. They will be positively better off, in respect of their own satisfaction, under the rule of reason than when left to themselves. And conversely, if either of the lower parts usurps control, not only does it force the others to pursue false pleasures, but it does not even find the truest satisfaction of which it is itself capable. In this respect the lowest is the worst. A life dominated by unchecked sensual indulgence is the least pleasant of all.

Hence it appears that we are not to think of the soul as divided into reason, a thinking part, on the one side, and irrational appetite on the other; or of the internal conflict as between passionless reason, always in the right, and passion and desire, usually in the wrong. That analysis would point to an ascetic morality of the repression and mortification of the flesh, the extinction of passion and desire, leaving only dispassionate contemplation. Much of the *Phaedo* suggests a morality of that type; but there what is called 'the soul' is only the highest of the three parts, which alone is immortal; the other parts are called 'the body' or the flesh. The *Phaedo* is concerned with death and its significance for the perfect man. For him philosophy is a rehearsal of death, and death is deliverance from the flesh. But the *Republic* is concerned with this life and the best that can be made of our composite nature, in which all three forms of desire claim their legitimate satisfaction. Hence the conception of virtue is centred in the notion of a harmony of desires—a condition in which each part pursues its appropriate pleasure and finds its truest satisfaction, without thwarting or perverting the others. There is for each type of man one best possible balance or harmony of various desires. The condition may not be perfect; but it is more stable and happier than any other.

Beyond this lies an ideal solution, which would produce the perfect individual. In the later books of the *Republic* that solution is stated on the intellectual side. There is a higher education which might end in perfect knowledge and fashion the only type of man who ought to take control of human society—the philosopher-king. But the process is not purely intellectual; it involves the education of desire. This aspect is developed in the *Symposium*, in the theory of Eros, the name for the impulse of desire in all its forms. We are now to learn that the three impulses which shape life are not ultimately distinct and irreducible factors, residing in three separate parts of a composite soul, or some in the soul, some in the body. They are manifestations of a single force or fund of energy, called Eros, directed through divergent channels towards various ends. This conception makes possible a sublimation of desire; the energy can be redirected from one channel to another. The flow can be diverted upwards or downwards. The downward process is analysed in the eighth and ninth books of the *Republic*. It leads to the hell of sensuality in the tyrannical man. The upward process is indicated in the *Symposium*.

I must pass over the earlier speeches, which contribute suggestions about the nature of Eros that are either taken up or criticised in the discourse of Socrates. Last of the six speakers, Socrates follows after Agathon, the poet, who has given a sentimental and euphuistic panegyric of Eros as personified by the artist's imagination. Agathon professes to describe 'the nature of Eros himself', the most blessed of the gods, fairest and youngest, delicate and soft in form. He has every virtue: he is just, as neither doing nor suffering injustice; temperate, as the master of all pleasures, for no pleasure is stronger than Love; brave, for Ares himself cannot resist him; and wise, transforming anyone whom he touches into a poet.

Socrates then opens with a conversational criticism of Agathon. By a masterstroke of delicate courtesy he avoids making his host look foolish. He pretends that he himself had spoken of Eros in similar terms to Diotima, a wise priestess of Mantinea, and he represents the criticism as administered by Diotima to himself. This is a sufficient reason for the invention of Diotima. Socrates, moreover, can put forward the whole doctrine not as his own, but as hers, and so escape professing to know more about Eros than his fellow-guests.

Agathon's description of Eros as graced with every beauty and virtue is not a description of Eros at all, but of the object of Eros. Beauty and goodness are attributes, not of desire, but of the thing desired. This criticism points to a curious phenomenon of personification. The representations of Aphrodite and Eros in highly developed art, as an ideally beautiful woman and youth, are representations of the desirable, not of Desire—of the lovable, not of Love. Henceforward it will be assumed that the object of Eros, in all its forms from lowest to highest, is something that can be called either the beautiful or the good, indifferently. Beauty and goodness may be manifested in a variety of forms, ranging through the whole scale of being. It is this variety of forms that distinguishes the several kinds of desire; but the passion itself is fundamentally the same.

Diotima had put the same argument to Socrates: that desire must lack that which it desires; but she had added that, if Eros lacks beauty and goodness, it does not follow that he is ugly and bad. He may be neither good nor bad. In mythical terms, Eros is neither god nor mortal, but a *daimon* intermediate between the two —one of those spirits through whom intercourse between the divine and mortal worlds is maintained. For the object of Eros is to be found in both worlds, the seen and the unseen; here there is visible beauty, a likeness of the invisible beauty yonder; and Eros lends to Psyche the wings that will carry her across the boundary. But the point here is that desire, in itself, is neutral, neither good nor bad; it takes its value from its object.

This object is first described in general terms: Eros is the desire for the possession of beauty and goodness, that is to say, of happiness. This desire is universal: 'All have a passion for the same things always.' The name Eros has been wrongly restricted in common speech to what is really only one form of this universal desire. Just as the word 'making' (ποίησις) really means creation of any kind, but has been misappropriated to one species—metrical composition, poetry—so the name of Eros is misappropriated to one species of passion, but really means 'any and every desire for good things and for happiness'. Diotima next alludes to the three types of life. Those who turn to seek it in many other directions, some in getting wealth, some in athletic pursuits, others in the pursuit of wisdom, are not called 'lovers' nor said to be 'in love'; the name has been usurped by those whose energy passes into one special form.

From this conception of a common fund of moving force Plato elsewhere draws an inference, based on experience. The amount of energy directed into one channel is withdrawn from the others, as if only a limited quantity were available. In the *Republic* (588B) the soul is imaged as a composite creature, part man, part lion, part many-headed monster. One who praises injustice is saying that it is profitable to feed and strengthen the multifarious monster and to starve and enfeeble the man, so as to leave him at the mercy of the other two. Again (485), where the language of Eros is used to define the philosophic nature by its essential passion for truth, the metaphor of channels is used. 'When a person's desires are set strongly in one direction, we know that they flow with corresponding feebleness in every other, like a stream whose waters have been diverted into a different channel. Accordingly when the flow of desires has set towards knowledge in all its forms, a man's desire will be turned to the pleasures which the soul has by itself and will abandon the pleasures of the body, if his love of wisdom be not feigned.' Socrates then goes on to explain how the whole character is shaped by this master passion.

We can now see more clearly how virtue of the ordinary kind, the harmony of desires in the complex nature, is effected by the readjustment of natural impulses. During this life the energy must flow along all the channels in due measure. Some part must go to preserve mortal life. The pleasure attached to bodily functions attracts the necessary force, and is innocent, if controlled and not mistaken for the end of life. Another part must go into the interests and duties of civic life. So the love of power is satisfied and rewarded with the honours bestowed by society. And the love of truth and goodness will be satisfied in the exercise of prudence or practical wisdom. The harmony of the three elements will be achieved by a right distribution of the available energy.

But this is not the end of the matter, or of Diotima's discourse. She now defines the common object of all desire as the possession of the good, with the significant addition 'for ever'. How can this be attained by the mortal creature? By means of the characteristic operation of love, generation. In all human beings there is the urge to bring to birth children, whether of the body or of the mind. The end is not the individual's immediate enjoyment of beauty, like a birth-goddess, giving release from travail. Procreation is the divine attribute in the mortal animal. Eros is, in the last resort, the desire for immortality.

Even in its lower forms Eros betrays this divine quality, whereby it reaches out to something beyond its immediate and apparent object—beyond any personal happiness that can be achieved and enjoyed during the individual's life. At its lowest level, in the animal form of sex-passion, its aim is the immortality of the species. 'Have you not perceived', says Diotima, 'that all animals are strangely affected when the desire comes upon them to produce offspring? They are all distraught with passion, first for union with one another and then for rearing the young creature: and for its sake the weakest will fight with the strongest and lay down their lives, or they will starve themselves to feed their young; there is nothing they will not do.' The reason is that the mortal nature seeks, within the limit of its power, to exist for ever and to be immortal. This it can achieve, not in its own person, but by leaving behind a new thing in place of the old. All mortal life is a perpetual renewal and change, not unchanging like the divine. This is the only immortality possible for the mortal race.

Discussing marriage regulations in his last work, the *Laws*, Plato writes: 'It is a man's duty to marry, remembering that there is a sense in which the human race by nature partakes of immortality—

a thing for which the desire is implanted in man in all its forms; for the desire to be famous and not to lie nameless in the grave is a desire for immortality. The race of man is twinborn with all time and follows its course in a companionship that will endure to the end; and it is immortal in this way—by leaving children's children, so that the race remains always one and the same and partakes of immortality by means of generation' (721 B).

This passage mentions the desire for the immortality of fame. Diotima passes on to this: 'If you consider human ambition, you will marvel at its irrationality, unless you reflect on what I have said, and observe how strangely men are moved by the passion for winning a name, and laying up undying glory for all time.' This form of Eros is characteristic of the passionate or spirited part of the soul. Usually we think of the ambitions of this part as directed to the worldly success and advancement of the individual. But here also desire reaches out to an immortality which the individual can never enjoy, and for this he will sacrifice all that he can enjoy and life itself.

There is, moreover, a third way in which the individual can perpetuate something of himself, namely by begetting children, not of his body, but of his mind. Of this kind are poets and creative artists, whose works survive and carry their thoughts to posterity. Still more the educator begets children of a fairer and more lasting kind, by planting his thoughts in living minds, where they will live again, to beget yet other generations of spiritual children. And with the educator is ranked the lawgiver—Lycurgus or Solon— who leaves laws and institutions as permanent means of training his fellow-citizens in virtue.

At this point Diotima pauses and says: 'Into these lesser mysteries of Eros, you, Socrates, may perhaps be initiated; but I know not whether you are capable of the perfect revelation—the goal to which they lead. I will not fail, on my part, to express it as well as I can; you must try to follow, to the best of your power.' I incline to agree with those scholars who have seen in this sentence Plato's intention to mark the limit reached by the philosophy of his master. Socrates had been the prince of those educators who can beget spiritual children in others' minds and help them to bring their own thoughts to birth. Had he gone further? Immortality in all the three forms so far described is immortality of the mortal creature, who may perpetuate his race, his fame, his thoughts, in another.

The individual himself does not survive; he dies, and leaves something behind. This is immortality in time, not in an eternal world. All that is contained in the lesser mysteries is true, even if there be no other world, no enduring existence for any element in the individual soul. The disclosure of the other world—the eternal realm of the Ideas—is reserved for the greater mysteries that follow. If I am right in believing that Socrates' philosophy was a philosophy of life in this world, while Plato's was centred in another world, here is the point where they part company.

The line which here divides the lesser from the greater mysteries corresponds to the division between the two stages of education described in the *Republic:* the lower education in gymnastic and music of the earlier books and the higher education of the philosopher in Book VII. In the *Republic* the transition is obscured by a long intervening discussion of other matters; the *Symposium* supplies the link. The end of that lower musical education was to produce in the soul reasonableness, harmony, rhythm, simplicity of character. These are likenesses, existing in individual souls, of the eternal Ideas of Temperance, Courage, and the other virtues. Such an image is, for him who can discern it, the noblest object of contemplation, and also the loveliest: it inspires Eros in the musical man, the love of the individual person in whom these images of goodness dwell. So music ends, where it should end, in the passion for beauty, not a passion for sensual pleasure. From this point the greater mysteries of the *Symposium* start. They describe the conversion of Eros from the love of a single beautiful and noble person to the love of the Beautiful itself. They correspond to the higher intellectual education of the *Republic*, where the eye of the soul is converted from the idols of the Cave to the upper world of sunlight and finally to the vision of the Good. In this last transformation Eros becomes a passion for immortality, not in time, but in the region of the eternal.

There are four stages in this progress. The first step is the detachment of Eros from the individual person and from physical beauty. The individual object is lost sight of in the realisation that all physical beauty is one and the same, in whatsoever individual it may appear.

The passions [writes Mr. Santayana], in so far as they are impulses to action, entangle us materially in the flux of substance, being intent on seizing, transforming, or destroying something that exists; but at the same time, in so far as they quicken the mind, they are favourable to the discernment of essence; and it is only a passionate soul that can be truly contemplative. The reward of the lover, which also chastens him, is to discover that, in thinking he loved anything of this world, he was profoundly mistaken. Everybody strives for possession; that is the animal instinct on which everything hangs; but possession leaves the true lover unsatisfied: his joy is in the character of the thing loved, in the essence it reveals, whether it be here or there, now or then, his or another's. This essence, which for action was only a signal letting loose a generic animal impulse, to contemplation is the whole object of love, and the sole gain in loving.[1]

Next, we must learn to value moral beauty in the mind above beauty of the body, and to contemplate the unity and kinship of all that is honourable and noble—a constant meaning of τὸ καλόν—in law and conduct.

The third stage reveals intellectual beauty in the mathematical sciences. Eros now becomes the philosophic impulse to grasp abstract truth and to discover that kind of beauty which the geometer finds in a theorem and the astronomer in the harmonious order of the heavenly bodies. By now we have lost sight of individual objects and the temporal images of beauty, and we have entered the intelligible world.

The final object—beyond physical, moral, and intellectual beauty—is the Beautiful itself. This is revealed to intuition 'suddenly'. The language here recalls the culminating revelation of the Eleusinian mysteries—the disclosure of sacred symbols or figures of the divinities in a sudden blaze of light. This object is eternal, exempt from change and relativity, no longer manifested in anything else, in any living thing, or in earth or heaven, but always 'by itself', entirely unaffected by the becoming or perishing of anything that may partake of its character. The act of acquaintance with it is the vision of a spectacle, whereby the soul has contact with the ultimate object of Eros and enters into possession of it. So man becomes immortal in the divine sense. As in the *Republic*, the union of the soul with Beauty is called a marriage—the sacred marriage of the Eleusinia—of which the offspring are, not phantoms like those

[1] G. Santayana, *The Realm of Essence* (London, 1928), p. 116.

images of goodness that first inspired love of the beautiful person, but true virtue, the virtue which is wisdom. For Plato believed that the goal of philosophy was that man should become a god, knowing good from evil with such clearness and certainty as could not fail to determine the will infallibly.

The final act of knowledge is described as an immediate intuition in which there is no longer any process of thought. The eye of the soul directly contemplates reality. We may, and perhaps must, conjecture that the description is based on some experience which Plato had at privileged moments. There is no warrant in tradition for supposing that he ever passed into a condition of trance or ecstasy. The Neoplatonists would have seized eagerly on any such tradition, had it existed in the school. He uses the language of the Eleusinian mysteries because it is appropriate to a sudden vision led up to by a long process of instruction and initiation. But the revelation at Eleusis, of course, no more involved ecstasy than does the elevation of the host. Perhaps Plato's experience should be called metaphysical, rather than religious—a recognition of ultimate truth. On the other hand, it is not purely intellectual, but a conversion of every element in the soul by the last transfiguration of Eros: and at that point the distinction between the metaphysical and the religious may become meaningless.

To return to the theory of Eros: the energy which carries the soul in this highest flight is the same that is manifested at lower levels in the instinct that perpetuates the race and in every form of worldly ambition. It is the energy of life itself, the moving force of the soul; and the soul was defined by Plato precisely as the one thing that has the power of self-motion. The Platonic doctrine of Eros has been compared, and even identified, with modern theories of sublimation. But the ultimate standpoints of Plato and of Freud seem to be diametrically opposed. Modern science is dominated by the concept of evolution, the upward development from the rude and primitive instincts of our alleged animal ancestry to the higher manifestations of rational life. The conception was not foreign to Greek thought. The earliest philosophical school had taught that man had developed from a fish-like creature, spawned in the slime warmed by the heat of the sun. But Plato had deliberately rejected this system of thought. Man is for him the plant whose roots are not in earth but in the heavens. In the myth of transmigration the lower animals are deformed and degraded types, in which the soul which has not been true to its celestial affinity may be imprisoned to work out the penalty of its fall. The self-moving energy of the human soul resides properly in the highest part, the immortal nature. It does not rise from beneath, but rather sinks from above when the spirit is ensnared in the flesh. So, when the energy is withdrawn from the lower channels, it is gathered up into its original source. This is indeed a conversion or transfiguration; but not a sublimation of desire that has hitherto existed only in the lower forms. A force that was in origin spiritual, after an incidental and temporary declension, becomes purely spiritual again. The opposition to Freud is not merely due to misunderstanding and prejudice. It is due to the fact that the religious consciousness of Christianity has been, almost from the first, under the influence of Plotinus.

I adopted the view that Diotima's words to Socrates on the threshold of the greater mysteries, where she doubts if he can follow her further, indicate that Plato is going beyond the historic Socrates. It has been objected that this interpretation makes Plato 'guilty of the arrogance of professing that he has reached philosophical heights to which the historical Socrates could not ascend'. But the best commentary on the *Symposium* is to be found in the *Divine Comedy*. Dante, as a man, was far more arrogant than Plato; but it was not arrogance that made him represent Virgil as taking leave of him at the threshold of the Earthly Paradise, before his flight from Earth to Heaven. Dante has passed the seven circles of Purgatory and is now purified of sin. Virgil, who has guided him so far, stands for human wisdom or philosophy, which can lead to the Earthly Paradise, but not to the Heavenly. The analogy is not complete. Dante's guide to the higher region is the Christian revelation, the divine wisdom symbolised by Beatrice—not a further development of human philosophy, but a God-given addition. But if there is some analogy, Plato might mean that his own philosophy, centred in another world, lay beyond the explicit doctrine of his master, though it might be implicit in his life and practice. That is not to deny that Socrates was the ideal philosopher, who lived (though he never taught) what Plato intends to teach. Nor is it to say that Plato claimed to be a greater philosopher than Socrates, any more than Dante claimed to be a better poet than Virgil.

However that may be, Virgil's farewell words exactly express the doctrine of Eros:[2]

[2] *Purgatorio*, Canto xxvii, lines 115 ff.

This day the sweet fruit which mortals seek on so many
branches will set thy hunger at rest.

The sweet fruit is happiness which men pursue under so many
guises. At these words,

Desire upon desire of being above so came to me that at
every step thereafter I felt my wings grow for the flight.

These are the wings which Psyche receives from Eros—the wings of
her own desire.

When the whole stair was passed and now beneath us, and
we were on the topmost step, Virgil fixed his eyes upon me,
and said: 'My son, thou hast seen the temporal fire and the
eternal, and thou art come to a place where, of myself, I see no
further. I have led thee hither with intelligence and art;
henceforward take thine own pleasure for guide; thou hast
come forth of the steep and narrow ways.
See there the Sun, which shines upon thy forehead; see
the tender grass, the flowers, the young trees which here the
Earth of herself alone brings forth.
While those fair eyes with joy are shining, whose weeping
made me come to thee, here mayst thou sit and walk among
them.
Await no more word or sign from me. Free, right and sound
is thine own will; and not to act according to its prompting
would be a fault.
Therefore I give thee, over thyself, the mitre and the crown.

The mitre and the crown are the signs of sovereignty, spiritual
and temporal. Dante, now purified, is subject to no external power;
because his own will has become right, sound and free, and cannot
lead him astray. Hence he is made priest and king over himself.
So the *Republic* calls the perfect philosopher 'the most royal of
kings, who is king over himself'; but not until he has climbed the
steep and narrow way out of the Cave, to see the Good, like a sun

shining upon his forehead, and has learnt what it is that makes man's life worth living.

Originally published in *The Unwritten Philosophy and Other Essays* by F. M. Cornford, edited by W. K. C. Guthrie (Cambridge University Press, Cambridge, 1950). Reprinted by permission of the Cambridge University Press and the editor.

8

THE DIALECTIC OF EROS IN PLATO'S *SYMPOSIUM*

R. A. MARKUS

Pondus meum amor meus: eo feror quocumque feror.
St Augustine, *Confessions*, XIII, ix, 10

St Augustine's famous phrase, and the position it epitomises, contains more than a remote echo of Plato. But St Augustine is a Christian Father of the Church and not a pagan philosopher in fourth century Athens; when he speaks of *amor*, his word has to be able to bear the whole weight of the love wherewith 'God so loved (ἠγάπησεν) the world that he gave his only begotten Son' (John iii, 16). The suggestion that St Augustine failed to see the radical difference between two things we call 'love'—the *agapē* of the crucified Christ and the *erōs* of passionate desire—need not even be considered. But could it not be that his 'philosophy of love', being cast in Platonic moulds and modelled on the pattern of *erōs*, should tend to blur this radical difference? This is, indeed, a suggestion often made. It is powerfully urged by Dr. Nygren (in his *Agape and Eros*), who sees in the seduction of Christian reflexion on love by Platonic influences the besetting temptation to which it has yielded, the corruption, sometimes amounting to betrayal, of the unique Christian *agapē* revealed in Christ.

So far as St Augustine is concerned, this charge has been adequately met by Professor Burnaby in his beautiful study, *Amor Dei*. But may it not be true, also, that the feeling we have on reading Plato's *Symposium* that the love there finally shown us is, at bottom, really so 'very Christian', is not wholly due to our being duped by the pervasive and corrupting influence of Platonic moulds in the tradition of Christian thought? This is the approach I want to explore here; to try to discern in the Platonic 'dialectic of love' the features which have recommended it to Christian thinkers like St Augustine and the pseudo-Dionysius and, through them, to St Thomas Aquinas; to find, within it rather than in our gullibility, the source of its perennial fascination to Christian minds. For I do not believe that the reason for the seductive attraction exercised on our minds by the *Symposium* is that we read into the dialogue the content of a long tradition so firmly established that we cannot think except in its terms; still less that Christians do not understand what the words 'love' and *erōs* mean. What I am going to suggest is that there are grounds within the dialogue itself for our impression.[1]

At the outset of the dialogue we are met by Socrates' insistence that 'love is the only subject that I understand' (177E)—a staggering claim, surely, from one who normally confined his rôle, in bringing to light truth, to that of a midwife. And yet, Socrates not only reiterates the claim when it is his turn to 'praise love next' (198D), but the characteristic Socratic method only makes a brief appearance in the dialectical cross-questioning of Agathon and is, apart from this, replaced by large-scale, continuous exposition by the participants, including Socrates. What then, if we take this claim seriously, is the 'truth about love' which Socrates claims to know and to impart to his audience?

I have used the word 'dialectic', and—objectionable as it is— used it advisedly. For the truth about love which Socrates knows is being shown us as mediated by Plato's account; and the subtleties of the dramatic structure in Plato's account evoke a movement, not only from the superficiality of Phaedrus' eulogy to Diotima's discourse initiating Socrates into the 'perfect revelation of love' (210A), but also a movement within Socrates' own statement. In both these movements—I shall hint at the way in which they constantly reflect each other—positions established, though they are continuously subjected to criticism and modification, are never *merely* discarded. Thus Socrates in his speech is made to cover the ground already covered by the other speakers, refining, qualifying and deepening their contributions; and not only theirs, but what is both more important and less obvious, also his own. The dialogue

---

[1] This essay makes no claim to summarize the argument of the *Symposium*. I can only hope that the signposts which I have tried to provide to its 'dialectical' structure make sense in the light of renewed reading of the dialogue. Quotations are for the most part taken or adapted from the translation by W. Hamilton (Penguin Classics). Still less have I been able to discuss Plato's 'philosophy of love' in general, and in particular, the striking parallels with the *Symposium* contained in the different imagery of the *Phaedrus*. On this last point I may refer to the late F. M. Cornford's illuminating discussion in *Principium Sapientiae* (particularly Chapter V).

as a whole, then, presents in a dramatic structure Plato's view of love. Only this view is not systematically stated, but allowed to emerge in what, failing a better term, I have called a 'dialectic', in which the contribution made by Socrates is but one, though the culminating stage. (I am inclined to agree with the suggestion that if we wish to draw a line between the views of the historic Socrates and the Platonic Socrates, it is to be drawn between the 'lesser' and the 'greater' mysteries into which Diotima initiates him in the dialogue.)

At the point in the dialogue where Socrates begins to take the lead, the following results can be regarded as having been established, in turn, provisionally:

(1) Phaedrus has drawn attention to the fact that we praise love 'for his effects': *erōs* is a principle which directs and is manifested in action.

(2) Pausanias now points out that not all love is praiseworthy, but that it is subject to moral standards for its assessment: love is ethically ambivalent.

(3) Eryxymachus extends the field of relevance by treating love as a cosmic principle of harmony. The commonplaces of a good deal of Greek thought have gone to the making of his speech, sententious though it is out of all proportion to its content. Behind it there stands the world as seen by Heraclitus, in terms of an 'attunement of opposites'; it must have suggested to his audience the more primitive world of Hesiodic myth, in which 'love' (*erōs*), contrasted with 'hateful strife' (*eris*), is 'the oldest of the gods' and all-powerful. Again, his speech would have recalled the more philosophical treatment which these ideas received in the cosmology of Empedocles: where love (*philia*) is the agency which brings together opposites and makes for cohesion among the parts constituting a whole. Above all, his speech would have carried conviction by enlisting the support of the one genuinely empirical science known to his hearers, that of medicine. For the medical writers, too, health consisted in the equilibrium of opposing 'powers' in the body, and their art claimed to provide just the attunement of affinities and diversities as required. Eryxymachus—himself a doctor—adds nothing but the name *erōs* for the cohesive force to the nexus of affinities in terms of which his profession saw the world.

(4) Aristophanes, carefully made to *follow* Eryxymachus, gives

an *approfondissement* of this cosmic notion of love. The originally human conception, projected into nature and rediscovered there as a pattern for human imitation—like so many Greek moral concepts—is now, without restricting its cosmic application, considered as exemplified in man. What Aristophanes' myth is meant to illuminate is the same cosmic force which had been superficially described by Eryxymachus; we are now shown it from within, as it can be experienced only in human longing for union with an object loved and, perhaps, only dimly known (192C–D). Love is identified with this desire for completion; its object, which may be otherwise unknown, is defined simply by being the 'complement' (*symbolon* is the word Plato puts in Aristophanes' mouth, 191D) of the lover's need.

(5) Agathon follows this profound joke of Aristophanes—perhaps the profoundest statement in the dialogue of love thought of as a need or lack—with a speech aptly described by the exchange between himself and Socrates at the close of the ensuing cross-talk:

> Agathon then said: 'It looks, Socrates, as if I didn't know what I was talking about . . .' 'Never mind, Agathon, it was a pretty speech all the same . . . (201B–C).

His speech, simply ignoring what Aristophanes has said, reaffirms what has been quite lost sight of since the first speech, that by Phaedrus: the 'perfection' of love. Since then, the tendency, culminating in Aristophanes' speech, has been to lay all the stress on the relational quality of love: the principle of affinity of a part for its counterpart, the cohesive force which unites them in a complete whole. Agathon now asserts—and it is, except in rhetoric, a bare assertion—that 'love is, in the first place, supreme in beauty and goodness, and in the second place the cause of like qualities in others' (197C).

This statement of Agathon's, is, of course, incompatible with the Aristophanic account, so far unchallenged, and Socrates pounces on it in his cross-questioning of Agathon. This bit of the genuine Socratic method is intended to reintroduce into the discussion the relational quality of love and adds nothing to the substance of what Aristophanes has already said except Agathon's easily won consent. The upshot of the discussion is that 'love' is a word which can only be used meaningfully in phrases like 'love of . . .'; but 'love of . . .'

necessarily involves 'desire for . . .' and 'desire for . . .' is incompatible with 'possession of . . .' Agathon is tactfully reduced to silence, but the stress which his speech had placed on the 'perfection' of love at this stage in the dialogue served as a reminder of something that risked being forgotten. We shall see that the reminder was by no means wasted on Socrates, and that it is not to be treated as a mere foil to his dialectical skill.

One new point does, however, appear as a by-product of this discussion. It is not dwelt on, but, although it may be no more than the result of a simple logical development of the ideas voiced by Aristophanes, this is the first time it is explicitly faced. On the Aristophanic view of love, as Socrates shows the bewildered Agathon, where union with the beloved is achieved, and desire satisfied, the 'need' met by its 'complement', we are driven to saying either that at this point love ceases or that desire continues. Socrates chooses the second course out of this dilemma and explains that love is compatible with possession of its object, since desire continues even after its fulfilment: it is desire for *continued* possession of the object loved. He does not consider the consequences of this expedient, which he has been led to adopt in order to enable him to speak of love as capable of surviving the attainment of union with its object. It calls for two remarks: first, on this view, once you've got what you've wanted, 'love' means '*wanting* to hang on to what you've got'; but if 'wanting' here means anything at all, it means 'being afraid of losing what you've got'. Are we then to call love a kind of fear? But more important than this empirical, psychological inappropriateness is the logical dilemma still involved in this position: for either perfect happiness (which consists in perfect possession of the good and the fulfilment of all desire—cf. 204E) is impossible of attainment; or love must cease, since it must, by definition, involve unsatisfied desire, on the attainment of perfect happiness. There is no escape between the horns of this dilemma short of re-defining 'love' in a way which loosens its logical connexion with 'unsatisfied desire'.

Now it seems to me that at the back of his mind Plato was aware of the weakness of this makeshift position he makes Socrates adopt. Why then did he not say so, and accept one or other horn of the dilemma, or, alternatively, abandon the position which led to it? We shall not be in a position to see the reason until the conclusion of this analysis; indeed, the only evidence for my suggestion lies in whatever plausibility it may possess as an account of the 'philosophy' of the *Symposium*. To state it here, in a preliminary fashion, the reason is, I think, this: the Aristophanic account of love, complete with the resultant dilemma, is a sufficient and acceptable account of 'love' understood in a limited sense as 'passionate love'; that is to say, of *erōs* according to its precise meaning in Greek. But instead of saying so and leaving the matter at that—as a lesser man interested in mere formal coherence might have done—Plato goes on to develop a 'philosophy of love' in the language of *erōs* but with an interest and a scope far transcending the 'erotic'. 'Words strain, crack and sometimes break under the burden', and Plato makes the word *erōs* bear a burden far in excess of anything it had ever been made to bear; and the 'love' which he goes on to portray strains the language of *erōs* almost out of recognition.

This, it seems to me, is the 'problem' of the *Symposium*, and up to now the dialogue has been concerned with its statement. The first few steps Socrates is now taken by Diotima (in his own account) are identical in substance with the ground traversed by Agathon under Socrates' guidance. We are being given to understand that we are to start at the beginning: we are well within the world of *erōs* as universally understood, of love thought of as a want, as desire for its own fulfilment. But the horizon now widens rapidly. The conclusion is first of all drawn that if the longing for happiness (which consists in possession of the good, which is identical with the beautiful—an identification axiomatic for Plato, first stated in this dialogue by Agathon, 197C; cf. 201C, 204D–E) is common to all men, as it is, then all men are always in love, and it is only the convention of common usage which denies them the name of 'lovers', which has become appropriated to a special sort of lover. The *Leitmotif* of the whole dialogue, that love is the universal principle of everybody's and everything's activity, defining, so to speak, the agent's orientation with regard to other things in a world of which it and they are parts—in an unusually literal sense of 'part'—here appears particularly clearly. This is the general conception of love to which Plato wants to adhere, and in the interests of which he is prepared to deal pretty drastically with *erōs* as strictly understood.

The crisis of *erōs* takes place towards the conclusion of the portion of the discussion between Diotima and Socrates which is to lead to the generalization of the love-formula: 'Love is desire for perpetual possession of the good' (206A). 'The good', hitherto left undefined, has simply stood for 'what satisfies desire', that is to say, that in virtue of which particular good things are desired. But desire for 'the good' is not like desire for money or for physical prowess or for (homo-)sexual satisfaction or even for knowledge, only differing from all these in having the 'good' for its object. It differs from all these desires in being 'desire' in a very different sense, in the same way as 'the good' is not one among a lot of good things and is not 'good' in the same sense as they are 'good'. This is forcibly insisted on by Plato when he makes Diotima allude to the Aristophanic theory with the staggering discrimination which marks a whole change of perspective in the dialogue:

> There is indeed a theory, she continued, that lovers are people in search of the other half of themselves; but according to my view of the matter, my friend, love is not desire either of the half or the whole, *unless that half or whole happens to be good* (205E).

'Love,' henceforth, is to mean not *only* the whole complex of passions, desires and impulses directive of all activity; it is also directive of these passions, desires and impulses themselves. Love is not *only* subject to ethical criteria for its assessment, but at the same time provides these criteria and performs the activity of assessment. Though adhering to the basic notion of love as the directive principle of all activity, Plato has now passed well beyond the limits of the original conception of *erōs*.

This radical change of perspective is marked by Plato's abandoning the picture of love in terms of which the discussion has hitherto proceeded, the picture appropriate to *erōs*, of an incompleteness seeking completion by its complement. The new picture which henceforward becomes the dominant one, is that of love as a begetting or procreating. Though it is at first grafted onto the original metaphor of desire-and-fulfilment, it very soon achieves independence. Procreation is first brought into the desire-fulfilment picture as a 'sign' wherein lovers manifest the intensity of their desire (206B *et seq.*) for *perpetual* possession of the good. But let us observe the strain that results as a consequence in the original picture: it is not desire for possession of its object that begetting satisfies, but some quite distinct desire. As Diotima puts it:

> All men, Socrates, are in a state of pregnancy, both spiritual and physical, and when they come to maturity they feel a natural desire to bring forth, but they do so only in beauty and never in ugliness (206C).

This 'desire'—if we may still call it such—is now of a being already complete or 'perfect' (in a cosmological and etymological sense), indeed, complete to overflowing; no longer is it thought of as a lack. This 'desire' is not for something to be obtained—the beloved—but for giving something from itself; and the beloved is not its object but becomes, in the course of the immediate sequel (206D), the beautiful or good in the presence of which the lover performs his creative bringing forth. The strain in the Aristophanic love-picture is indeed so serious that the picture has to be abandoned unless it is to break altogether. So Plato doesn't use it henceforth, because he doesn't want it broken. For not only had it provided him with a model which revealed something of 'love' in its more extended meaning, and revealed it with unrivalled force in its inwardness; but in the final scene between Socrates and Alcibiades it is also to provide the clue to Alcibiades' love for Socrates —a 'love' whose claim to the name Plato is not prepared to dispute.

The 'divinity' of love had originally been asserted by the non-reflective Phaedrus; it was then, by implication, ruled out of court by Aristophanes' insistence on the longing for fulfilment which it involves, again to be reasserted at the close of the discussion just prior to Socrates' entry by Agathon. It was the *fulcrum* of Socrates' confutation of Agathon, and Socrates' denial of love's perfection was reinforced by Diotima's authority at the beginning of her discourse. It is appropriate that in the new perspective now established, its rehabilitation on a deeper level should come from Diotima's lips. Continuing her discourse she describes love's 'participation' in divinity:

> There is something divine about the whole matter: in pregnancy and bringing to birth the mortal creature is endowed with a touch of immortality (206B).

The conclusion is now quickly drawn that in virtue of its quest for immortality (i.e. participation in divinity) the whole of nature is 'haunted by eager desire and love' (208B).

By now we are prepared for the final revelation, beyond the 'lesser mysteries of love' into which Diotima initiates Socrates (210A). The nature of *erōs* has undergone the preliminary transformation required in order to talk about love for, and desire for αὐτὸ τὸ καλόν [the beautiful itself], the absolute subsistent beauty in which all other beautiful things participate. We know by now that desire for this is 'desire' in a very queer sense: it is desire to give rather than to receive, a kind of generosity rather than a kind of need. It culminates in togetherness with the object loved and in a creative bringing forth in its presence from the lover's superabundance. At the end of its gradual ascent through dim and fragmentary intimations the soul is united with the perfect archetypal beauty in a blaze of light wherein it beholds 'the things that are' (to borrow the language of the *Phaedrus*—249E); and the offspring produced in the union is wisdom and true virtue. It is not by accident that at this point, in approaching the final revelation of 'the greater mysteries of love', Plato makes Diotima speak in the language of the Sacred Marriage borrowed from the Eleusinian Mysteries. For here, too, the lover is possessed by the 'madness' of divine inspiration—analysed at length in the *Phaedrus*—a 'madness' which merges into 'memory' of the archetypal realities, into insight and prophetic vision, and which speaks the language of poetry and myth.

It is unnecessary to dwell on the wealth of subtle dramatic detail in the last part of the dialogue, subsequent to the arrival of Alcibiades, to see this dialectic of love displayed in the concrete. What the discussion began with is the passionate love exemplified in Alcibiades. This is the love—the love which Socrates finds a burden (Cf. 213C–D)—which conforms most precisely to the literal meaning of *erōs* and its analysis by Aristophanes: and not the 'completeness' of Socrates which Alcibiades feels as an impact not only soliciting his reverence for Socrates, but as challenging his own sort of *erōs*, and as a demand for his own integrity. And yet, it is Socrates' 'indifference' which Plato is presenting to us as an instance—as *the* instance—of the 'love' which finally emerges from the dialectic of the *Symposium*. But it is being presented with a delicacy so sure that there is not so much as a hint that the claim of Alcibiades' passion to the name of 'love' is being impugned.

Indeed, if my reading of the argument of the *Symposium* as a whole is right, Plato could not have disputed the claim of this kind of ego-centric passion to the name of *erōs*. For—philological appropriateness apart—this had been the starting-point and the ostensible subject of the whole discussion. I have tried to take seriously the implications of Socrates' insistence that, in this case at least, he knows what he is talking about. This is what I have tried to do in suggesting an interpretation such that the development of Socrates' view of love, with all its inconsistencies, reflects the dramatic movement of the dialogue as a whole. His seeming contradictions become phases in the dialectical growth of a notion which, in the course of development, outgrows the language in which it is being talked about, whose terminology necessarily continues to carry the deposit of undertones appropriate to its original field of application. One might, of course, suggest that for the sake of clarity and consistency Plato should have adopted some other word for 'love', say *philia* or *agapē* at the point where he saw that *erōs* would no longer bear the weight he was to put on it. He might have done so, and would, in that case, perhaps have left us with a valuable catalogue of differences between two things which no Greek could have mistaken for each other. (*agapan* best reveals its meaning in the vocabulary of hospitality: 'to welcome', 'to be pleased to receive'; more generally, 'to approve of', 'to prefer', 'to have a regard for'; *philein* likewise, though meaning 'affection' in a wider sense, has not got the connotation of passionate longing characteristic of *erōs*. There is, of course, inevitably, a limited possibility of overlapping margins.) But to do this would have been to do something quite different from the task he had set himself in the *Symposium;* and it would have been to undertake a lexicographical rather than a philosophical enquiry. We are apt to forget the profound insight summed up in our having one word in English for *erōs*, *philia* and *agapē*.[2] But in order to make this concealed insight explicit, what we have to do is something very much like translating 'love' into its Greek equivalents; or at any rate, to distinguish within its scope distinct and perhaps incompatible realities to which the word nonetheless applies. What I am suggesting is that Plato, who had three perfectly good words for these realities, achieved some-

---

[2] In Latin the case is more complex. A vestigial distinction remains in the fact that neither *dilectio* nor *caritas* translate *erōs*; but otherwise *amor*, *dilectio* and *caritas* have all undergone too much theological development to preserve the outlines of whatever distinct meanings they might once have possessed.

thing both like and more than this insight in his attempt so to extend the scope of *erōs* that it could do the work of the English 'love'. But where the *Symposium* does more than simply coin a new word to include in its meaning those of the other words for 'love' is in that it utilizes one of these words itself for the purpose. Thereby it illuminates all that we call 'love' by means of a particular and narrowly restricted sort of love, that of impulse and desire. In treating all that we should call 'love' in terms of *erōs* Plato is far from wishing to obliterate the distinction between the love of impulse and desire and the free, spontaneous love of choice. He is trying to discern a single and more fundamental reality which at bottom—but only at bottom—these *different* things manifest.

What he saw, at this level, is that love is involved in what a thing is, its nature, and is determinative of its activity and passivity in relation to other things. He discovered, moreover, that this is also true of man, who is capable of so many different sorts of love. He is the only creature who is not only what he was made to be but also what he makes himself; and whose love, likewise, is what inclines him to seek not only what he was made to seek, but also to seek what he makes himself seek. As we have seen, this insight cost Plato an expansion of the category of desire such as to enable him to talk in terms of desire about the sort of love which, as Kierkegaard reminds us in his great work, *The Works of Love*, is a duty: the love of the neighbour. (Who is 'the neighbour'? He whom I love *as* my neighbour, is Kierkegaard's answer; here it is not the object that defines the love, but the nature of the love that defines its object. If I have this sort of love, every man is my neighbour.) And here Plato shows us love both as passivity subject to ethical evaluation and as the activity which performs this evaluation; as natural impulse and inclination as well as free, self-imposed inclination or duty. This is the duality of love which St Augustine has in mind when he speaks of a love which is itself to be loved, and a love which is not to be loved, and of human virtue as the *ordo amoris* (Cf. *de Civ. Dei*, XI, 28, XV, 22), the right order freely imposed on human love by human love itself.

Plato may certainly not have known all that lay behind the love the Gospel tells of; but he certainly knew something of the category of duty, and was conscious of straining language almost to the breaking point in analysing the love which is a duty in terms of passion, impulse and desire. He had not, it is well to remind ourselves, at his disposal Aristotle's conception of intellectuality which was to enable St Thomas to think of spiritual creatures as a unique sort of two-level being: in virtue of his reflexivity man can impose desires on himself, that is to say, is capable of recognizing duty, to respond freely to 'presences' encountered; his 'openness' enables him to enter into a togetherness which merges 'I' and 'Thou' in an inclusive 'We' without compromising their individual 'integrities' or wholeness. St Thomas' reflexion on love doesn't make sense outside the context of his conception of intellectuality; but it is worth remembering that it is precisely in the sort of analyses which we encounter in the *Symposium* that such a conception of intellectuality originates. Is it then a matter for surprise that Platonic modes of thinking and expression should disclose their fullest content in a much later, but nonetheless not wholly alien context?

Originally published in the *Downside Review* 73 (1955), 219–30. Reprinted by permission of the *Downside Review* and the author.

9

PLATO AND THE RULE OF LAW*

GLENN R. MORROW

The name of Plato has been figuring rather prominently in our recent warfare of ideologies. Hardly had the National Socialists come into power when academic apologists in Germany began pointing out the similarities between Plato's state and the program of the Third Reich.[1] A famous philosopher at the University of Berlin is reported to have announced that now for the first time the Platonic idea of the state was about to be realized. There is evidence that in Russia also official thinkers like to consider Plato as their ideological ally. A story in the *New York Times* of October 18, 1938, reported that a Professor Skatkin of the Moscow Electrical Institute had aroused the indignation of his students by his declaration that Plato was the founder of Fascism. A week later the same newspaper reported the dismissal of Professor Skatkin because of his declarations concerning Plato (and related assertions). "This action", the story continues, "was followed by a full faculty meeting at which both the Communist Party and the Young Communist organization were represented. . . . The directorate of the Institute was rebuked for not exercising better control over the faculty."[2] The inference is clear that Moscow will not allow the name of Plato to be taken in vain. On this side of the Atlantic, however, a contrary phenomenon has been taking place. Whether because of the adoption of Plato by the totalitarians, or for independent reasons, there has been something like a revulsion against him in liberal quarters. Professor Rader names him along with Machiavelli, Fichte, Hegel, Treitschke, and other intellectual precursors of the ideologies of

* The presidential address to the Western Division of the American Philosophical Association, Ohio State University, April 26, 1940.

[1] *Cf.* Joachim Bannes, *Hitlers Kampf und Platons Staat*, 1933; K. Hildebrandt, *Platon, der Kampf des Geistes um die Macht*, 1933; Scheliha, *Dion*, 1934; Grunsky, *Seele und Staat*, 1935.

[2] I am indebted to Professor Ronald B. Levinson for this interesting item.

oppression today.[3] And another of our American philosophers has recently called the *Republic* "the original philosophical charter of fascism" and "one of the most dangerous items in the education of the western world".[4]

Now the heart and center of the Nazi and Communist admiration for Plato, and of the American liberal's repudiation of him, is of course the idealization of absolutism in the *Republic*, the doctrine that government is a high art that can only be entrusted to an élite group, who must not be hampered in their policies by the rules that men call laws. I am by no means sure that Plato intended to say just this in the *Republic;* certainly he intended it to be taken with important reservations which are usually left out of account.[5] For when he took a hand in practical politics in Sicily, which happened first about the date of the *Republic*, the advice he gave the young Dion does not seem to have been a counsel of absolutism. According to the *Seventh Letter*, the chief reform he urged upon Dion, and later upon the young Dionysius, was to restore the constitution of Syracuse, which had fallen into abeyance during the tyranny : in short, to replace absolutism with a government of laws.[6] If we regard this account as accurate, then it is clear that Plato's fondness for absolutism, even at the time of the *Republic*, must be taken with decided reservations. Even if he held to it as a counsel of perfection, he was not willing to advocate it as a practical expedient in Syracuse. And it may be that his actual proposals for Syracuse give us a better understanding of what he meant by the rule of philosophy than the abstract exposition in the *Republic*.

But the *Republic* is not the only work that Plato wrote on politics. The Plato of my title is the Plato of the *Laws*, a Plato who has been very much overshadowed in modern times by his younger self. Whatever he may have believed when he wrote the *Republic*, in his later years Plato would not have agreed even in theory with the advocates of power untrammelled by law. Of the many ringing declarations on this point in the *Laws* I mention only a few. There is no mortal soul, Plato declares, that can bear supreme and irresponsible

---

[3] Melvin Rader, *No Compromise*, 1939.

[4] Edward O. Sisson, in *Phil. Rev.* (March 1940), p. 143.

[5] It is only fair to say that Professor Rader, in the book above mentioned, does not leave them out.

[6] *Ep. VII*, 334C–D, 336A, 324A–B; *Ep. VIII*, 354A, 354C, 355E; *Ep. III*, 315D.

power without losing his wisdom and integrity (691 C). No absolute ruler can avoid interpreting the public good in terms of his private interest (875B). Unless the laws are sovereign, and the rulers servants of the laws, the state is on the road to destruction (715D). The highest of all the civic virtues, and the highest qualification for office, is obedience to the laws (715C). Every judge and every officer must be responsible for what he does as judge or officer (761E). Finally, the highest officers of the state are to be called Nomophylakes, Guardians of the Law, ministers of the sovereignty they do not themselves possess.[7] Thus in his old age, if not in his youth, Plato is at one with the tradition of his people in distrusting everything savoring of absolute and irresponsible power, and in placing the sovereignty of law at the very basis of political theory.

But what precisely did Plato mean by the rule of law? And what agencies would he set up for making it effective? These are the questions that I wish to examine with you this evening. The sovereignty of law cannot be realized merely by a declaration that the law is sovereign, or by moral exhortations to the citizen to obey. If Plato's *Laws* contained only this, we might praise his intentions, but doubt the will or intelligence to fulfill them. But Plato sees that if the rule of law is to be more than an empty aspiration, procedures must be set up to give effect to the substance of rights and duties; and these procedures must be geared to human motives so as to be sure of being called into play when necessary. A great part of the *Laws* is concerned with this practical and humble task of devising instruments of law-enforcement. It is into the details of this law-enforcing process that I wish us to follow him . . .; for in no other way can we form a proper estimate of what the rule of law would mean for a citizen of Plato's state, and in no other way can we gauge the degree of kinship between his and our way of thinking.

---

[7] *Cf.* Aristotle, *Politics*, 1287A 21: "And if it is better that certain persons rather than others should rule, let them be established as guardians and servants of the laws (νομοφύλακας καὶ ὑπηρέτας τοῖς νόμοις)". The title and the institution of νομοφύλακες were not invented by Plato. Νομοφύλακες existed in a number of Greek states in his day, and the office became more common in the century after his death. *Cf.* Aristotle, *op. cit.*, 1298B 29, 1323A7; Xenophon, *Economics*, IX, 14: Cicero, *De Leg.* III, xx, 46; Gilbert, *Handbuch der Griech. Staatsaltertümer*, I, 172, 178; II, 337–38.

Plato's ideas of the rule of law and of the means for achieving it did not arise in a vacuum, nor are they altogether novel, when we consider the practices of his people. Consequently I shall refer frequently to the historical counterparts or parallels to Plato's proposals, for without this background they can hardly be properly understood. As Goethe says,

> Wer den Dichter will verstehen
> Muss in Dichters Lande gehen.

Now the distinctive feature of the administration of justice at Athens in the fifth and fourth centuries was the supremacy of the popular courts, or dicasteries. These courts, as we all know, were large bodies, consisting normally of 500 members, sometimes of as many as 2500, selected by lot immediately before the opening of the trial. Justice had not always been so administered at Athens. These courts were a development of the democratic movement of the fifth century, and replaced older and smaller tribunals made up of officials or magistrates. Some of these older tribunals persisted alongside the popular courts, notably the Areopagus. But the tendency was for the popular courts to acquire a constantly wider range of judicial powers at the expense of the older tribunals. Only the Areopagus was immune. After its political powers had been taken away in the fifth century, no serious attempt seems to have been made to restrict its venerable prerogatives over homicide and certain other capital offenses. In fact, it seems to have held the esteem of all parties in the state. The popular courts, on the other hand, were a center of controversy. Their defects were caricatured by Aristophanes, pointed out dispassionately by Thucydides, hinted at cautiously by the orators (who had to plead before them); but they were defended by the democratic party as the bulwark of the democracy, a claim which the enemies of democracy freely admitted.

Long before the writing of the *Laws* Plato had taken a hand in this controversy. The *Apology*, though primarily a defense of Socrates, may be read also as a subtle indictment of the system under which Socrates was condemned to death—before a court indecently eager to get its business over with, so disorderly at times that the defendant could scarcely make himself heard, and withal left to its own devices for distinguishing between what was relevant to the formal charge and irrelevant appeal to personal prejudice. The *Gorgias*, treating of the sham art of rhetoric, also treats of the sham art of justice which it serves; for the purpose of rhetorical skill, as Gorgias states it, is "persuasion in the dicasteries and in other mobs" (454B). The *Republic* is sprinkled with caustic observations, such as the reference to the "sleepy dicast" nodding on his bench during the proceedings (405C), and the unforgettable picture of the "Great Creature", who shows his most stupid and brutal side when sitting in judgment on those who displease him (429ff).[8] In the *Eighth Letter*, written to the friends of Dion in answer to their request for advice, Plato advances some proposals for the reform of the courts, among others the proposal to set up a court of select judges to pass on accusations of treason and other capital offenses (356D–E). In short, the defects of the popular courts is a topic that engaged Plato's attention throughout his lifetime. He sees their susceptibility to flattery and other appeals to their emotions; their helplessness before the specious advocate; the ease with which they can be manipulated by leaders in party strife; and the anonymity of their voting, rendering the dicasts individually immune to criticism or attack (*Laws*, 876B). Above all, such courts violate the fundamental principle of social well-being, the principle of "doing one's own business". "In our state a pilot will be a pilot and not a shoemaker also; and a farmer will be a farmer and not a dicast also" (*Rep.* 397E).

Nevertheless, when Plato in the *Laws* faces the problem of setting up a system of courts, he does not, as we might expect, do away with the popular courts. We find him, in fact, asserting two somewhat inconsistent principles. On the one hand, he says that judgment should be rendered, wherever possible, by a few carefully selected judges. "A multitude cannot easily give judgment, nor a few when they are incompetent" (766D). This corresponds to his fundamental principle of social well-being, the assignment of important functions to persons especially competent to perform them. To this general justification the *Laws* adds another: it is easier for a small court to get at the bottom of a case; they will be able to question the parties and their witnesses, whereas the judges in a large court will be merely passive listeners to the speeches of the

---

[8] It is important to remember that the "Great Creature" symbolizes the demos in dicastery as well as in ecclesia.

litigants (766D). But at the same time Plato asserts with equal insistence that the people should have a share in the administration of justice. He has not changed his mind with respect to the faults of the popular courts. "It is a very grave evil in the state", he declares, "when the judges are disorderly and noisy, as in a theatre, clapping and hooting in turn this or that orator."[9] Why then does he retain the popular courts? In the first place, they are immune to certain species of corruption.[10] You cannot bribe 500 or more judges, especially if you do not know in advance which of the thousands of jurymen assembled on any given day will be chosen to try your case. And it would be still more difficult to intimidate a jury of that size. As Grote remarks, the popular courts at Athens were able to do what has always been difficult for any system of justice: they were able to bring wealthy and powerful offenders to account.[11] But there is another reason upon which Plato puts greater emphasis. "He who is without the right of sitting with his fellows in the courts of law thinks that he is excluded from citizenship" (768B). The thought here, as is so often the case, finds its commentary in Aristotle's *Politics*. What constitutes the citizen? asks Aristotle. Not residence in a particular place, for then metics and slaves would be citizens; not access to the courts, for foreigners may have that granted them by treaty. He concludes that the special characteristic of the citizen is that he shares in the administration of justice and in access to office, particularly the "indefinite office" of ecclesiast and dicast.[12] But after having reached this definition, Aristotle proceeds to say that it is applicable in the strict sense only to the citizen in a democracy. When therefore Plato insists that the people should share in administering justice, he is relying upon a conception of citizenship worked out in the Greek democracies and in its full sense practised only by them.

Thus these two principles represent, one the aristocratic, the other the democratic idea of how justice should be administered. Plato is not willing to renounce either one; instead he devises a system in which both popular participation and selected competence

[9] *Laws*, 876B. Jowett's translation.

[10] A feature of these courts recognized by Aristotle (*Constitution of Athens*, XLI, 2; *Politics* 1286A 32) and apparently referred to by Plato in *Laws*, 768B.

[11] *History of Greece*, VI, 27 (Everyman's edition).

[12] *Politics*, 1275A.

find a place. He does this by developing a procedure which was known but not fully utilized at Athens, the procedure of appeal. The result is three grades of court, courts of first instance and two stages of appeal. The courts of first instance are bodies variously called "neighbors" (762A, 766E, 768C, 915C) or "arbitrators" (920D, 956B); next above them stand the popular courts, constituted in all essential respects like the familiar Athenian dicasteries; and above them all is the Court of Select Judges, as it is called, whose decision is final in all matters coming before it (766E–767B; 956B–D).

This system, viewed as a whole, is a highly original construction, though almost all the parts which make it up are taken from Athenian practice. In the courts of first instance, the courts of neighbors or arbitrators, Plato has adapted to his purposes one of the most interesting and admirable features of the Athenian judicial system. Every private suit at Athens was first assigned by lot to a public arbitrator, a man of experience, who endeavored to bring about an agreement between the parties; but if this proved impossible, he was authorized to make an award on the basis of the arguments and the evidence presented. This was a cheap and quick and reasonable method of settling disputes, and there is almost no criticism of it in antiquity. Plato's proposal differs but slightly from the Athenian practice; he provides that the arbitrators shall be selected by the parties to the dispute, rather than being selected by lot from a list of public arbitrators.[13] These arbitrators, Plato evidently thought, would ordinarily be personally acquainted with the litigants and familiar with the circumstances giving rise to the dispute (766E).

A litigant who is not satisfied with the decision rendered in the court of arbitrators has the privilege of appealing his case to one of the popular courts, subject to a penalty if the original verdict is sustained. These popular courts are variously called "common courts" (762B, 846B, 847B), "courts of villagers and tribesmen" (956C), or more often simply "tribal courts" (768B–C, 915C, 920D, 921D). Some of these designations are misleading and the interpreters of the *Laws* have hitherto failed to recognize that they refer to popular

---

[13] It was possible also at Athens for the parties to select their own arbitrator; but from the decision of such a private arbitrator there was no appeal. Plato's system therefore combines features of both Athenian types of arbitration.

courts on the Athenian model.[14] Plato says very little about the constitution or selection of these courts, but what he does say makes it quite clear that he is thinking of large popular courts, chosen by sections and tribes (hence the designation "tribal courts"), and selected by lot as occasion demands and immediately before the opening of the trial. This is essentially the method used at Athens for selecting the dicasteries. The theory behind it was that in this fashion a court would be set up embodying a representative cross-section of the whole citizen body, and therefore competent to exercise the judicial function inherent in the demos. Plato does not go into details of selection, leaving such matters, as he says, to the "younger legislators" (956E; 846C). There seems to have been considerable tinkering with the procedure at Athens during Plato's lifetime, in the hope of making it proof against intrigue and corruption. What is important is that Plato does not propose any departure from familiar practice in the selection of these courts.

But he does place certain important restrictions upon their jurisdiction and procedure. In the first place, their competence does not extend to capital offenses. For these a separate court is set up which I shall describe later. At Athens, as we know, the power of the popular courts was not thus restricted. It was before a popular court that Socrates was tried. Again, the pleading before these courts is restricted in a fashion unknown at Athens. Plato forbids the "party oath", *i.e.*, the oath taken by the litigants at the opening of the case as to the truth of their contentions. "It is a terrible thing to think", says Plato, "that where many lawsuits are going on in a state almost half the people one meets are perjurers" (948E). Plato also forbids the "challenge to the oath", a relic of trial by ordeal and in practise merely a maneuver for distracting attention from the evidence (948A–C). What is most important, the speakers are required to stick to the issue ($\tau\grave{o}$ $\delta\acute{\iota}\kappa\alpha\iota o\nu$), and the presiding officials are authorized to call a speaker back if he digresses (949B). No such power seems to have been enjoyed by the presiding magistrates in the heliastic courts at Athens. It is true that in Aristotle's day the litigants in private suits took an oath to confine their pleading to the matter at issue,[15] but this regulation was either very recent or very ineffective, if we can judge by the extant speeches of the

---

[14] Ernest Barker (*Greek Political Theory: Plato and His Predecessors, 337*) sees that these are popular courts, but mistakes them for local courts.
[15] Aristotle, *Constitution of Athens*, LXVII, 2.

orators. Elsewhere Aristotle tells us that in "well-governed states" there were rules of procedure that excluded irrelevant pleading, and he mentions the Areopagus as one court in which such rules were put into effect. His silence as to the heliastic courts is eloquent.[16]

But Plato's greatest innovation is the denial of final authority to these popular courts with the setting up of a higher court, the Court of Select Judges, to which cases heard in the popular courts may be appealed. This court is elected annually by the full body of officials of all ranks. They meet under solemn auspices in a temple and select from each office in the state that magistrate whom they consider to be the most competent in his group. A further stage of scrutiny after the preliminary election affords an opportunity for rejecting any one already named and replacing him with a more suitable choice (767C ff.). The size of the court is not explicitly stated, but if one person is to be chosen from each office, the total number will be something less than a score.

Since this is the court which is to embody the principle of special competence, it is important to notice the way in which this special competence is obtained. In the absence of a professional class of lawyers or jurists, Plato turns to those who have had experience in administering the laws, *viz.*, the magistrates. It is not a passing fancy. An identical proposal for selecting such a high court is set forth in his letter to the friends of Dion in Syracuse (*Ep. VIII*, 356D–E). And it had its parallels in current Greek usage. In many Greek states, notably in oligarchies such as Crete and Sparta, the highest judicial functions were discharged by a court composed of ex-officeholders. The Areopagus at Athens was such a court, consisting of ex-archons sitting for life. But Plato's court differs from these historical models in several respects. It contains members from all grades of office in the state, lowest as well as highest. Membership in it is a matter of election, not a privilege automatically enjoyed by those who have held office. And lastly, its members hold office for one year only, not for life. Though there is no stated bar to reëlection, yet it is clear that the membership will be subject to frequent and radical changes. We are left to infer the reasons for these specific provisions. One obvious result is to prevent this high court from attaining a position of entrenched power. Again, the court will always be in close touch with the problems of

---

[16] *Rhetoric* I, 1354A 16; 1355A 2.

administration at all points in the government. These are advantages, and perhaps they are advantages that Plato deliberately seeks. A disadvantage that cannot escape the attention of the modern reader is that the short tenure of office, for one year only, would prevent the development of anything like judicial competence, as we understand the term, and would hinder the development of a judicial tradition. Plato's court will be essentially a court of amateurs, as judged by our standards, and will therefore possess all the disadvantages, as well as the undoubted advantages, of the non-professional administration of justice.

In giving this court power to hear cases on appeal from the popular courts, Plato is departing radically from the theory and practice of Athenian democracy. The appeal was known at Athens, but it meant invariably an appeal from magistrates or arbitrators to the popular courts; from the sovereign people there was no appeal. Plato's proposal therefore would take away from the people that judicial supremacy which was regarded by friends and foes alike as the most typical feature of a democratic constitution. The hatred of the oligarchs for the popular courts is notorious, and one of their first acts, in both the revolutions that took place toward the end of the fifth century, was to suspend them; just as the democracy was equally prompt in reëstablishing them after its return to power. It is characteristic of Plato's compromising spirit in the *Laws* that he does not side with either group of extremists. He deprives these courts of judicial supremacy, but he assigns them an important place in his system. Their verdicts would undoubtedly put an end to many of the cases that come before them, since an appeal to the higher court involves a penalty if unsuccessful. Not only that, but we must also take into account the influence of the lower court on the higher one, an influence that may be more or less great according to the political structure of the state, but can never be altogether negligible.

We may observe also that the compromise Plato sets up seems to have been highly original. We know of many Greek states in which there were no popular courts of the Athenian type. We know also of states other than Athens in which the popular courts were judicially supreme. But of states in which there were popular courts restricted in competence and subject to reversal by a higher court we have no evidence until a later time, when the Greek cities had lost their independence and their judicial as well as their administrative acts were subject to review by their Macedonian overlords.

III

Let us turn now to Plato's treatment of a more difficult question involved in the rule of law, the problem of preventing arbitrary and illegal action by officials in the discharge of their duties. The problem presented is a most delicate one, as even the layman can see; and success or failure in solving it determines whether or not the rule of law, in the strictest sense of the term, prevails.

The Athenians, like Plato, were well aware of the importance of this problem, and in the fifth and fourth centuries they had powerful constitutional devices for preventing the abuse of official power. In the first place, every newly designated official, before taking office at Athens, had to pass a scrutiny (δοκιμασία), or official examination before the Council and the popular courts. In the second place, every office-holder at the end of his term of office had to undergo an official review (εὔθυναι) of his acts in office, and was subject to fines and other penalties if he was judged guilty of having acted contrary to the laws. And lastly, at any sovereign meeting of the Assembly, that is ten times a year, a vote (ἐπιχειροτονία) could be taken on the conduct of any official and he could be suspended forthwith if the vote was unfavorable. By these three devices the actions of public officials seem to have been kept well within the law, at least within the law as understood by the popular courts and the assembly.

Of these three typically Athenian institutions, Plato intends to retain at least two, the scrutiny and the review; but he retains them with important modifications. At Athens both these functions lay in the hands of the popular courts, but Plato would evidently entrust them to smaller and more responsible bodies. This intent can be inferred, I think, as regards the scrutiny;[17] and it is clearly evident with respect to the review. For this function he creates a special board of Examiners (εὔθυνοι) to review the conduct of all officials, both during and after their terms of office, and at intervals to make a report of their findings (945B–948B). Where malfeasance is discovered, they have the power to impose a fine or other penalty. But the power they wield is responsible; for an official who is in-

---

[17] The scrutiny is mentioned in connection with almost all the offices in the state, but usually without any details as to how it is to be conducted. Where the examining body is mentioned, it is a group of officials, not the popular courts (766B, 767D). For the procedure at Athens, see Aristotle, *Const. of Athens*, LV, 2–3.

dicted by them may carry this case to the court of Select Judges, subject to a double penalty if he loses; but if he succeeds in vindicating himself, he may bring legal action in the courts for the removal or punishment of the Examiner who indicted him (946D).

Besides this powerful instrument for keeping officials in the path of rectitude, Plato provides another remedy to which he makes numerous references, and which is in some respects so original, as compared with both ancient and modern law, that some of these references should be quoted in full.

> As to the rural magistrates, if they abuse the authority they have, by imposing inequitable levies upon the farmers, or seizing and taking away their goods or implements without their consent, or if they receive gifts or render unjust judgments . . . let the injured man bring suit in the common courts. 761E ff.

By "common courts" Plato means, as other passages show, the popular courts already described.

> If any magistrate appear to have delivered an unjust judgment he shall be liable for double damages to the injured person. Whoever wishes may bring suit in the common courts against the magistrates for unjust decisions rendered in cases brought before them. 846B.

These and other texts show clearly that any person who considers he has been wronged by an official may bring a suit for damages against the offending official. Now this procedure has certain obvious advantages lacking in the review. It is an immediate remedy and one that can be invoked by the person who considers himself injured. It has close analogies with the civil suit against an officer which is allowed by our law. It seems also as if the texts intended to grant the right of action not merely to the injured person, but also to any other person who wishes to prosecute on his behalf; for the language used (ὁ βουλόμενος, "whoever wishes") is exactly the same as the Attic legal term employed in describing a γραφή or action that could be initiated by persons other than those whose interests were directly affected. Such a privilege might be of great importance, for example if the official act complained of was such as to incapacitate its victim, or otherwise hinder him from prosecuting.

But the most striking feature of Plato's proposal is yet to be noted. Plato makes an official liable to prosecution for the abuse of the judicial as well as of administrative powers. The officials in Plato's state almost always have judicial as well as administrative functions.[18] This is especially marked in the minor officials, such as the Rural Magistrates (ἀγρονόμοι) or the Market Officials (ἀγορανόμοι). Not only may they impose fines for violations of the ordinances they are charged with enforcing, but they also have power to hear and settle private claims involving injury to person or property or breach of contract up to three hundred drachmae. This was a sizable claim, when we consider that a drachma was the normal day's wage in the fifth century.[19] It is partly against the abuse of their powers by these magistrates that the remedy we are discussing is directed. But it is provided not merely against these lesser magistrates with their incidental judicial powers, but also against judges in the stricter sense of the word. With few, if any, exceptions, all judges are subject to prosecution under this law.[20] This is the most striking and unusual feature of Plato's conception of official liability. One can hardly imagine a more dramatic remedy against judicial injustice than a suit for damages against the judge; and there is, so far as we know, no historical counterpart in the procedure of any Greek state, not even Athens, and but few analogies. It may be that we have here an original Platonic invention. Judges may shake their heads at this proposal. For it makes the judge render judgment at his peril, and thus may incline him

[18] The texts are too numerous to list in full. The most important are 763C–D, 764B–C, 761D–E, 842E–844D, 845D–E.

[19] In the fourth century prices, and probably wages also, were somewhat higher.

[20] The statement in 761E immediately before the law above quoted, is puzzling: "No judge or ruler ought to be exempt from liability (ἀνυπεύθυνος) for what he does as judge or ruler, except those whose judgment is final, such as kings." The relevance of this exception is not clear. There are no officials in Plato's state that are immune to prosecution and removal. Either this is a statement of principle which was later revised, or Plato is stating the principle broadly enough to include states which, unlike his own, have kings. *Cf.* [Plat.] *Def.* 415B: βασιλεὺς ἄρχων κατὰ νόμους ἀνυπεύθυνος [King ruling with laws but not accountable]. Yet for Syracuse in 352 Plato proposes an ἀρχὴ ὑπεύθυνος βασιλική [accountable royal rule] (*Ep. VIII*, 355E).

to consider the personal consequences of his decision rather than the law and the facts of the case to be decided. On the other hand it is probable that a similar objection might be raised on *a priori* grounds to the now familiar practice of holding officials liable to prosecution for their administrative acts; but in practice it does not seem to have had any serious effects upon the efficiency of administration. I confess to a secret fondness for Plato's proposal, because it strikes at a defect in the administration of justice to which our Anglo-Saxon lawyers seem to be congenitally blind, *viz.* the abuse of judicial power. For the rule of law, as it has worked out in our legal institutions, means the rule of judges, and this kind of rule, like any other, can become tyranny unless properly safeguarded. In the last few weeks there have occurred some striking instances of what looks like judicial ὕβρις, against which our law provides only devious and uncertain remedies.

Plato applies this remedy against abuse of power in essentially the same fashion to all grades of offices, high as well as low. Thus an indictment may be brought against a member of the Court of Select Judges, if any one thinks he has been guilty of injustice (767E). In this case the trial takes place before the Guardians of the Law sitting as a court, not before the ordinary tribunals. This modification of procedure is obviously necessary, since the Select Judges are the highest of the ordinary courts. Again, a Guardian of the Law is subject to prosecution by any qualified citizen for negligence or wilful injustice in the conduct of his office. An action of this sort is brought before the Select Judges, apparently without going through the lower courts (928B). As to the other body of high officials, the Examiners, we have already seen that not only may their findings be disputed in the courts, but they themselves may be prosecuted by any qualified citizen and if found guilty removed from office. The trial of an Examiner comes before a special court consisting of the Guardians of the Law, the Select Judges, and the other Examiners (946D–E, 948A).

Evidently the intention of these provisions is to confer upon each of these bodies a judicial check upon the others. Here we have another original invention, and the most influential perhaps of all Plato's suggestions. The distribution of the judicial power it involves is without a parallel in any constitution of Plato's day, so far as we know. It differs from the procedure of the democracies, for in them the popular courts were judicially supreme. It differs likewise from the practice of the oligarchic states and from the program of the oligarchic party at Athens. In the oligarchies we always find a hierarchy of officials leading to a group at the top who cannot be called to account by any other body, such as the Spartan Gerusia, or the Athenian Areopagus in the days before Solon. And the oligarchic conservatives of Plato's day invariably sought to create some such supreme judicial body, usually by enlarging the powers of the Council. But the Council in Plato's state has no judicial powers at all. Thus Plato has rejected both the oligarchic and the democratic theories as to the locus of judicial supremacy; and in proposing to divide the judicial power so that every group of high officers is legally liable to another and independent body, he gave expression to an idea destined to make its fortune in the world. It is an old story how Plato's invention of a "mixed state", designed to achieve stability by a balance of opposing tendencies, lived on in Aristotle, Polybius and Cicero as the essence of political wisdom; and how it was rediscovered in modern times by Locke and Montesquieu. Perhaps we should add that Plato not only conceived the idea of a mixed state, but also anticipated some of the checks and balances necessary to maintain it.

Before we leave these remedies for the correction of private and official wrong-doing, let me call your attention to a striking feature common to them all, *viz.* the freedom of prosecution possessed by the private citizen. There is no public prosecutor in Platonic law, any more than there was at Athens. When a man has been wronged, it is he who takes legal action against the offender. Moreover, the private citizen has the right (and also the duty) to prosecute for offenses against the public,[21] or for wrongs to third parties too weak or timid to take legal action themselves.[22] These are familiar principles of Athenian procedure and constitute that "freedom of prosecution" so much prized at Athens. Such a system of volunteer prosecutors may seem primitive to us, accustomed as we are to public prosecutors. Yet we know all too well how an incompetent or dishonest public prosecutor can defeat the ends of justice by failing to take action against a criminal, or by changing the charges against him to a less serious category, or by other tricks

[21] Here the texts are legion. Typical examples are 767B, 745A, 856C, 919E, 943A–B, 948A.

[22] 928B, 932D, 954E–955A. Homicide was an exception. Both in Platonic law and in Attic law prosecution for homicide must be instituted by a relative of the victim.

known to that office. Nothing like this could happen at Athens. A voluntary prosecutor might be bought off, but some one else would probably press the charges in his place. This freedom of prosecution may bring evils of its own, as is shown by Athenian history. Peaceful citizens do not like to be prosecuted, even if they are innocent and can prove their innocence; and law-abiding Athenians were often subject to blackmail through threat of prosecution. Nevertheless the Athenians thought these inconveniences were not too great a price to pay for the certainty that the unauthorized use of power would bring retribution. And Plato seems to agree. He does endeavor, however, to prevent the abuses of the system by imposing penalties for unfounded accusations and for persistent litigiousness (938B–C, 948C).

IV

We come finally to the procedure set up for dealing with capital offenses.[23] The list of offenses punishable by death in Plato's state is a long one, as it was at Athens, including among others, temple-robbing (854D–E), sedition (856 C), treason (856E, 857A), premeditated homicide (871D), and certain cases of impiety

[23] To get a complete picture of the administration of justice in Plato's state one would have to consider many other details of his courts and legal procedure; but much has to be omitted here for obvious reasons. There are special courts—*e.g.* military courts and family courts—for certain offenses; but the most important of the courts not mentioned in the text is the Court of the Demos, consisting of the whole body (πλῆθος) of citizens, which judges offenses against the public (767B–E). So far as one can judge from the scanty account given, it corresponds to the ecclesia at Athens, which occasionally sat as a court to judge cases brought before it by way of εἰσαγγελία—a type of procedure which was as much political as judicial, since the offenses against the public which it dealt with were but vaguely defined (and in earlier days not defined at all) by the law. Such an institution is a powerful instrument for keeping the actions of officials in line with the public sense of the common welfare, and seems to be adopted by Plato for that reason. Plato places two restrictions upon the Court of the Demos which were unknown at Athens: (1) it is without competence to impose the death sentence; and (2) "only the beginning and the end of such trials shall come before the people; the examination (βάσανος) of the case must be entrusted to three of the chief magistrates whom the prosecutor and the defendant shall agree upon" (768A). The provisions forbidding the use of the oath and irrelevant pleading would doubtless apply here also, as well as to the other popular courts we have described.

(910C–D). Neither Plato nor his countrymen seem to have had any special feeling against capital punishment. Plato did feel, however, that the judgment of such cases should be entrusted to a special court. At Athens these offenses were judged, some by the Areopagus, and some by the heliastic courts and the assembly. No fault seems to have been found with the handling of its cases by the Areopagus, but many of the capital cases tried by the popular courts became *causes célèbres*, notably the trial of the generals after the battle of Arginusae before the assembly, and the trial of Socrates. It is not surprising therefore that Plato would have capital offenses passed on by a select court. This court is to consist of the Select Judges together with the Guardians of the Law (855C), a court which in its constitution, as well as in its functions, bears a striking resemblance to the Areopagus, particularly the Areopagus of the days before Pericles, when its members still had important executive as well as judicial powers.

There is no appeal from the decisions of this court, and no provision for pardon;[24] but Plato devotes special attention to procedure.

> The voting shall be public. During the hearing the judges shall sit next one another in order of age and directly before the defendant and prosecutor; and all citizens who have the time shall attend. . . . Each party shall make one speech, first the prosecutor and then the defendant. After these speeches the eldest of the judges shall begin the examination and make a thorough inquiry into what has been said. And after the oldest has concluded, all the others shall proceed in order to address whatever questions they like to either of the parties with regard to what they have said or failed to say. . . . Whatever has been said that the judges deem to be relevant shall be set down in writing, and after being signed by all the judges shall be sealed and deposited on the altar of Hestia. On the next day they shall come together again and go through the examination of the case in the same manner and set their seals upon what has been said. And when they have done this a third time and examined thoroughly all the evidence and witnesses, each one shall give his solemn vote . . . and thus they shall put an end to the case (855D–856A).

[24] Unless we assume that the assembly, as at Athens, is intended to have the power of pardon.

Note the use of the inquisitorial proceeding, which Plato regards as one of the advantages of a small court. We should note also the requirement of publicity for the hearings and for the votes of the individual judges. This provision runs counter to the current practice at Athens. In the heliastic courts the proceedings were private and the votes of the individual judges secret. The Areopagus also seems to have excluded the public from its hearings, but whether the votes of the judges were known to one another we do not know.[25] Plato is guarding against an obvious danger, the danger of Star Chamber proceedings (*cf.* 876A–B); besides, public proceedings and open voting are necessary if the judges are to be held responsible. Of greatest interest is the requirement that the proceedings shall extend over three days. This may be regarded as in a sense the substitute for the appeal in civil cases. The haste with which capital cases were disposed of by the heliastic courts in a single day must have been something of a scandal. It is well to recall Socrates' dignified protest in the *Apology:* "If there were a law at Athens, as there is in other cities, that a capital cause should not be decided in one day, then I believe I should have convinced you" (37A; Jowett's translation). All readers of the *Apology* in Plato's day would have caught the implication of these remarks. We know that at Sparta such a trial would have come before the Gerusia and would have extended over several days.[26] Even at Athens, if Socrates had been charged with homicide, instead of impiety, the case would have been handled with more deliberation; it would have come before the Areopagus, which could render final judgment in capital cases only after three successive hearings.[27] Evidently these proposals of Plato's are charged with bitter memories.

v

"In determining a nation's rank in political civilization", says Sidgwick, "no test is more decisive than the degree in which justice as defined by the law is actually realized in its judicial administration."[28] What is the quality of Plato's state as measured by the standard Sidgwick lays down? It is evident, at least, that Plato adheres very closely to that conception of the rule of law which is a

[25] Demosthenes XXV, 23; LIX, 79 ff.
[26] Gilbert, *Handbuch der Griechischen Staatsaltertümer*, I, 89.
[27] Gilbert, I, 433.   [28] *Elements of Politics*, 481.

cherished part of our political heritage. All the persons in his state, whatever their rank or condition, are subject to the ordinary laws of the state and are amenable to the jurisdiction of the ordinary courts. Executive actions can always be brought before the courts for examination. Plato has even gone beyond us in the variety of his provisions for calling officials to account, most strikingly in the remedy he proposes for the abuse of judicial power. In his generous provisions for appeal in civil cases he has improved upon the best level of Athenian justice, and the famous idea of a mixed state, with its balancing of powerful forces, lives today embodied in our tradition and practice. But without dwelling further upon these positive merits, I should like, in conclusion, to point out certain respects in which Plato's conception of the rule of law differs from that which has become orthodox in later theory.

The first point concerns the close connection between judicial and executive functions in Plato's state, and the consequent lack of a distinct and independent judiciary. "There is no liberty", says Montesquieu, "if the power of judging be not separated from the legislative and executive powers." But when Plato looks for persons especially qualified to administer justice, he invariably turns to his officials, or to persons who have had official experience. Sometimes this leads to a situation fraught with grave peril for the accused, as when he puts his Guardians of the Law, probably the most powerful executive officers in his state, on the Court of Capital Offenses, with power to judge treason and sedition. Why Plato follows such a dangerous principle is perhaps intelligible if we take a glance at the development of the judicial process in Greece. In the earliest times, judicial and administrative functions were uniformly exercised by the same persons, an aristocracy of birth. The later centuries brought about a double change: public offices became elective or subject to the lot, and the administration of justice was more and more taken from the officials and put in the hands of the people. In time the wheel went full circle; in the advanced democracies the people in their courts began to exercise administrative as well as judicial powers, so that once again there was a union of the two functions in the same hands. Those who saw the dangers of such a situation invariably turned to the remedy suggested by the past; they sought to reinvest in the officials a portion of the judicial power that had been taken from them. The creation of a trained judiciary, separate in personnel from executive officials and relatively independent in their tenure of office, was an expedient which did not occur, so far as we know, to any Greek thinker.[29] It could hardly have come about in fact before the rise of a separate legal profession; and this was contrary to the amateur spirit which pervaded practically all spheres of civic life in Greece. Plato was one of the first to challenge the competence of the amateur; but he failed to see the special kind of competence required for the judicial function.

Another respect in which Plato's conception of the rule of law fails to meet a requirement regarded as axiomatic today is the absence of any theory or process of legislation. Our idea is that the law must adapt itself to changes in public opinion, through representative law-making bodies, or otherwise. Plato believes that public opinion must adapt itself to the law, and all the forces of art, religion and education are directed to this end. He does occasionally suggest the possibility of changes in the laws, but such changes are obviously to be rare events, and the manner in which they are to be brought about is left exceedingly vague. The same way of thinking was traditional among his conservative countrymen. There was, of course, provision for legal change at Athens, but the procedure was exceptional, and always surrounded with special precautions. It is a striking fact that in Aristotle's description of the constitution of Athens, otherwise so detailed, there is not a single sentence concerned with legislation, and but little more in the *Politics*.[30] There could be no better evidence that legislation was not generally recognized as one of the normal functions of government, at least in the circles to which Aristotle and Plato belonged.

Again we may ask, who are they who benefit by the law's protection? I have confined my discussion for convenience to the citizen class only. But in Plato's state, as in practically all Greek states in historical times, there would be foreigners as well as slaves. Is the law intended to protect them as well as the citizens? It must be said that in Plato's state the law has little to offer the slave. The slave looks to his master; only on rare occasions may he invoke the

---

[29] Aristotle's recognition of τὸ δικάζον [the judiciary] (*Politics*, 1298A 3) as a separate part of the state distinct from the deliberative and the executive does not mean a separate and independent personnel for the discharge of this function.

[30] Aristotle does not even mention the νομοθέται, whose existence and activity in the second half of the fourth century are well attested by texts and inscriptions.

law's protection in his own right. But Plato evinces a special interest
in the legal rights of foreigners. So far as one can judge, they are on
an equality with the citizen as respects access to the courts for
redress of wrongs. In most states in Greece the foreigner's legal
rights were defined by treaty, or (in the case of resident aliens)
could only be exercised through a citizen patron. There is no trace
of this in Platonic law. A fair indication of Plato's attitude is his
law prescribing the same penalty for the murder of a foreigner as
for the murder of a citizen (872A; *cf.* 871A). Even at Athens there
was a difference: the one offense involved the death penalty, the
other exile. To complete the picture of the range of protection
afforded by Plato's law we should add other details of his legislation, such as his proposals for increasing the legal rights of women
and for protecting wards and orphans. When all the evidence is
considered I venture the opinion that the "sharers in the law", to
use the expressive Greek phrase, will be found to be more numerous
in Plato's state than in any historical Greek state we know.

We are encroaching on substantive law and must call a halt.
How well Plato's law measures up to modern standards of equity in
the substantive rights it gives the citizen, the foreigner, and the
other persons affected by it cannot be considered here. It is essential, however, to realize that in any system of law, procedure (in the
broad sense of the word) is as important as substance; and that in
insisting on the rule of law as I have outlined it, even with its defects, Plato has set forth some of the primary conditions of freedom
and justice.

> We must not make our officials big and savage; for we want
> our city to be free and wise and full of fellow feeling (693B.).

Assuredly this doctrine, so congenial to us who still speak the
language of democracy, has little kinship with the totalitarian
glorification of irresponsible "leadership". Whatever may be said
of the *Republic*, the *Laws* does not countenance personal sovereignty.
It may be that the younger Plato did not see, as clearly as the Plato
of the *Laws*, the dangers of absolutism, or the difficulty of finding
that union of wisdom and integrity required for the exercise of an
imperium legibus solutum. If so, Plato himself has passed judgment on
his own lack of insight, in the words of the Athenian Stranger.

> "A state in which the law is subject and without authority is
> ripe for destruction; but when the law is sovereign over the

rulers, and the rulers servants of the law, then, as I see it, the state is secure."

"Excellent, stranger!" says Cleinias: "You have sharp eyes for an old man."

"In matters such as these," replies the Athenian Stranger, "a man's vision is at its dullest in his youth and keenest in his old age"(715D).

Originally published in the *Philosophical Review* 59 (1941), 105–26. Reprinted by permission of the *Philosophical Review* and the author.

10

WAS PLATO NON-POLITICAL?[1]

WAYNE A. R. LEYS

I

Did Plato develop a mature political philosophy, or was he non-political? In raising this question I shall direct your attention to at least three problems: (1) the merits of the arguments of the past generation concerning Plato's alleged totalitarianism, (2) the meaning of "politics" and the proper use of any definitions that may be given for words like the word "political," and (3) the task of political philosophy.

The first problem is to determine whether Plato can properly be called a fascist or a totalitarian. This appears to be a factual problem, and many of the scholars who have taken positions on the matter have had scientific or literary training. Teachers of philosophy entered the controversy typically when they believed that one of their favorite authors was being misinterpreted by selective quotation. Even when a philosopher, such as Levinson or Wild, entered the controversy, the argument remained an argument about fact. The philosopher called attention to some of Plato's statements that had been overlooked by Popper, Chapman, or Crossman.

The factual problem of what Plato said and advocated is not a new one, but during the 1930's the successes of Hitler and Stalin made it seem important and, to some extent, novel. Had Plato idealized a totalitarian state? Were the strong-arm tactics and the centralized bureaucracies of the Third Reich and the Soviet Union anticipated by this ancient Greek philosopher?

In the quarter-century following 1930, Plato's "enemies" contended that the harsh brutality of Plato's political philosophy had been ignored by modern expositors. In Britain, for example, the Cambridge Platonists, More and Cudworth, said very little about Plato's politics, concentrating their attention upon questions in theology, metaphysics and personal ethics. The leading English

[1] This paper was presented to the Illinois Philosophy Conference, October 24, 1964.

translators and Interpreters of Plato in more recent times (Jowett, Nettleship, Barker, etc.) have had more interest in the Philosophy of the State, but their comments were expressed in language that made the most dictatorial proposals sound like the "generous suggestions of a benevolent paternalist."

Plato's "defenders," contrariwise, emphasized the contrasts between Plato's ideal and the totalitarian actuality. Plato did not advocate a police state; he made no provision for secret police, for concentration camps, for cruel and unusual punishments. There was no intent to rule by terror. Furthermore, the rulers were to be guided, not by expediency, but by a perfect ideal, a rational plan. Indeed, Plato was represented as the fountainhead of the natural-law philosophy, a point of view credited with resistance to numerous tyrants.

On another occasion, when I had to take a position in this controversy, I ventured to suggest that it was a mistake to identify Plato either as an advocate or as an opponent of totalitarianism. Plato seemed to me to be antipolitical. Although he has much to say about "the state," Plato never approves of institutions that I would call "political." His polemic against the persuaders (in *The Republic, The Gorgias* and other dialogues) is only one bit of evidence to this effect. In *The Statesman* and in *The Laws*, where Plato describes second-best states, there is a grudging recognition of the need for laws; but there is never an admission that persuaders or politicians are necessary. Nor do we find in any of the dialogues a plan whereby action may be taken in the face of unresolved disagreements among organized factions. There is, in *The Laws*, a treatment of crime and punishment; but underlying this discussion is the assumption that there is really no question as to what the law and public policy should be.

I find no basis for comparing Plato to Cicero, Aquinas, Locke, Machiavelli, or Hegel as a political philosopher. He seems more like the non-political philosophers—Descartes, for example, who found the product of a single mind always superior to the products of committees. Plato is more comparable to the modern economist than to the modern political scientist. He is concerned with the best means to ends that are regarded as good rather than the disposition of unresolved conflicts over what is good. Plato is like the non-political scientist, technician, and plain citizen: he is always asking about the merits of policy disputes. Plato is not like the lawyer, the politician, or the military strategist, who ask what can be done in the face of failure to secure general agreement on the merits.

Karl Popper was correct when he asserted that Plato did not like an "open society." The political institutions of an "open society" maintain the conditions under which there is some possibility of achieving a majority consensus (by persuasion, by trading, or by exhaustion). But Popper was wrong when he suggested that Plato was approving the sort of regime which in our time we call "totalitarian." The totalitarian recognizes the political problem, the existence of disagreement and conflict. He proposes to solve the political problem by suppressing all except one faction. Plato, on the other hand, was preoccupied with the prescription of institutions that had no political problems. His ideal society was troubled by individual malefactors and by enemy states, but not by organized factions within the community in ultimate disagreement over goals and policies. Plato should not be likened to the twentieth-century dictators or their theorists, Rosenberg, Rocco, Lenin. He bears more resemblance to the people who say, "Let's keep this, that, or the other issue out of politics."

II

In calling Plato non-political or antipolitical, I have, of course, assumed the propriety of a definition of the word "political." I define as political any activity, institution, or issue that pertains to a division of opinion and aspiration within a population that has some dealings with one another despite that division.

I use the word "political" in about the same way that Croce did, when he said that some men have political sense and some do not. In deciding which problems should be called "political," I follow the tradition of Machiavelli and Hobbes, which culminates in the writings of Carl Schmitt. Schmitt contended that the distinction between friend and foe is the essential political distinction. Thus, a person who has political sense is one who thinks about the opposition and also about the support, actual and potential, that may be connected with any idea, activity, or institution.

In adopting this definition of the political, I do not intend to indorse the policies and attitudes which the neo-Machiavellians advocated as solutions of political problems. I merely agree with them in the meaning which they assign to the word "political." And it was with this meaning in mind that I suggested that Plato was non-political or antipolitical. The propriety of adopting and using such a definition is, in our time, a seriously debated philosophical issue. The ancient Greek practice of seeking characteristics that can be called essential or defining characteristics has been under attack by logical positivists, pragmatists, existentialists, and ordinary language philosophers.

To avoid the objections of these varied schools to my use of a definition of the word "political," I now make a series of disclaimers.

1. To assert that Plato did not develop a political philosophy because he was concerned with the avoidance of disagreements rather than with what to do about them is not to deny that Plato had a political philosophy in some other sense. The use of the Machiavellian definition of "political" merely clarifies a thesis which stands or falls on textual evidence, namely, that Plato—despite much talk about the state and rulers—has little to say about living with conflict and few, if any, proposals for action in a society that is divided into factions. The definition is not being used as a proof or as a persuasive device; it merely clarifies what is being looked for in the Platonic texts.

2. To define "the political" as "that which pertains to divisions, disagreements and conflicts" is not the same thing as asserting that political institutions, as a matter of fact, have no other function than that of dealing with conflicts; nor is there any normative implication that all other activities of political institutions should be subordinated to the activities that relate to conflict. I believe that what we call government is more political than the enterprises we call religion, business, and the fine arts; but a definition of "the political" merely defines a characteristic that is especially prominent in government. It does not prove that government may not carry on service activities of a non-political nature or that other institutions may not be to some extent political.

3. To follow the Hobbesian and Machiavellian practice of viewing politics as the art of the possible (in view of actual and potential conflicts) is to make the conflict of power-possessing groups an essential characteristic of anything that is called "political." This practice is contrary to the Platonic usage, according to which "the political" always has some reference to the common good, the order, or harmony that is desirable in a community. But this modern practice does not commit one to the opinions of Machiavelli or Botero or Clausewitz as to what is possible. It does not en-

tail acceptance of the opinions of Thrasymachus or Marx or Bentham regarding the nature of human conflict. To make conflict an essential property of "the political" means only that, whenever one asks whether some fact or problem or situation is political, one looks for disagreements that affect what is happening and sets some limitations upon what can be done.

In these disclaimers I have tried to recognize the reasonable objections of contemporary philosophers to what may be called the abuse of definitions in classical philosophy. But, if one refrains from proposing any general definitions of such words as "politics," as some of our contemporaries do, the result will be a studied neglect of many of the most interesting and pressing philosophical problems.

III

What are the tasks of political philosophy? What are the jobs to be done? Are they merely the clarification of what the ancients had to say? Or a disentangling of fact and value in common discourse? I venture the suggestion that political philosophy, like other branches of philosophy, should not be limited to such analytic work, important as that may be.

Equally important is the relating of generalizations that are based upon different varieties of experience: political, religious, scientific, and so on. If "the political" is defined as "that which refers to human conflict and disagreement," "political philosophy" consists of those principles, proverbs, or values that seem to make sense of our experiences of conflict. Such principles as "religious toleration," for example, or "majority rule" or "inalienable rights" are grounded in experiences of conflict and in efforts to do something about conflict.

But, as soon as a collection is made of such principles (with the aid of a definition of "the political"), it is obvious that the descriptive and normative generalizations of political philosophy are not entirely the same as the generalizations of the philosophy of religion or the philosophy of science or of ethics or of aesthetics. "Majority rule" is nonsensical as a rule of logic. "Compromise," "log-rolling," and "give-and-take" are repugnant as procedures for making religious commitments. Strikes, boycotts, shows of force, and other tests of strength are irrelevant in the determination of scientific questions. There are many practices, policies, and beliefs that help in the solution of political problems that we reject in non-political situations. One of the issues of political philosophy is how we reconcile these political beliefs and practices with other beliefs and practices. And the point that I am trying to make is this: that the reconciliation of political and non-political beliefs cannot even be formulated unless there is a fairly general definition of "the political."

Let us return now to our original thesis. Plato has an incomplete political philosophy for the reason that he avoids approving any institutions that are specifically intended to deal with political problems, that is, with problems of action in the face of conflict and disagreement. His ideal state and his second-best state are pictures of societies that have no political problems. Organized oppositions are prevented from arising by education (in *The Republic*) and by wise legislation (in *The Laws*). Hence, there are no distinctively political institutions to reconcile with the scientific, economic, and morale-maintaining beliefs.

In a sense, preoccupation with non-political ideals is a philosophy of politics. It is as much of political philosophy as is possessed or done by many persons who hate opposition and the practices that opposition makes necessary. It is a political philosophy in the sense of an attempted escape from politics. It is comparable to the philosophy of religion of a man who contends that, given the right diet and the right toilet training, men will not have emotional or morale problems. Or it is comparable to the "logic" of a man who says that there are no orderly ways of testing arguments; that all you can do is rely on hunch.

If "political" is defined as necessarily referring to actual and potential conflicts within a society, "political philosophy" must deal with the following kinds of data:

a) Judgments of the nature and extent of conflict
b) Information about the agreements and acquiescences in conflict-settling institutions
c) Judgments of the feasibility of various kinds of behavior under the above-mentioned conditions
d) Judgments of the extent to which politically feasible behavior is consistent with morality, religion, etc.

These elements are largely missing in Plato's writings. By contrast, let me mention a few political philosophers who do wrestle with these data. John Locke, for example, looks at the religious wars and comes up with the suggestion that theological beliefs ought to be regarded as private matters, the truth of which shall never be publicly determined. Aristotle looks at the tendency of various forms of government to go to reaction-provoking extremes and suggests an untidy mixed polity. Hobbes sees the political value of arbitration and recognizes that this value is in conflict with popular religious commitments. John Stuart Mill looks at the potential follies of representative government and argues for absolute rights of free speech, which are scarcely compatible with his inherited utilitarianism. W. D. Ross looks at the existing customs and agreements and argues for the logical independence of the right and the good.

Here are the kinds of problems that Plato does not face. He was capable of the sort of philosophical solutions which the political philosophers adopted: epistemological doubts, metaphysical speculations, etc., but he does not employ them to rationalize anything but an abstinence from politics in actual society.

Among the philosophers who take politics seriously I believe you will always find an awareness of the difficulty of reconciling the right and the good, the virtuous and the sacred, the moral and the logical. Such tensions in a philosophy indicate that the philosopher is aware of the unique quality of political experience and of what appear to be reasonable demands of the political predicament. In our time such a tension is often evident in the problem of reconciling institutional loyalties. It is also apparent in the incompatibility of due process and humanitarian goals.

In Plato I find no such tension. The political values that enable man to deal with organized opposition are represented as a corruption, alien to all right thinking. Plato has no reason for trying to distinguish between the better and the worse within the realm of controversy. He sets the style for those who solve the political problem by declaring that there need not be a political problem. He is the godfather of those who find only nonsense in political palaver. He is the saint of those who see only evil in their opponents and in the institutions that require concessions to opponents.[2]

---

[2] In the first draft of this paper I went on to assert that Plato should not be called the fountainhead of Western political philosophy. Dr. Donald Verene criticized this assertion as an underestimate of Plato's historical importance. I recognize that Dr. Verene's criticism is just.

I have implied, in these characterizations of Plato, my own conception of the task of political philosophy; it is to make some kind of sense of political experience and to develop standards by which some political practices may be adjudged better than others. This conception of political philosophy is comparable to widely held conceptions of other branches of philosophy. The epistemologist does not assume that all inferences are valid or that they are all invalid. He assumes that, among the conclusions reached by intelligent men, some are valid and some are invalid. He undertakes to articulate standards appropriate to his material. The philosopher of religion similarly does not assume that all religious experience and all theologies are buncombe, nor does he accept them all at face value; he seeks some orderly way of interpreting what is otherwise a miscellany of confusing claims. So, also, I suggest, the political philosopher assumes that the political enterprises, which have claimed the thought and effort of many able men, are not to be rejected or accepted in an all-or-none fashion, but that it may be possible to find reasons for preferences, good reasons for some and not for others.

BIBLIOGRAPHY

Aristotle. *The Politics*.

B. Croce. *Politics and Morals*. Philosophical Library, 1945.

R. Levinson. *In Defense of Plato*. Cambridge, Mass., 1953.

W. Leys. "Platonic, Pragmatic, and Political Responsibility," in C. Friedrich, *Responsibility*. Atherton Press (Nomos Series), 1960.

Plato. *The Republic, The Gorgias, The Protagoras, The Statesman, The Laws, The Epistles*.

K. Popper. *The Open Society and Its Enemies*. Princeton, 1950.

C. Schmitt. "Der Begriff des Politischen," *Archiv für Sozialwissenschaft und Sozialpolitik*, Vol. LVIII (1928).

J. Wild. *Plato's Modern Enemies and the Theory of Natural Law*. Chicago, 1953.

However, Plato's historical importance for political philosophy lies in the fact that he articulated non-political ideals (moral, economic, logical, religious ideals) so clearly that later generations could not ignore the contrasts between political wisdom and other kinds of wisdom.

Originally published in *Ethics* 75 (1965), 272–76. Reprinted by permission of The University of Chicago Press and the author.

11

PLATO AS ANTI-POLITICAL THINKER

F. E. SPARSHOTT

Professor Leys stigmatizes Plato's thought as non-political, even anti-political.[1] He defines as political "any activity, institution, or issue that pertains to a division of opinion and aspiration within a population that has some dealings with one another despite that division." The context suggests that what he means is as follows: Within any community or association there will be groups or individuals whose interests conflict or who have incompatible opinions about what the whole community or association should be doing. Such issues are to be thought of as political insofar as they do not disrupt the community or association into smaller independent units, and a method of handling such issues is political insofar as it respects the divergent interests and opinions as legitimate and devises means whereby those who continue to hold them may remain members of the same community or association. Non-political methods would be those which do not presume that divergent opinions and interests are equally legitimate or which treat such divergence as incompatible with joint membership of a single group. In that sense Plato, who is notoriously impatient of such continuing divisions, is plainly non-political in the general tendency of his thought. It remains only to supplement Leys' characterization by clarifying the nature, ground, and extent of Plato's abstention from political solutions. What follows is a sketch for such a clarification.

In what situations are political solutions called for? Leys's own reference to "division of opinion and aspiration" suggests the following analysis. Such situations occur (1) when different groups have incompatible aims ("aspirations") and (2) when they have different opinions about how agreed aims are to be achieved—or, to put the same thing the other way around, when they differ as to what the actual results of a given proposed action will be. Differ-

[1] Wayne A. R. Leys, "Was Plato Non-Political?" *Ethics* LXXV (1965), 272–76, reprinted above, pp. 166–73.

ences in aspiration may be either (1.1) reflections of different ideals, different ideas as to what form the institutions of a society as a whole should take, or (1.2) expressions of the different interests of different groups. The latter differences may arise out of either (1.21) false or (1.22) true readings by the various groups of their own interests and those of others. If a reading is false, the obvious remedy is to correct it rather than accommodate it; if it is true, the resulting difference may be either (1.221) capable or (1.222) incapable of resolution. If it is irresoluble, the resulting division may be handled by (1.2221) persuasion or (1.2222) compromise or (1.2223) conflict. So much for differences about ends. Differences of the other kind, differences about what means will actually bring about an admittedly desirable result, may be either (2.1) resolved or (2.2) left unresolved. If the former, they may be resolved either by (2.11) substituting knowledge for opinion or by (2.12) agreeing on whose opinion shall be accepted; if the latter, the resulting division may be handled by (2.21) persuasion or (2.22) some sort of compromise or bet-hedging or (2.23) force. However, the use of force here seems inappropriate (as opposed to its appropriate use in differences about ends), and we shall not consider it further. For all these differences, a "political" solution in Leys's terms is one that allows the difference to continue: a "non-political" solution is one that prevents or terminates it. Let us now see which of the foregoing possibilities Plato recognizes and how he addresses himself to each.

1.1 *Different ideals.*—The requirements of political constitutions are determined by the various needs and interests of different types of human being (cf. *Statesman* 306A–311C). A valid political ideal must thus rest on a valid comparative psychology (*Republic* II–IV). But Plato notoriously tends to think that mutually incompatible ideals cannot both be valid, since valid ideals are determined by eternal "Forms" (e.g., *Phaedo* 75, 100; *Republic* 494, 497, 499); it is thus supposed that such a comparative psychology will uniquely determine a social organization. Rival ideals are represented as mere projections of personal weaknesses, reflecting the unhappy experiences of those who hold them (*Republic* VIII–IX). On the objective side, only two political ideals other than that schematically determined by Plato's theoretical assumptions are represented as more than mere expressions of sectional interests: the militaristic Spartan type and the democratic. Of these, the former rests on a mere respect for public order without any regard to the rational ends that such an order might subserve (*Republic* 547–49); the latter rests on an immature preference for immediate gratifications over long-term interests, for the gaudy over the substantial (*Republic* 557–62; cf. *Gorgias* 521–22). These are both merely familiar forms of stupidity and thus fall under the rubric of 2.1 below. Conclusion: Plato holds that all political ideals except one are, in principle, demonstrably mistaken.

1.21. *Interests wrongly thought to diverge*—False ideas about differences of interest may be put right by explanation and experience: people may have wrong ideas about what they will like, but not about what they are actually enjoying now (*Philebus* 32–40), except that (*a*) they might enjoy something else even more if they tried it and (*b*) they may not like the consequences of what they like (*Philebus* 40–42). The commonest sort of error about one's interests is represented by greed (*pleonexia*, more literally, "wanting more"), the supposition that appetites are best satisfied by unrestricted gratification. That is false: experience shows that moderation yields more satisfaction (*Republic* 586–87). To want "more," as such, is a sign of folly: since there is always "more" to be desired, such a desire actually precludes its own satisfaction (*Gorgias* 491–94). Members of a community may all be able to "keep up with" each other but cannot all "get ahead of" each other. Conclusion: Plato thinks that many apparent divergences of interests rest on simple mistakes and that such mistakes are in principle quite readily corrigible.

1.221. *Real but resoluble divergences of interests.*—Interests of different groups may be rendered really incompatible by the social order to which they belong. In such cases the obviously best solution is to modify the social order so that the incompatibility is removed. Such solutions are called non-political by Leys, but are favored by Plato, and it is fair to note that constitutional arrangements are treated by Aristotle as one of the two fundamental kinds of political question (*Nicomachean Ethics* 1141B25). But such constitutional accommodations may seldom be possible.

The commonest type of divergence of interest, and that least amenable to constitutional engineering, is the competition among groups for goods and services. Such competition can only express itself in attempts at exploitation, and Plato thinks such attempts incompatible with the idea of a single community (*Republic*

351C–D). The community can be saved only if the competing parties unite against a richer adversary to increase the available supplies (*Republic* 422) and thus make competition unnecessary. But Plato's preferred solution is to modify the desires rather than to arrange for their joint gratification, by providing a social system that educates against greed. Conclusion: Plato thinks that many actual divergences of interests can be removed by social engineering, by consumer education, or by foreign wars.

1.2221. *Handling divisions by persuasion.*—Plato assumes that no one in his sane senses ever prefers another's interest to his own (cf. *Gorgias* 468); such preferences can only be induced by the hypnotism of oratory (cf. *Gorgias* 456 and *passim*), never by reasoned argument. And although persons or groups may be inveigled into embracing a policy, they cannot be thus hoodwinked into liking what its consequences actually turn out to be (see 1.21 above and *Theaetetus* 177C ff.). Conclusion: Plato thinks that such persuasion cannot be lastingly effective.

1.2222. *Handling divisions by compromise.*—Law-abiding behavior is commonly represented as a compromise among selfish people: one escapes fraud and violence at the price of abstention from fraud and violence (*Republic* 358–59). But such compromises are unstable, since it is obviously more advantageous to secure the escape without the abstention, if one can get away with it (*ibid.*). It would thus be pointless to establish elaborate mechanisms for arbitrating conflicting interests, since neither party would abide by the terms of such arbitration any longer than it found it expedient to do so.

It is interesting to see how Plato reconciles his rejection of self-sacrifice as a psychological possibility with his requirement that the Guardians of his imaginary society shall absent themselves from the researches which they enjoy and engage in administration, which they do not enjoy. He cannot represent this requirement (as we might represent it) as demanding that they sacrifice their own good to that of others. Instead, he says three different things. First, the good that their administration serves is not represented as that of "others" but as that of the whole community of which they themselves form one part (*Republic* 519–20); nothing is said of "service" in this context. Second, the compromise that they make is not one of those that can be evaded by stealth: the only alternative to really governing themselves is to be really governed by others (*Republic* 347C–D—the key word *anagkaion* at 347D1 reappears in almost the same phrase at 520E2). Third, and most significantly, the case is taken out of the realm of conflicting interests altogether and presented in terms of "justice": since their taste for scholarship is no chance growth but was inculcated by the state as a means of providing itself with dispassionate and wise officials, the very dispassionate wisdom thus inculcated will make them accept as "just" the requirement that they perform this task for which they are uniquely fitted by training and temperament (*Republic* 520A–E). The justice of this requirement lies essentially in the fact that their taking office is objectively the best solution to the problem of how good administration is to be secured; and their training is designed precisely to make them seek and favor the objectively best solutions to problems.[2] Conclusion: Plato thinks it psychologically impossible to acquiesce in a compromise conceived as such.

1.2223. *Handling divisions by force.*—Plato clearly takes the normal condition of Greek politics to be one in which conflicts of interest are settled by force (*Republic* VIII–IX, *Laws* 714D–715B). And the histories of Thucydides and Xenophon do suggest that the Greek cities of the fifth and fourth centuries had been at best intermittently successful at handling divergent aspirations through constitutional means. It follows from what was said in 1.2221 and 1.2222 that, so long as different social groups are truly or incorrigibly convinced that their interests diverge, rational political solutions are ruled out by Plato as impossible and irrational solutions as unstable. This mistrust of politics, for which Leys castigates Plato, seems at least defensible. One can certainly argue that the essential political problem, even in Leys's terms, is not one of devising institutions to work out compromises but rather, always one of getting people to accept compromises and to abide by the compromises they have formally acquiesced in. On the international level, one reading of Thucydides would suggest that the chief weakness in "political" relations between Greek cities of the time was not that no machinery existed for entering into treaties, or even that treaties were not made, for treaties were indeed often entered into and the requisite formulas were well understood: the difficulty was that treaties, once made, were not kept. Insofar as this is the case, the political problem is one of education, one of producing a

---

[2] The implications of the concept of justice in this connection are explored at length in my "Socrates and Thrasymachus," *Monist* L, No. 3 (July, 1966).

frame of mind in which shared interests bulk larger than divisive interests. That is, of course, precisely how Plato sees the political problem: political machinery is converted into educational machinery (*Republic* 423E–425E). The fact that he applies this machinery to an ideally non-divisive situation does not lessen the importance of his thesis.

If education is neglected violence must be accepted, and one can only hope to mitigate the effects of such violence. And Plato does indeed offer reasoned recommendations on the conduct of civil wars—"political" recommendations of precisely the kind that Leys praises Locke for making and upbraids Plato for not making (*Republic* 469–71). Leys has presumably failed to notice them because he has not noticed the importance of violence both in Plato's thought and in the political life of his day. And it is possible that he has not noticed that the limitation of conflict is among the leading political concerns of our own "one-world" era. Conclusion: Plato thought that if divergent interests are not reconciled the divergence must issue in conflict and that the political activities of his own place and time were forms of conflict.

2.11. *Knowledge as resolving differences about means.*—Notoriously, a key point in Plato's antipolitics is that most supposed differences in interests are really only differences of opinion: what is taken for a difference in ends is in fact a difference about means. We have touched on this theme under 1.21. Everyone, it is argued, really wants "what is best" for himself, and what he concretely seeks is sought always under the guise of "what is best" or as a means thereto (*Gorgias* 467B ff.). The theme is still familiar to us in a religious context, though not in a political one: a prudent man petitioning a supposedly omniscient and benevolent being will hedge his requests with the proviso, "if that shall be best for me." Many political disagreements arise and persist because even where there is no significant divergence of interest or ideal it is not clear what policies will in fact secure the common welfare; and, more concretely, there is often no agreement about what the actual consequences of adopting a given policy will be and how to achieve a given objective.

Where knowledge is known to be possible, no one is content with opinion: even political assemblies defer to expert testimony on obviously technical questions (*Protagoras* 319B). Normal political procedures rest on the assumption (*ibid.*) that questions of policy are non-technical. Plato's thesis is that such questions are, in principle, technical: if it were possible to determine with certainty and precision what the outcome of a given line of action would be (through knowledge of causal laws of economics, etc.) and what would prove acceptable to what social groups (through knowledge of sociological and psychological laws), there would be no point in *arguing* about what to do. The *Republic* is a sustained exploration of the hypothesis that such knowledge is in principle accessible: and the hypothesis is explicitly that administrators endowed with this knowledge are beings on a quite different intellectual plane from those whose affairs they run (*Statesman* 274E–75C, *Laws* 713C–E). Conclusion: Plato thinks that most if not all differences in politics are ultimately differences about means rather than ends and that such differences can always in principle (though seldom in practice) be resolved by ascertaining the truth about the relevant matters of present and future fact.

2.12. *Accepted authority as resolving differences about means.*—Existing practice shows that the authority of knowledge extends to its possessors when it and they are recognized (*Protagoras* 319C). Beyond that, Plato recognizes that agreement on who shall take decisions is the basis of social harmony (*Republic* 431D–432A); but the *Republic*, being devoted to exploring the implications of certainty, shows little interest in how such agreement is to be reached in that absence of certain knowledge that is normally taken to be the condition of political life (*Republic* 488B–C, *Protagoras* 319A– 320D). This apparent lack of interest is among the things that make Plato seem an anti-political philosopher. He does, however, remark that opinions in general acquire authority only from intelligence or from argument or from experience (*Republic* 582A); the proposal of the *Republic* is that the opinions of those pre-eminent in these re- spects should be allowed to prevail, although the issue is obscured in that dialogue by the complicating hypothesis that their pre- eminence should amount to certainty. In the later *Laws*, however, that additional supposition is not made, and we have there a most elaborate set of provisions for the selection of authorities. All offices are to be elective, with the more important offices filled by a com- plex system of successive ballots (*Laws* 735C–D, 945E–946C), the principle apparently being, as Professor Morrow points out,[3] that

[3] Glenn R. Morrow, *Plato's Cretan City* (Princeton, N.J., 1960), p. 162.

even men of no particular merit tend to be sound judges of merit in others (*Laws* 950B). The claims of experience to authority are met by making the legality of the proceedings of the lesser magistracies subject to review by boards (themselves elective) whose members enjoy mature years and long tenure. Similar boards are charged with introducing constitutional reforms (769E–771A) and are to appoint roving commissioners to visit foreign lands from whose practice legal and educational reforms might be derived (951A–952A). The chief task of the popular assembly is apparently to conduct the elections of these officials and boards. These proposals seem designed to accommodate two apparently irreconcilable principles, that authority must rest on consent and that opinions must be given the authority they objectively deserve. The arrangements by which Plato proposes to meet these requirements come closer to the practice of modern representative government than to that of Plato's own place and time, and perhaps for that reason are somewhat neglected in modern accounts of his political thought. Whatever their merits, the proposals are thoroughly political in Leys's sense. The fundamentally non-political nature of Plato's thinking is doubtless shown in his failure to say anything at all about how these boards themselves might reach agreement or what forms of persuasion might lead to the nomination and election of one set of officials rather than another. The constitutional proposals are elaborate, but Plato shows no interest in the actual dynamics of the politicking within the constitutional framework. If it be said that this is unsurprising in a work whose explicit aim is the formulation of constitutional proposals, the reply must be that Plato's non-political mind shows itself in his failure to devote any work to the decision-making procedure. It is not easy to see how the deficiency could be supplied, since a practice once formalized becomes itself part of the framework and hence apparently in Leys's terms non-political. But perhaps the situation is covered by the remark made in another context (*Republic* 425D–E) to the general effect that if you get a watchdog you need not bark yourself, that if you appoint competent men you need not prescribe their procedures. And it is surely on this point that Plato would join issue with Leys: if there is one place where the philosopher as such has nothing to contribute it is to the actual wheeling and dealing in smoke-filled rooms. Conclusion: Plato thinks that, though there can be no direct criteria of the merits of opinions where certainty is unobtainable, objective and readily applicable indirect criteria may be found in the qualifications of those who hold the opinions; and similar considerations apply to the selection of decision-making procedures.

2.21. *Settling differences of opinion by persuasion.*—Plato frankly regards as sinister the use of non-rational means of persuasion to support policies whose merits are objectively uncertain: to use them is necessarily to give opinions more weight than they are known to deserve (*Gorgias* 455A–456C, 458E–459C). Two palliative considerations may be noted, however. One is that non-rational support is as available to a sound opinion as to an unsound one (*Gorgias,* 456C–457C, *Statesman* 303E–304E); in fact, since not everyone can appreciate the true merits of all opinions, a sound opinion (even a demonstrable truth) needs such backing no less than an unsound one (cf. *Republic* 402A, 414B–415D). The other palliative is that the very same knowledge of human psychology that is necessary to form a sound opinion on what policy will produce most happiness will also enable the persuader to make his persuasion effective (*Phaedrus* 270A–272B). Thus knowledge has an advantage over ignorance even in the use of non-rational means, and the soundest statesman should also be the most effective politician. It is this dual function of psychological knowledge that forms the essential basis of Plato's dream of a "scientific" politics. Conclusion: Plato recognizes the need for winning people over to the support of policies whose advantages are not at once apparent but condemns the use of such means without relation to the merits of the policies for which support is canvassed.

2.22. *Settling differences of opinion by compromise.*—The art of practical politics is no doubt in large measure to minimize the consequences of unavoidable error. Modern multiparty democracies with their provision for periodic reversals of controversial policy make provision for this: Plato knows no such devices and does not recognize a need for them. He would not have his officials "bethink them that they may be mistaken." It is this neglect to keep the way open for overridden views, together with the deep pessimism about the possibilities of abnegation noted under 1.2223, that is the measure of his failure as a political philosopher in Leys's sense. Conclusion: Plato makes no provision for minority rights as such.

General conclusion.—Philosophy, for Plato, is exclusively concerned with knowledge and its applications (*Republic* 475–87). The philosopher as such can therefore have nothing to contribute to situations where knowledge is not available: specifically, he can make no useful contribution to practical politics (*Republic* 592 and *passim; Gorgias* 462–63, 521–22). Practical politics is based exclusively on memory of what in the past has proved effective and acceptable (*Republic* 516C–D, *Gorgias* 462–65) and thus neither needs nor can use the philosopher's special skills.

Our examination of the various possibilities has shown, however, that knowledge may potentially eliminate all disputes except those based on a real conflict of interests; and Plato tries to show that in a properly organized society no such conflicts are real. What are taken to be such arise from the unwise indulgence of appetites as opposed to their rational gratification—that is, from failure to recognize one's own best interests. This is as true of international as of interpersonal conflicts (*Republic* 373E).

We have seen that Plato does in fact make suggestions that are political in Leys's sense, some of them of considerable historical importance. But he believes that such proposals are rendered ultimately unworkable by the very social context of continuing antagonism that makes them necessary. His preferred solutions to political problems are therefore directed rather toward changing the social context itself; and, conversely, his preference for such solutions doubtless leads him to a quite unrealistic pessimism about the workability of ordinary political devices. In this sense his thought is certainly antipolitical. But the systematic elaboration with which he develops his antipolitics itself constitutes a major, even if a formally negative, contribution to political philosophy. Certainly his arguments do not earn him the name that Leys calls him, "the saint of those who see only evil in their opponents."

Originally published in *Ethics* 77 (1967), 214–19. Reprinted by permission of The University of Chicago Press and the author.

12

AN AFTERTHOUGHT

WAYNE A. R. LEYS

The emphasis which Professor Sparshott places on the problem of knowledge is greater than the emphasis which I had given it in my interpretation of Plato. Professor Sparshott's emphasis is supported by the Platonic texts, and I am grateful for this criticism. At the same time I am not sure that, between us, we have yet achieved an altogether defensible view of Plato's relation to modern statecraft and its preoccupation with opposed powers and conflicting rights.

When so much stress is placed on the knowability of the public good, Plato might be regarded as simply quarreling with emotivists, non-cognitivists, irrationalists or ideologists. I believe that philosophical readers may need to be shown that the difference between Plato's "common good politics" and much of modern political theory is not simply a difference in epistemology. I suspect that a statement on this point is needed, because philosophers like to locate as many important questions as possible on that level of abstraction.

Of course, it's true that Plato is an ethical cognitivist, and it's also true that many political scientists are now non-cognitivists. But Thrasymachus and the other persuaders in Plato's dialogues were usually represented as cognitivists. Thrasymachus, it may be recalled, agreed that the holders of power might not know what was in their own best interest, and he was represented as treating this admission as damaging to his case.

Furthermore, Locke and some of the other political philosophers (whom I have contrasted with Plato) were also ethical cognitivists. They believed that there was such a thing as moral knowledge. Their reason for expecting factionalism to persist was not that they had come to regard the good as unknowable. Many modern theorists have agreed with Plato's contention that political conflicts are rooted in mistakes, the mistakes that men make in judging what is good for themselves and for society. Sometimes they have made statements that are stronger than Plato's, as when Louis

Brandeis said, "Behind every controversy is somebody's ignorance."

Why, then, do so many moderns resign themselves to the persistence of controversy? Why do they even welcome adversary proceedings? And why do they try to improve on "the wheeling and dealing in smoke-filled rooms"? It is not because they are convinced that all differences in politics are about undebatable ends. It is not because they would not, in many cases, agree with Plato that differences about means are, in principle, capable of resolution.

I think that anyone much experienced in the life of large and complex states recognizes the *practical* difficulties in research, in communication, and in education. In a populous nation-state and, still more, in an international market, the cost of getting information and disseminating it to all concerned is staggering. The competition for public attention is fierce. In order to enlighten the whole population (or all the "influentials") on a single issue, it would be necessary to mobilize all available resources. And a complex society has hundreds of important issues.

Hence, cognitivists (who study the difficulties of fact-finding and communication) join with non-cognitivists in assuming that many important differences will not be resolved and that government must undertake somehow to enable unreconciled factions to coexist. From this point of view Plato jumped from the theoretical intelligibility of social life to the assumption that a consensus could actually be achieved.

I am arguing that Plato's non-political point of view depends upon a second premise, in addition to his belief that more adequate knowledge of the good is possible. That premise is that everyone can be correctly informed or guided by someone who is correctly informed.

In trying to explain how Plato could fail to take seriously what has become the distinctively political problem of our era I do not want to be misunderstood as arguing for the total politicization of human life. I believe that many conflicts can be resolved by understanding them. To the extent that pressure group leadership becomes skillful, the immediate objective of much politicking and litigating should be the securing of agreements whereby factions are brought to an acceptance of expert rule-making and adjudication. But I also sympathize with people who have been pushed around by so-called experts, experts who understand one small part of collective life and then make pronouncements that presuppose omniscience. I agree with the slogan of democratic public administration: "The expert should be on tap, not on top."

Professor Sparshott is quite aware of what I call the political problem of large and complex societies, and I want to make it clear that I do not attribute a non-political point of view to him. What has evoked these argumentative comments is Professor Sparshott's accurate account of the importance of Plato's theory of knowledge in his prescriptions for community life.

The only point on which I would disagree with Professor Sparshott is his suggestion that the philosopher has nothing to contribute to the actual wheeling and dealing. I agree that a philosopher is not very likely to invent a major political settlement. Nevertheless, the philosopher can remind people who are intent on non-political enterprises *that* there are issues which require political treatment, just as the philosopher reminds people who can think of nothing but politics *that* there are matters that need not and should not be the subject for wheeling and dealing. Philosophical instruction should provide each generation with a schema, if not a *Weltanschauung*, that enables men to walk into the unknown future, ready for radically different kinds of problems.

This selection has not been previously published.

13

PLATO'S POLITICAL ANALOGIES

RENFORD BAMBROUGH

Recent work on the origin of philosophical problems and doctrines has been done mainly in the fields of epistemology and ethics. The concepts of mind, knowledge, belief, perception, right, good, will, intention, responsibility, and some of the concepts of mathematics and the advanced natural sciences, have received the careful and almost the exclusive attention of those philosophers who have trodden the trail blazed by the classical English empiricists, and walked in the more freshly-printed footsteps of Moore, Russell and Wittgenstein.

But in the last few years there have been signs that, in spite of the gloomy prognostications of diehard opponents of the linguistic school, and in spite of the youthful exaggerations of some of its early adherents, its methods can be used outside the areas in which they were at first so effectively applied. The second and third generations of linguistic philosophers are seeking new fields to plough. It is no longer considered either over-ambitious or unrespectable for a linguistic philosopher to apply his techniques to the discussion and characterizing of modes of discourse in which his predecessors were, on principle, not interested. The result is that we can now see in a new light some of the most celebrated of the doctrines that have traditionally been called philosophical; we may not agree with the authors of the doctrines as to their precise characters and effects and consequences; we may believe that their authors seriously misconceived the logic of the doctrines; but philosophers of to-day are increasingly free from the delusion that a doctrine has been finally scotched when it has been shown that it is not what it seems, or not what its author supposed it to be. We are learning that an ugly duckling may be an entirely satisfactory swan.

There are two distinct ways in which philosophers have shown their new and refreshing broadmindedness. In the first place there has been a revival of interest in the philosophers of the past, and

such books as that of Mr. Stuart Hampshire on *Spinoza* are likely to
appear more frequently in future: books which are written from
the standpoint of a modern critical philosopher, but which interpret, sympathetically as well as with penetration, ethical and metaphysical doctrines built in an earlier manner and style. The second
way in which philosophers are showing the widening of their interests is by devoting philosophical time and attention to new kinds of
questions, and, in particular, by examining the vocabulary and the
grammar of historical, political and religious discourse. Among recent work under these heads may be mentioned Mr. T. D. Weldon's
book, *The Vocabulary of Politics*, Mr. Patrick Gardiner's account of
The Nature of Historical Explanation, and Professor John Wisdom's
essay on the logic of *Gods*.

The present essay on Plato's use of analogies in his discussion of
politics is an attempt to combine the two new types of interest: to
set out as accurately and fairly as possible how Plato was led to his
characteristic doctrines in political philosophy, and also to make
certain comments upon those doctrines, and upon his manner of
supporting them, which may be able to establish points about the
nature of political philosophy in general, and what, and by what
means, it may be expected to achieve. Although only Professor
Gilbert Ryle seems to have acted on it, there is a growing belief
that the interpretation of Plato and the elucidation of philosophical
questions and doctrines can profitably be combined.[1] The following
pages have the dual purpose of making Plato's doctrines clear and
making a contribution to the understanding of the logic of political
theories.

It will prevent misunderstanding, and the awakening of expecta-
tions that this essay will not satisfy, if the following points are
stressed at the outset:

(*a*) It is a commonplace that for Plato and Aristotle the relation
between ethics and politics was so close as to make them virtually
one inquiry. No attempt will be made here to force on Plato a
distinction which could only lead to distortion of his doctrines.

(*b*) There will be no discussion of Plato's concrete and particular
political recommendations, but only of the general principles
according to which he claimed to show the necessity for his concrete
proposals.

(*c*) Attention will be concentrated on certain analogies, pictures,

[1] G. Ryle, 'Plato's Parmenides', *Mind* (1939).

parallels and metaphors which recur repeatedly in Plato's writings on ethics and politics. An attempt will be made to show:

(i) That these analogies were very influential in shaping and directing Plato's political thought.

(ii) That they are in themselves very plausible, and that they continue to influence philosophical and semi-philosophical thinking on politics.

(iii) That they are, nevertheless, if taken too seriously and pressed too far, radically misleading as to the character of political thinking and political action and decision.

(iv) That it does not follow from conclusion (iii), even if it can be adequately established, that the analogies concerned are entirely vicious and unilluminating. Still less does it follow that analogies must be avoided in writing and thinking philosophically about politics (as, for example, Miss Margaret Macdonald in her article 'The Language of Political Theory' might seem to be suggesting).[2]

*

The analogies which are most characteristic of Plato's way of thinking about ethics and politics are those between the established arts, crafts and branches of knowledge and a supposed art, craft or branch of knowledge whose exponents would be uniquely qualified to pronounce infallibly on questions of value in ethics, politics and aesthetics. They are derived from a characteristically Socratic mode of argument. Socrates was in the habit of asking his listeners to whom they would go for a new ship or a new pair of shoes. When they said, 'To a shipbuilder, to a shoemaker', Socrates would go on to ask to whom they would turn for an ethical or political decision. The only answer that would satisfy him was that political and ethical decisions must be made by political and ethical specialists or experts. Justice seemed to him to be a *techne* like medicine, mathematics, music, or agriculture. In the shoes and ships of which Socrates was for ever talking we have the origin of Plato's conception of the philosopher-king, and of the virtue that is equated with knowledge. In the *Republic*, the *Politicus* and the *Laws*, as well as in the ethical dialogues which deal less prominently with the political aspects of virtue, Plato consistently maintains that the true states-

---

[2] M. Macdonald: 'The Language of Political Theory', in Flew, ed., *Logic and Language*, 1st Series, Oxford, 1951.

man must be thought of as the possessor of the knowledge of good
and evil, an expert physician of the soul whose prescriptions for
spiritually diseased men and cities carry with them an absolute
and unchallengeable authority. The average citizen and even the
politician of long and wide experience is no better than a layman
or a quack doctor in comparison with the philosopher. We insist
on having our shoes and ships made by skilled specialists: surely it
is unreasonable to rely on our own untutored judgments, or on
those of any unskilled amateur, for commodities infinitely more
valuable than any material goods?

All such expressions as 'the body politic' and 'the ship of state',
which we now use so freely and easily that we are barely conscious
that they are metaphorical, are derived ultimately from these
Platonic analogies between politics and the specialized arts, crafts,
trades and professions. The word 'government' itself is based on a
transliteration of *gubernator*, which is in turn a translation of
κυβερνήτης—the helmsman who was one of the favourite illustrations of Socrates and Plato. When Plato used them in his dialogues
to elaborate a portrait of the politician as a qualified specialist,
these metaphors were striking poetical pictures, which had been
used by some of the poets but which were still new and suggestive
as the basis for political theorizing. The conception of politics that
they could most naturally be used to express, and the only one to
which they could lead if they were regarded as more than *mere*
figures of speech, was firmly opposed to that of the majority of
Plato's fellow-citizens in his own and in the preceding century.
Plato puts into the mouth of Protagoras a story which presents the
democratic view that all citizens are equally entitled to have
political and ethical opinions and to exercise political influence. Although some men have special faculties and skills which others lack,
a sense of right and wrong was, by the command of Zeus to his
messenger Hermes, given equally to all men. It follows that it is
reasonable and right to adopt the Athenian practice of entrusting
to skilled and trained specialists the building of ships and the treatment of disease, while at the same time reserving to the whole citizen body all questions calling for political decision.[3] The same
political principle is embodied in the Funeral Speech of Pericles as
given by Thucydides.[4] Not every citizen can be in charge of his

[3] *Protagoras*, 320C–328D, especially 322A–324C.
[4] Thucydides, II, 40.

city's affairs, but he is competent and he is entitled to criticize the policies of those who govern him.

Against this democratic view Plato set a theory of ethics and politics whose practical consequences would be radically different. If the royal art of politics is analogous to the art of the healer or the skill of the navigator, then it follows that it can be practised only by the small minority who have the native ability and the training necessary to master its subtlety and complexity. As Plato says in the *Politicus*, even draughts-players of distinction are few and far between in any community, and so it would be foolishly optimistic to expect to find more than a very few men in any place at any time who were qualified to be true statesmen.[5] It is therefore misguided to entrust the government of a city to the whole body of the citizens, or to any minority party among them, or to any individual man who is not qualified by the possession of true political wisdom.

Even the most severe critics of this Platonic political doctrine have acknowledged that it is very plausible. Many commentators have succumbed to its fascination without resistance. What no commentator appears to have done is to do full justice to its plausibility without accepting too many of its implications, or to subject it to the necessary criticisms without being excessively severe. Disputes about the value of these Platonic political analogies share with many other philosophical disputes a chronic unsettleability which has led men of equal discernment as philosophers and commentators to take up diametrically opposed positions about them. What seems to be needed, if it can be obtained, is a neutral account of the logic of the dispute between Plato and his critics, which may be able to show that the dispute is to be ended, not by a victory of one party or the other, but by a setting out of the just claims of both sides.

A feature which distinguishes this dispute from many others of the same general type is that its unsettleability arises not only from the complexity of the logic of such expressions as 'art', 'science', 'branch of knowledge', when they are used in a variety of metaphorical senses, but also from the fact that very much more is at stake than the application of these words. This is not to say that all disputes about the application of words are trivial. The inclination or disinclination to apply a particular word often goes with no ability or inability to see things in a particular light or from a

[5] 292E.

particular point of view, and there may be scope for sustained rational discussion, for argumentation, between the inclined and the disinclined. But disputes which are at the same time about practical issues are both more bitter and less amenable to resolution by neutral analysis. The dispute about Plato's political analogies is such a dispute. We have seen that Plato's aristocratic and monarchical principles can be derived from his analogies, and that a Protagorean criticism of Plato's imagery can contribute to the defence of democratic institutions. In all disputes about the value of particular political analogies the issue is liable to be not only theoretical (logical) but also practical (political) in character, and the task of the logician is to elucidate and to evaluate the arguments that may be urged on both sides, and not to take up the position of one side against the other. Part of this task of elucidation will consist in showing which concrete political proposals are logically related to the acceptance or rejection of particular metaphorical and analogical ways of speaking about politics and politicians. To call for a neutral account of the logic of political analogies is not to suppose that the account, when given, will be equally acceptable to both parties in a dispute about the analogies; nor is it to ask that the logician, in his capacity as citizen, should refuse to favour one side rather than the other. His analysis would be unacceptably tendentious if it were conditioned by his allegiance, but it would, on the other hand, be useless if it were prevented from issuing in allegiance. The remainder of this essay will be an attempt to set out the logic of Plato's political analogies in the manner here suggested.

*

The doctrine that political wisdom is analogous to a special skill is nowhere more clearly and succinctly expressed than in the Parable of the Ship in the *Republic*, which it will be convenient to quote in full:

> Imagine this state of affairs on board a ship or a number of ships. The master is bigger and burlier than any of the crew, but a little deaf and short-sighted and no less deficient in seamanship. The sailors are quarrelling over the control of the helm; each thinks he ought to be steering the vessel, though he has never learnt navigation and cannot point to any teacher under whom he has served his apprenticeship; what is more, they assert that navigation is a thing that cannot be taught at

all, and are ready to tear in pieces anyone who says it can. Meanwhile they besiege the master himself, begging him urgently to trust them with the helm; and sometimes, when others have been more successful in gaining his ear, they kill them or throw them overboard, and, after somehow stupefying the worthy master with strong drink or an opiate, take control of the ship, make free with its stores, and turn the voyage, as might be expected of such a crew, into a drunken carousal. Besides all this, they cry up as a skilled navigator and master of seamanship anyone clever enough to lend a hand in persuading or forcing the master to set them in command. Every other kind of man they condemn as useless. They do not understand that the genuine navigator can only make himself fit to command a ship by studying the seasons of the year, sky, stars, and winds, and all that belongs to his craft; and they have no idea that, along with the science of navigation, it is possible for him to gain, by instruction or practice, the skill to keep control of the helm whether some of them like it or not. If a ship were managed in that way, would not those on board be likely to call the expert in navigation a mere star-gazer, who spent his time in idle talk and was useless to them?

I think you understand what I mean and do not need to have my parable interpreted in order to see how it illustrates the attitude of existing states towards the true philosopher.[6]

Before attempting to criticize the suggestions contained in this parable it will be advisable to set them out with all possible clarity and precision. In the first place it is clearly implied that there is a body of knowledge which is indispensable to the ruler in precisely the sense in which the knowledge of 'the seasons of the year, sky, stars, and winds', is indispensable to the navigator. This body of knowledge is recognized to be indispensable by all rulers who are worthy of the name. Only a ruler who was ignorant of it would deny that it was relevant and necessary to the purposes of government, and his ignorance would make his denial of no account, since *either*

(*a*) He knows that the knowledge which he lacks is necessary, and he *dishonestly* denies that it is necessary, *or*

(*b*) His ignorance of the knowledge that is necessary blinds

[6] VI, 488A–489A, translated by F. M. Cornford.

him also to its necessity, and he *ignorantly* denies that it is
necessary.

The knowledge required by the ruler, like the knowledge required by the navigator, can be passed from master to pupil. Just
as we should refuse to entrust our safety at sea to a man who had no
training or experience in navigation, so ought we to entrust the
government of our cities only to the accredited expert in the art
of government. Political conflict, whether it is carried on by force
of arms or by rhetoric, is both irrational and wicked, since it consists in attempting to settle by force or by mere persuasion a
question which is capable of being settled by rational means, and
which must be settled by such means if we are not to be criminally
misgoverned. The tyrant, the oligarch or the democratic leader
who induces men to accept his rule is an impostor: his desire for
political power implies the claim that he has mastered a science of
which he is in fact ignorant. Such skill as he has is a mere cleverness
which deserves the name neither of knowledge nor of art.

The parable presupposes a distinction between knowledge and
skill, or between knowing *that* and knowing *how*. The knowledge
of times and seasons and stars and winds, and the knowledge of the
routes by which particular destinations can most quickly and safely
be reached, together form an indispensable part of the equipment
of the navigator, but he must also know how to make use of the
knowledge at his disposal. Similarly the statesman's qualifications
will consist of both science and skill, of theoretical knowledge
and the ability to apply it in practice.

*

This analogy is sound at so many points that Plato and many of
his readers have been misled into supposing that it is sound at all
points. The clearest way of showing its fatal limitation is to amend
the analogy so as to make it wholly accurate. As soon as we do this,
we are able to see at once that the analogy, properly understood,
can be held to count against the point of view which Plato expresses
through it and claims to derive from it. Plato takes the crucial step
in the wrong direction when he draws a parallel between a gover-
nor's choice of a policy and a navigator's setting of a course, and
this move is all the more dangerous because it is so tempting. The
true analogy is between the choice of a policy by a politician and
the choice of a destination by the owner or passengers of a ship. The

point can be put in the familiar terms of ends and means. Plato represents a question about what is to be done (as an end) as if it were very like a question about what is to be done (as a means) in order to achieve some given or agreed end. He obscures the fact that, in politics as well as at sea, the theoretical knowledge and the practical ability of the navigator do not come into play until the destination has been decided upon; and although navigators may have their own preferences for particular destinations, these preferences have no special status, and are neither better nor worse than those of their masters. It follows that the democrat can state his anti-Platonic case in terms of Plato's analogy. Plato's claim that there is a special *techne* by which the political expert may reach infallibly sound decisions can be disposed of by putting it accurately into the terms of Plato's own picture. He is like a navigator who is not content to accept the fares of his passengers or the fee of his master, and then to conduct them where they wish to go, but who insists on going beyond his professional scope by prescribing the route and the destination as well as the course by which the route can best be traversed and the destination most suitably reached.

This criticism reduces the power of the 'ship of state' parable, but it does not leave it quite powerless. Provided that we do not use it for a purpose which it can only serve when it is tendentiously stated, the parable is an illuminating one. Our governors certainly do need special qualities and qualifications if they are to govern well. Not every citizen in a democratic country is equally suitable to be Prime Minister; and those who are suitably gifted need training and experience before they can safely be entrusted with high political office. But it cannot be shown that these special qualities and qualifications amount to knowledge of an absolutely and universally correct set of ultimate political objectives, or to a special skill at selecting such objectives. There is no body of knowledge such that from it can be derived infallible or even fallible decisions about ultimate political objectives. The bus-driver has his special skill and training, but they do not entitle him or enable him to choose the route along which he is to drive. The decisions which a politician is specially qualified to make are decisions about how a given objective is to be reached. Although it is tempting, it is also misleading to pass from one sense to another of the ambiguous proposition that a politician is specially qualified to make decisions. If this means that he has a certain skill and experience at deciding which measures will produce which desired effects, then it is acceptable and unexciting. But if it means that he is entitled to decide which *ultimate* effects are desirable, then it is spectacular and unacceptable. Plato's version of the parable of the Ship of State commits him to the second sense of this proposition, and to the view that there can be and ought to be accredited experts to answer our questions about moral and political values, wise men who will speak with true authority where actual politicians speak only with the authority of force or rhetoric to back them.

*

This suggestion that there can be knowledge of what is good, and therefore experts at determining what is good, both for individual men and for communities, is explicit in Plato's recurrent use of the analogy from which all talk of 'the body politic' is ultimately derived; an analogy between justice and bodily health, and between the politician or moralist and the physician.[7] The basic features of this comparison are very like those of the parable of the ship, but it deserves a full and separate treatment because it is so frequently used by Plato and by theorists who are under his influence, and also because some of its consequences are subtly different from those of the analogy between politics and navigation.

The dualism of body and soul was well established in Greek language and thought before the time of Socrates, but Socrates and Plato sharpened the opposition between them, and used the contrast as the basis for a picture of man from which they derived their conception of the philosopher-statesman as a 'doctor of souls', a physician qualified to prescribe remedies for the spiritual ills of men and cities. The argument may be summarized as follows. When we are sick in body we entrust ourselves to qualified medical practitioners, who have learned their *techne* from qualified teachers. We do not presume to set up our own untrained judgments against those of the specialist whose business it is to know the difference between health and disease, and who has learned by what specifics health may be preserved or restored, and disease cured or avoided. We very properly mistrust the unqualified quacks who fraudulently set themselves up as physicians. But in matters of spiritual health, or justice, which is infinitely more important than mere bodily health, we do not behave so rationally. We either totally neglect our spiritual ailments, or we write out our own untrustworthy pre-

---

[7] E.g. *Gorgias*, 463B ff.; *Politicus*, 293A.

scriptions, or we trust to some demagogue or sophist who has had no training in spiritual medicine, and who does not know, but only pretends to know, under what laws and by what policies a city may be well governed, and by what rule of life an individual man may be made upright and virtuous. An ignorant orator may be able to persuade an ignorant mob that he knows what is good for them and their city, and that the true philosopher is a rogue or a visionary. But the demagogue is in reality no better than a confectioner who persuades a crowd of children to prefer his own wares to the unpalatable drugs of the physician who really has their welfare at heart and who knows how to minister to their needs.[8]

The persuasive force of this elaborate analogy resides mainly in the insistence that actual politicians have not undergone a special course of training in order to learn the nature of the good and to master the methods by which it may be attained. It is perfectly true that none of us, whether a politician or not, has gone through such a course of training. But it is only in the context of the parallel between ethics-and-politics and medicine that we can be induced to feel ashamed of this deficiency. Because it is obvious that a physician who had no special knowledge and no special skill would be no true physician, we are induced to feel that a politician who has not had an analogous training to that of the physician, leading to the possession of an analogous body of knowledge, is no true politician, but a fraudulent pretender to a science that he lacks. It is only when we free ourselves from the toils of the analogy that we can see why politicians lack the special training which Plato wishes to prescribe for them. It is not, as Plato suggests, because they are lazy, or morally perverse, or neglectful of a clear duty, but because there is no such special training, no body of political knowledge, analogous to the medical knowledge of the physician, to which the politician could aspire. The complaint that our governors do not know their job has great force because it suggests that we could go further and specify the knowledge that they regrettably lack. The complaint loses its power as soon as we recognize that no such specification is possible. The physician can learn from other physicians how to preserve and restore our health, and he can teach his art and craft to his successors, because within well-known limits there are agreed standards for determining whether a body is healthy or diseased. When the diagnosis has

[8] *Gorgias*, 521 E.

been made, it then becomes possible for the doctor to apply the
remedies which experience has shown to be beneficial in comparable cases in the past. But the diagnosis and treatment of
spiritual ills is not on such a firm theoretical or experimental basis.
There are no agreed standards for determining whether a soul or a
city is healthy or diseased, just or unjust, and this is not because
spiritual medicine is an under-developed science, but because it is
not a science at all. The lack of agreed standards of justice, which is
Plato's main reason for pressing the analogy between justice and
health, is also the decisive reason against accepting the analogy.
Plato's aim is to suggest that he himself *knows* what is ultimately and
absolutely good. If we accept this suggestion, then politics and
ethics become, for us, sciences like medicine, learning by experiment and experience how to embody in law and policy the given
standards of justice and virtue. But we cannot accept the analogy
unless we can accept the suggestion, and we cannot accept the
suggestion because Plato can say nothing in its defence that could
not equally be said by a rival claimant to ultimate and absolute
knowledge of the good, in defence of a different set of 'absolute'
standards. Only if there were some conclusive tests by which we
could adjudicate in a dispute between Plato and his absolutist rival
would it be proper to speak of ethical and political knowledge in
the sense required by the Platonic analogies between ethics-and-
politics and the *technai* of medicine, navigation, shoemaking and
shipbuilding: and there are no such conclusive tests. Ethical and
political disagreement is different in logical kind from medical disagreement or disagreement between navigators. Ethical and political disagreement is radical and interminable in a sense in which
scientific disagreement, or disagreement about the means for
achieving an agreed end, is terminable by recognized procedures,
such disagreement remains terminable in principle even when it is
not terminated in fact. But ethical and political disagreement in its
most characteristic forms is interminable, because it is not about
means, but about ends.

This is not to say that none of the disagreements which are
commonly and properly called ethical and political are about
means rather than ends. The fact that there are such disagreements
is one of the main sources of the Platonic doctrine, and is indeed
one of the important truths that the doctrine embodies. Still less is it
to say that ethical and political discussion is useless or irrational:
and it is here that the greatest positive value of the Platonic analo-

gies is to be found. What the analogies teach us, at the cost of certain distortions and exaggerations which may mislead us on other points, is the important lesson that there is scope for sustained rational discussion about the choice of ends and purposes. If we see the analogies at their true value, giving them neither too much nor too little weight, we shall avoid making each of two serious errors:

(i) *The Platonic error:* the error of supposing that, since ethical and political questions are proper themes for rational discussion and inquiry, and in this respect are like questions of fact, they must also be like questions of fact in the further respect that the answers to them will embody *knowledge*, and that to each of the questions there will be one incontrovertibly true or correct answer, if only it can be found.

(ii) *The anti-Platonic error:* the error of supposing that, since the answers to ethical and political questions do not embody knowledge, and are not such that to each of the questions there is one incontrovertibly true or correct answer, and in this respect ethical and political questions differ from factual questions, they must differ *toto caelo* from factual questions, and must be incapable of being rationally discussed and satisfactorily answered.

To see that both these errors are errors is to learn important lessons about the logic of ethical and political questions, statements and disputes, and it will therefore be appropriate to consider generally, and not only in direct connection with the Platonic analogies, certain questions about the logic of choice and decision which a discussion of the analogies has raised. But first it will be convenient to complete the account of the analogies themselves by making some comments on those which have not been considered at length.

*

Besides navigation and medicine, Plato illustrates his conception of ethics and politics by reference to mathematics and music, to the arts of manufacture, such as shoemaking, shipbuilding and weaving, and to the tendance of animals. None of these calls for a full and separate treatment, since the comments made above on the analogies with medicine and navigation apply, *mutatis mutandis*, to all the analogies in general. It will be sufficient to indicate those features of each *techne* which make it an unsuitable model for the supposed *techne* of ethics and politics.

The importance of mathematics and music for Plato's purpose is that they are disciplines in which, *par excellence*, we find questions to which there are precisely correct answers, and experts who can find and give those answers as men speaking with authority. For Plato, as for Locke, mathematics was the paradigm of certainty and accuracy to which morals and politics were required to conform.[9] But the ambition is a hopeless one precisely because of those features of ethical discourse of which Plato complained, and without which ethical discourse would not be ethical discourse. We accept the expert's solution of a mathematical problem because we know from experience that he agrees with other experts, and he agrees with other experts because the problem can be precisely stated and there are approved methods of solving it. These conditions do not hold in ethics and politics. There are not even any adequate neutral criteria for determining who are the experts, so that an attempt to appeal to experts simply transforms an ethical or political dispute into an equally unsettleable dispute about who are the ethical or political experts. In such a case as this it has become misleading to speak of experts at all, since it is an important part of the meaning of the word 'expert', in its standard uses, that an expert is a man who can be appealed to by the ignorant or puzzled layman.

The practical skill of the shoemaker, the shipbuilder, or the weaver seems at first sight to be a more promising model for the practical skill of the politician, but here again, as in the cases of navigation and medicine, it is found that Plato has obscured certain important dissimilarities between the original and the alleged copy. Just as we were allowed to forget that it is the passengers and not the navigator who choose the destination and the route of a ship, although it is the navigator's skilled task to set and steer the course, so are we allowed to forget that the skill of the craftsman is an instrument which serves the purposes of his patron. The craftsman's function is a mastery of the means by which a given end can be achieved; the choosing of the end is no concern of the craftsman *qua* craftsman. There is certainly some analogy between the craftsman's skill and the skill and experience of the politician at managing men and affairs, but the parallel breaks down at the crucial point, since there is wide general agreement on the purposes to be served by shoes or ships or clothes, while there is no such agreement on the ends to which men and affairs are to be manipulated. As

---

[9] Locke: *Essay Concerning Human Understanding*, Pringle-Pattison's edition, p. 277.

soon as we cease to assimilate the choice of ends to the choice of means we also cease to ask that ends should be chosen as only means can be chosen. When the Platonic analogy is fully and accurately stated it no longer inclines us to accept the doctrine it was designed to support, for we then see that it is the unskilled customer who decides, and the skilled craftsman who acts on his instructions. Ethical and political disagreements are disagreements between the customers, and ethical and political skill, in the only sense in which the phrase can properly be used, is incapable of composing such disagreements.

Similarly, the shepherd and the goatherd are skilled at tending flocks and herds for well-known and well-agreed purposes. Their skill at feeding and fattening animals is instrumental to their own or their masters' desire for wool or milk or meat or money; it is a skill not at choosing, but at serving purposes. The shepherd of men is less favourably placed. There is no agreement about the ends to which his skill must be applied, and it is not only his fellow-shepherds, but also the sheep themselves, who justly feel entitled to be taken into his counsels. Despotism is the only political system which can be favoured by those who take this analogy seriously, and even if we mistakenly take the analogy as a valid argument in favour of a despotic form of government, we shall still be faced with all the questions which the analogy was intended to answer. These questions will now take the form, 'Who is to be the despot?' and 'To what ends is the despot to use his power?' To say that philosophers should rule is not to answer those questions *de finibus bonorum et malorum* which Plato claimed to be answering, since they all arise again as questions about the selection and training of the philosophers. The answer is acceptable only so long as it is vacuous; as soon as it acquires any content it is tendentious: and it is dangerously easy to fail to notice the transition from the platitude to the dogma that can be expressed in the same form of words.

Wherever Plato turns among the *technai*, although the word covers a wide variety of skills, studies and pursuits which no modern language would call by one single name, he cannot find what he is seeking, a skill at determining which ends ought and ought not to be pursued. He is conscious of this difficulty, and he attempts to overcome it by distinguishing between the standard, instrumental arts, and a higher, prescriptive art, the kingly art of politics.[10] All

[10] See e.g. *Politicus*, 260C.

the lower arts are means to ends; the royal art, as practised by the true philosopher, prescribes to the lower arts the ends they are to serve. But this is to stop an unbridgeable gap with an empty name. There is no such prescriptive *techne*, not because civilization is in its infancy, but for the inescapable logical reason that anything which can properly be called a *techne* will be by its very nature instrumental, and the decision about the purpose for which it is to be used will lie outside its own scope.

*

A critical account of Plato's political analogies has led us to diagnose and treat the Platonic error of over-assimilating questions about ends to questions about means, of demanding that there should be neutral and definitive answers to deliberative questions as well as to questions of logic and questions of fact. But if we take an overdose of the antidote we shall commit the anti-Platonic error of underestimating the similarities between deliberative questions and other kinds of questions. It is not for nothing that they are all called questions, and that the grammatical form of a question of fact is often indistinguishable from the grammatical form of a deliberative question. This similarity in name and form is the prime source of the Platonic error. It seems natural to expect that the question 'Which is the highest mountain on earth?' should be as logically similar as it is grammatically similar to the question 'Which is the best life on earth?' But when we look closely at the methods we adopt in answering these two questions, and at the language in which we conduct and describe our search for the answers, we see the important differences as clearly as we saw at first sight the important similarities. Questions about what is the case are answered by investigation leading to discoveries which are recorded in sentences which are both grammatically and logically indicative. Questions about what is to be done are answered by a process of deliberation leading to decisions which are recorded in sentences which are sometimes grammatically indicative, but whose logical mood is imperative rather than indicative.

The difference in the logical moods of the answers to the different kinds of questions is connected with differences in the logic of the questions themselves. It is also connected with differences in the logic of the procedures and the concepts we use in seeking for and recording the answers. When we have seen that the logic of factual questions both resembles and is different from the logic of deliberative questions, we shall be prepared to find that the logic of any concept which is used in dealing with both types of question will be appropriately different for each type of question; but we shall then need to guard against the danger of taking the differences too seriously, and denying that both types of questions are proper questions. The Platonic error and the anti-Platonic error have a common source in the error of supposing that all proper questions are to be answered in the logical indicative, that all proper questions are questions about what is the case. Plato recognizes that deliberative questions are proper questions and therefore supposes that they must be questions about what is the case. The anti-Platonist recognizes that deliberative questions are not questions about what is the case and therefore supposes that they are not proper questions.

To accept the Platonic analogies unconditionally is to suppose that the concepts of knowledge, truth, right answer, speaking with authority, expert, have the same logical roles in ethics and politics as they have in science and mathematics. To reject the Platonic analogies unconditionally is to suppose that none of these concepts has any place in the logic of ethics and politics. To give due weight to the Platonic analogies is to recognize that some of these concepts have a place in the logic of ethics and politics, but that the logical roles they play in ethics and politics are different from those they play in science and mathematics.

In science one expert agrees with another about the answers to most questions within their field, and the answers on which they agree are usually the right answers. The experts speak with authority, and the answers that they give are the map of a field of knowledge. It would be rash and unreasonable of a layman to disagree with an expert about the shape of the earth or the size of the sun or the ecology of orchids. Even when the experts disagree, they agree at least on the methods by which their dispute could be settled. They know what it would be like for the truth to be discovered, for one of them to be proved wrong. Even if they are both equally right they will not both be right to the same degree on the same question; they may be right about different questions in a cluster of questions; but as long as they are really contradicting each other only one of them can be right. Science is to this extent neat and tidy and safe. To one question, one answer; to one question of fact, one fact.

But in ethics and politics the experts disagree so much and so radically that we hesitate to say that they are experts. The Prime Minister and the Leader of the Opposition disagree as violently as the untutored laymen who sent them to Parliament. Whatever our own political views we shall have experts on our side and experts against us, even if we think that politicians are amateurs and we turn to those dons who *really* know about these things. But how can they know? They cannot all be right, and yet it seems that however long and hard we try we can never show that any of them is wrong. Perhaps they are all really amateurs, even the dons and the ministers, and we need a philosopher-king to teach them. Perhaps we ought to follow Plato and Mrs. Barbara Wootton to that 'entirely new and exciting country' where science is science and politics is also science and where they have a proper disrespect for unprofessional political judgment'. In this happy land 'controversies on matters on which at present reasonable men may differ will eventually fall into the category of arguments about the flatness or roundness of the earth'.[11]

But this will never do: and we see why it will never do when we see that the relation of decisions to deliberative questions is different from the relation of discoveries to questions of fact. There is nothing to which my decision must correspond in order to be a reasonable decision in the way that my belief must correspond to what the world is like in order to be a true belief; and so there is nothing to prevent your decision and my decision from both being reasonable although your decision is different from mine. In ethics and politics we can differ and go on differing and still be reasonable men. But of course some men are unreasonable, and they make their decisions without sufficient thought and knowledge, without looking far enough back upon experience or far enough forward to the consequences. Plato is right when he urges that we ought to be as careful in deliberation as we ought to be in investigation, even if he is wrong when he presses the point by saying that deliberation *is* investigation. Mrs. Barbara Wootton is right when she says that a good democracy is an educated and well-informed democracy, even if she is wrong when she presses the point by sketching an ideally educated democracy in which Parliament would be a fact-

[11] Barbara Wootton, 'The Social Sciences and Democratic Political Practice', in *Confluence*, vol. 3, no. 1.

finding commission and the Opposition would never earn their salaries.

In fields where the authorities not only do but *must* disagree, it is tempting either to choose one authority and say that he is the only authority, or to deny that there are any authorities at all: to forget that the great statesman or the great moralist has all the authority conferred by wide knowledge, long experience, clear thought, and above all the tolerant recognition that the search for the right solution to a practical problem can never be ended by a Q.E.D.

Originally published in *Philosophy, Politics, and Society*, edited by P. Laslett (Basil Blackwell, Oxford, 1956), 98–115. Reprinted by permission of the editor and the author.

14

PLATO AND THE IRRATIONAL SOUL

E. R. DODDS

There is no hope in returning to a traditional faith after it has once been aban-
doned, since the essential condition in the holder of a traditional faith is that he
should not know he is a traditionalist.

Al Ghazali

I propose here to consider Plato's reaction to the situation created
by the decay of the inherited fabric of beliefs which set in during
the fifth century. The subject is important, not only because of
Plato's position in the history of European thought, but because
Plato perceived more clearly than anyone else the dangers inherent in the decay of an Inherited Conglomerate, and because in
his final testament to the world he put forward proposals of great
interest for stabilising the position by means of a counter-reformation. I am well aware that to discuss this matter fully would involve
an examination of Plato's entire philosophy of life; but in order to
keep the discussion within manageable limits I propose to con-
centrate on seeking answers to two questions:

First, what importance did Plato himself attach to non-rational
factors in human behaviour, and how did he interpret them?

Secondly, what concessions was he prepared to make to the irrationalism of popular belief for the sake of stabilising the
Conglomerate?

It is desirable to keep these two questions distinct as far as
possible, though, as we shall see, it is not always easy to decide
where Plato is expressing a personal faith and where he is merely
using a traditional language. In trying to answer the first question,
I shall have to repeat one or two things which I have already said
in print,[1] but I shall have something to add on matters which I did
not previously consider.

[1] "Plato and the Irrational," *JHS* 65 (1945), 16 ff. This paper was
written before the present book was planned; it leaves untouched some
of the problems with which I am here concerned, and on the other
hand deals with some aspects of Plato's rationalism and irrationalism
which fall outside the scope of the present volume.

One assumption I shall make. I shall assume that Plato's philosophy did not spring forth fully mature, either from his own head or from the head of Socrates; I shall treat it as an organic thing which grew and changed, partly in obedience to its inner law of growth, but partly also in response to external stimuli. And here it is relevant to remind you that Plato's life, like his thought, all but bridges the wide gulf between the death of Pericles[2] and the acceptance of Macedonian hegemony. Though it is probable that all his writings belong to the fourth century, his personality and outlook were moulded in the fifth and his earlier dialogues are still bathed in the remembered light of a vanished social world. The best example is to my mind the *Protagoras*, whose action is set in the golden years before the Great War; in its optimism, its genial worldliness, its frank utilitarianism, and its Socrates who is still no more than life-size, it seems to be an essentially faithful reproduction of the past.[3]

Plato's starting-point was thus historically conditioned. As the nephew of Charmides and kinsman of Critias, no less than as one of Socrates' young men, he was the child of the Enlightenment. He grew up in a social circle which not only took pride in settling all questions before the bar of reason, but had the habit of interpreting all human behaviour in terms of rational self-interest, and the belief that "virtue," *aretē*, consisted essentially in a technique of rational living. That pride, that habit, and that belief remained with Plato to the end; the framework of his thought never ceased to be rationalist. But the contents of the framework came in time to be strangely transformed. There were good reasons for that. The transition from the fifth century to the fourth was marked (as our own time has been marked) by events which might well induce any rationalist to reconsider his faith. To what moral and material ruin the principle of rational self-interest might lead a society, appeared in the fate of imperial Athens; to what it might lead the individual, in the fate of Critias and Charmides and their fellow-tyrants. And on the other hand, the trial of Socrates afforded the strange spectacle of the wisest man in Greece at the supreme crisis of his life deliberately and gratuitously flouting that principle, at any rate as the world understood it.

[2] Plato was born in the year of Pericles' death or the year following, and died in 347, a year before the Peace of Philocrates and nine years before the battle of Chaeronea.

[3] Cf. *The Greeks and the Irrational*, chap. vi, nn. 31–33.

It was these events, I think, which compelled Plato, not to abandon rationalism, but to transform its meaning by giving it a metaphysical extension. It took him a long time, perhaps a decade, to digest the new problems. In those years he no doubt turned over in his mind certain significant sayings of Socrates, for example, that "the human *psyche* has something divine about it" and that "one's first interest is to look after its health."[4] But I agree with the opinion of the majority of scholars that what put Plato in the way of expanding these hints into a new transcendental psychology was his personal contact with the Pythagoreans of West Greece when he visited them about 390. If I am right in my tentative guess about the historical antecedents of the Pythagorean movement, Plato in effect cross-fertilised the tradition of Greek rationalism with magico-religious ideas whose remoter origins belong to the northern shamanistic culture. But in the form in which we meet them in Plato these ideas have been subjected to a double process of interpretation and transposition. A well-known passage of the *Gorgias* shows us in a concrete instance how certain philosophers— such men, perhaps, as Plato's friend Archytas—took over old mythical fancies about the fate of the soul and read into them new allegorical meanings which gave them moral and psychological significance.[5] Such men prepared the way for Plato; but I should

---

[4] Xenophon, *Mem.* 4.3.14; Plato, *Ap.* 30A–B, *Laches* 185E.

[5] *Gorgias* 493A–C. Frank's view of what is implied in this passage (*Platon u. die sog. Pythagoreer*, 291 ff.) seems to me right in the main, though I should question certain details. Plato distinguishes, as 493B7 shows, (*a*) τις μυθολογῶν κομψὸς ἀνήρ, ἴσως Σικελός τις ἢ Ἰταλικός, whom I take to be the anonymous author of an old Underworld Journey (not necessarily "Orphic") which was current in West Greece and may have been somewhat after the style of the poem quoted on the gold plates; (*b*) Socrates' informant, τις τῶν σοφῶν, who read into the old poem an allegorical meaning (much as Theagenes of Rhegium had allegorised Homer). This σοφός I suppose to be a Pythagorean, since such formulae are regularly used by Plato when he has to put Py-thagorean ideas into Socrates' mouth: 507E, φασὶ δ' οἱ σοφοί that there is a moral world-order (cf. Thompson *ad loc.*); *Meno* 81A, ἀκήκοα ἀνδρῶν τε καὶ γυναικῶν σοφῶν about transmigration; *R.* 583B, δοκῶ μοι τῶν σοφῶν τινος ἀκηκοέναι that physical pleasures are illusory (cf. Adam *ad loc.*). Moreover, the view that underworld myths are an allegory of this life appears in Empedocles and in later Pythagoreanism (Macrob. *in Somn. Scip.* I. 10.7–17). I cannot agree with Linforth ("Soul and Sieve in Plato's *Gorgias*," *Univ. Calif. Publ. Class. Philol.* 12 [1944], 17 ff.) that "the whole of what Socrates professes to have

guess that it was Plato himself who by a truly creative act transposed these ideas definitively from the plane of revelation to the plane of rational argument.

The crucial step lay in the identification of the detachable "occult" self which is the carrier of guilt-feelings and potentially divine with the rational Socratic *psychē* whose virtue is a kind of knowledge. That step involved a complete reinterpretation of the old shamanistic culture-pattern. Nevertheless the pattern kept its vitality, and its main features are still recognisable in Plato. Reincarnation survives unchanged. The shaman's trance, his deliberate detachment of the occult self from the body, has become that practice of mental withdrawal and concentration which purifies the rational soul—a practice for which Plato in fact claims the authority of a traditional *lŏgos*.[6] The occult knowledge which the shaman acquires in trance has become a vision of metaphysical truth; his "recollection" of past earthly lives[7] has become a "recollection" of bodiless Forms which is made the basis of a new epistemology, while on the mythical level his "long sleep" and "underworld journey" provides a direct model for the experiences of Er the son of Armenius.[8] Finally, we shall perhaps understand better Plato's much-criticised "Guardians" if we think of them as a new kind of rationalised shamans who, like their primitive predecessors, are prepared for their high office by a special kind of discipline designed to modify the whole psychic structure; like them, must submit to a dedication that largely cuts them off from the normal satisfactions of humanity; like them, must renew their contact with the deep sources of wisdom by periodic "retreats"; and like

---

heard from someone else . . . was original with Plato himself": if it were, he would hardly make Socrates describe it as ἐπιεικῶς ὑπό τι ἄτοπα [broadly speaking, a bit on the queer side] (493C) or call it the product of a certain school (γυμνασίου, 493D).

[6] *Phaedo* 67C, cf. 80E, 83A–C. For the meaning of λόγος ("religious doctrine") cf. 63C, 70C, *Ep.* vii. 335A, etc. In thus reinterpreting the old tradition about the importance of dissociated states, Plato was no doubt influenced by Socrates' practice of prolonged mental withdrawal, as described in the *Symposium*, 174D–175C and 220C–D, and (it would seem) parodied in the *Clouds:* cf. Festugière, *Contemplation et vie contemplative chez Platon*, 69 ff.

[7] See *The Greeks and the Irrational*, chap. v, n. 107.

[8] Proclus, *in Remp.* II.113.22, quotes as precedents Aristeas, Hermotimus (so Rohde for Hermodorus), and Epimenides.

them, will be rewarded after death by receiving a peculiar status in the spirit world.[9] It is likely that an approximation to this highly specialised human type already existed in the Pythagorean societies; but Plato dreamed of carrying the experiment much further, putting it on a serious scientific basis, and using it as the instrument of his counter-reformation.

This visionary picture of a new sort of ruling class has often been cited as evidence that Plato's estimate of human nature was grossly unrealistic. But shamanistic institutions are not built on ordinary human nature; their whole concern is to exploit the possibilities of an exceptional type of personality. And the *Republic* is dominated by a similar concern. Plato admitted frankly that only a tiny fraction of the population (φύσει ὀλίγιστον γένος) possessed the natural endowment which would make it possible to transform them into Guardians.[10] For the rest—that is to say, the overwhelming majority of mankind—he seems to have recognised at all stages of his thought that, so long as they are not exposed to the temptations of power, an intelligent hedonism provides the best practicable guide to a satisfactory life.[11] But in the dialogues of his middle period, preoccupied as he then was with exceptional

[9] As the Siberian shaman becomes an Üör after death (Sieroszewski, *Rev. de l'hist. des rel.* 46 [1902], 228 f.), so the men of Plato's "golden breed" will receive post-mortem cult not merely as heroes—which would have been within the range of contemporary usage—but (subject to Delphic approval) as δαίμονες (*R.* 468E–469B). Indeed, such men may already be called δαίμονες in their lifetime (*Cra.* 398C). In both passages Plato appeals to the precedent of Hesiod's "golden race" (*Erga* 122 f.). But he is almost certainly influenced also by something less remotely mythical, the Pythagorean tradition which accorded a special status to the θεῖος or δαιμόνιος ἀνήρ [divine or *daimonios* man] . . . . The Pythagoreans—like Siberian shamans today—had a special funeral ritual of their own, which secured for them a μακαριστὸν καὶ οἰκεῖον τέλος [a blessed and appropriate ending] (Plut. *gen. Socr.* 16,585E, cf. Boyancé, *Culte des Muses*, 133 ff.; Nioradze, *Schamanismus*, 103 f.), and may well have provided the model for the elaborate and unusual regulations laid down in the *Laws* for the funerals of εὔθυνοι (947B–E, cf. O. Reverdin, *La Religion de la cité platonicienne*, 125 ff.). On the disputed question whether Plato himself received divine (or daemonic) honours after death, see Wilamowitz, *Aristoteles u. Athen*, II.413 ff.; Boyancé, *op. cit.*, 250 ff.; Reverdin, *op. cit.*, 139 ff.; and *contra*, Jaeger, *Aristotle*, 108 f.; Festugière, *Le Dieu cosmique*, 219 f.

[10] *R.* 428E–429A, cf. *Phaedo* 69C.

[11] *Phaedo* 82A–B, *R.* 500D, and the passages quoted below from *Philebus* and *Laws*.

natures and their exceptional possibilities, he shows scant interest in the psychology of the ordinary man.

In his later work, however, after he had dismissed the philosopher-kings as an impossible dream, and had fallen back on the rule of Law as a second-best,[12] he paid more attention to the motives which govern ordinary human conduct, and even the philosopher is seen not to be exempt from their influence. To the question whether any one of us would be content with a life in which he possessed wisdom, understanding, knowledge, and a complete memory of the whole of history, but experienced no pleasure or pain, great or small, the answer given in the *Philebus*[13] is an emphatic "No": we are anchored in the life of feeling which is part of our humanity, and cannot surrender it even to become "spectators of all time and all existence"[14] like the philosopher-kings. In the *Laws* we are told that the only practicable basis for public morals is the belief that honesty pays: "for no one," says Plato, "would consent, if he could help it, to a course of action which did not bring him more joy than sorrow."[15] With that we seem to be back in the world of the *Protagoras* and of Jeremy Bentham. The legislator's position, however, is not identical with that of the common man. The common man wants to be happy; but Plato, who is legislating for him, wants him to be good. Plato therefore labours to persuade him that goodness and happiness go together. That this is true, Plato happens to believe; but did he not believe it, he would still pretend it true, as being "the most salutary lie that was ever told."[16] It is not Plato's own position that has changed; if anything has changed, it is his assessment of human capacity. In the *Laws*, at any rate, the virtue of the common man is evidently not based on knowledge, or even on true opinion as such, but on a process of conditioning or habituation[17] by which he is induced to accept and act on certain "salutary" beliefs. After all, says Plato, this is not too difficult: people who can believe in Cadmus and the dragon's teeth will believe anything.[18] Far from supposing, as his master had done, that "the unexamined life is no life for a human

---

[12] *Politicus* 297D–E, 301D–E; cf. *Laws* 739D–E.

[13] *Philebus* 21D–E.

[14] *R.* 486A.

[15] *Laws* 663B; cf. 733A.

[16] *Ibid.*, 663D.

[17] *Ibid.*, 653B.

[18] *Ibid.*, 664A.

being,"[19] Plato now appears to hold that the majority of human beings can be kept in tolerable moral health only by a carefully chosen diet of "incantations" (ἐπῳδαί),[20]—that is to say, edifying myths and bracing ethical slogans. We may say that in principle he accepts Burckhardt's dichotomy—rationalism for the few, magic for the many. We have seen, however, that his rationalism is quickened with ideas that once were magical, and on the other hand we shall see later how his "incantations" were to be made to serve rational ends.

In other ways too, Plato's growing recognition of the importance of affective elements carried him beyond the limits of fifth-century rationalism. This appears very clearly in the development of his theory of Evil. It is true that to the end of his life[21] he went on repeating the Socratic dictum that "No one commits an error if he can help it"; but he had long ceased to be content with the simple Socratic opinion which saw moral error as a kind of mistake in perspective.[22] When Plato took over the magico-religious view of the *psychē*, he at first took over with it the puritan dualism which attributed all the sins and sufferings of the *psychē* to the pollution arising from contact with a mortal body. In the *Phaedo* he transposed that doctrine into philosophical terms and gave it the formulation that was to become classical: only when by death or by

---

[19] *Ap.* 38A. Professor Hackforth, *CR* 59 (1945), 1 ff., has sought to convince us that Plato remained loyal to this maxim throughout his life. But though he certainly paid lip service to it as late as the *Sophist* (230C–E), I see no escape from the conclusion that the educational policy of the *Republic*, and still more clearly that of the *Laws*, is in reality based on very different assumptions. Plato could never confess to himself that he had abandoned any Socratic principle; but that did not prevent him from doing it. Socrates' θεραπεία ψυχῆς surely implies respect for the human mind as such; the techniques of suggestion and other controls recommended in the *Laws* seem to me to imply just the opposite.

[20] In the *Laws*, ἐπῳδή and its cognates are continually used in this metaphorical sense (659E, 664B, 665C, 666C, 670E, 773D, 812C, 903B, 944B). Cf. Callicles' contemptuous use of the word, *Grg.* 484A. Its application in the *Charmides* (157A–C) is significantly different: there the "incantation" turns out to be a Socratic cross-examination. But in the *Phaedo*, where the myth is an ἐπῳδή (114D, cf. 77E–78A), we already have a suggestion of the part which ἐπῳδαί were to play in the *Laws*. Cf. Boyancé's interesting discussion, *Culte des Muses*, 155 ff.

[21] *Ti.* 86D–E, *Laws* 731C, 860D.

[22] See *The Greeks and the Irrational*, chap. vi, p. 185.

self-discipline the rational self is purged of "the folly of the body"[23] can it resume its true nature which is divine and sinless; the good life is the practice of that purgation, μελέτη θανάτου. Both in antiquity and to-day, the general reader has been inclined to regard this as Plato's last word on the matter. But Plato was too penetrating and, at bottom, too realistic a thinker to be satisfied for long with the theory of the *Phaedo*. As soon as he turned from the occult self to the empirical man, he found himself driven to recognise an irrational factor within the mind itself, and thus to think of moral evil in terms of psychological conflict (στάσις).[24]

That is already so in the *Republic:* the same passage of Homer which in the *Phaedo* had illustrated the soul's dialogue with "the passions of the body" becomes in the *Republic* an internal dialogue between two "parts" of the soul;[25] the passions are no longer seen as an infection of extraneous origin, but as a necessary part of the life of the mind as we know it, and even as a source of energy, like Freud's *libido*, which can be "canalised" either towards sensuous or towards intellectual activity.[26] The theory of inner conflict, vividly illustrated in the *Republic* by the tale of Leontius,[27] was precisely

---

[23] *Phaedo* 67A, and cf. 66C, 94E, *Cra.* 414A. In the *Phaedo*, as Festugière has put it, "le corps, c'est le mal, et c'est tout le mal" (*Rev. de Phil.* 22 [1948], 101). Plato's teaching here is the main historical link between the Greek "shamanistic" tradition and Gnosticism.

[24] For a fuller account of the unitary and the tripartite soul in Plato see G. M. A. Grube, *Plato's Thought*, 129–49, where the importance of the concept of στάσις, "one of the most startlingly modern things in Platonic philosophy," is rightly stressed. Apart from the reason given in the text, the extension of the notion of *psyché* to embrace the whole of human activity is doubtless connected with Plato's later view that *psyché* is the source of all motion, bad as well as good (cf. *Ti.* 89E, *Laws* 896D). On the ascription in the *Laws* (896E) of an irrational, and potentially evil, secondary soul to the κόσμος see Wilamowitz, *Platon*, II.315 ff., and the very full and fair discussion of this passage by Simone Pétrement, *Le Dualisme chez Platon, les Gnostiques et les Manichéens* (1947), 64 ff. I have stated my own view briefly in *JHS* 65 (1945), 21.

[25] *Phaedo* 94D–E; *R.* 441B–C.

[26] *R.* 485D. Grube, *loc. cit.*, has called attention to the significance of this passage, and others in the *Republic*, as implying that "the aim is not repression but sublimation." But Plato's presuppositions are, of course, very different from Freud's, as Cornford has pointed out in his fine essay on the Platonic Eros (*The Unwritten Philosophy*, 78 f. [reprinted in this volume, pp. 119–31 above]).

[27] *R.* 439E. Cf. 351E–352A, 554D, 486E, 603D.

formulated in the *Sophist*,[28] where it is defined as a psychological maladjustment resulting "from some sort of injury,"[29] a kind of disease of the soul, and is said to be the cause of cowardice, intemperance, injustice, and (it would seem) moral evil in general, as distinct from ignorance or intellectual failure. This is something quite different both from the rationalism of the earliest dialogues and from the puritanism of the *Phaedo*, and goes a good deal deeper than either; I take it to be Plato's personal contribution.[30]

Yet Plato had not abandoned the transcendent rational self, whose perfect unity is the guarantee of its immortality. In the *Timaeus*, where he is trying to reformulate his earlier vision of man's destiny in terms compatible with his later psychology and cosmology, we meet again the unitary soul of the *Phaedo;* and it is significant that Plato here applies to it the old religious term that Empedocles had used for the occult self—he calls it the daemon.[31] In the *Timaeus*, however, it has another sort of soul or self "built on to it," "the mortal kind wherein are terrible and indispensable passions."[32] Does not this mean that for Plato the human personal-

---

[28] *Sph.* 227D–228E. Cf. also *Phdr.* 237D–238B and *Laws* 863A–864B.

[29] ἔκ τινος διαφθορᾶς διαφοράν (so Burnet, from the indirect tradition in Galen).

[30] The first hints of an approach to this view may be detected in the *Gorgias* (482B–C, 493A). But I cannot believe that Socrates, or Plato, took it over from the Pythagoreans ready-made, as Burnet and Taylor supposed. The unitary soul of the *Phaedo* comes (with a changed significance) from Pythagorean tradition; the evidence that the tripartite one does is late and weak. Cf. Jaeger, *Nemesios von Emesa*, 63 ff.; Field, *Plato and His Contemporaries*, 183 f.; Grube, *op. cit.*, 133. Plato's recognition of an irrational element in the soul was seen in the Peripatetic School to mark an important advance beyond the intellectualism of Socrates (*Magna Moralia* 1.1, 1182A15 ff.); and his views on the training of the irrational soul, which will respond only to an irrational ἐθισμός, were later invoked by Posidonius in his polemic against the intellectualist Chrysippus (Galen, *de placitis Hippocratis et Platonis*, pp. 466 f. Kühn, cf. 424 f.).

[31] *Ti.* 90A. Cf. *Cra.* 398C. Plato does not explain the implications of the term; on its probable meaning for him see L. Robin, *La Théorie platonicienne de l'amour*, 145 ff., and V. Goldschmidt, *La Religion de Platon*, 107 ff. The irrational soul, being mortal, is not a δαίμων; but the *Laws* seem to hint that the "heavenly" δαίμων has an evil daemonic counterpart in the "Titan nature" which is a hereditary root of wickedness in man (701C, 854B).

[32] *Ti.* 69C. In the *Politicus*, 309C, Plato had already referred to the two elements in man as τὸ ἀειγενὲς ὂν τῆς ψυχῆς μέρος and τὸ ζῳογενὲς'

ity has virtually broken in two? Certainly it is not clear what bond unites or could unite an indestructible daemon resident in the human head with a set of irrational impulses housed in the chest or "tethered like a beast untamed" in the belly. We are reminded of the naïve opinion of that Persian in Xenophon to whom it was quite obvious that he must have two souls: for, said he, the same soul could not be at once good and bad—it could not desire simultaneously noble actions and base ones, will and not will to perform a particular act at a particular moment.[33]

But Plato's fission of the empirical man into daemon and beast is perhaps not quite so inconsequent as it may appear to the modern reader. It reflects a similar fission in Plato's view of human nature: the gulf between the immortal and the mortal soul corresponds to the gulf between Plato's vision of man as he might be and his estimate of man as he is. What Plato had come to think of human life as it is actually lived, appears most clearly in the *Laws*. There he twice informs us that man is a puppet. Whether the gods made it simply as a plaything or for some serious purpose one cannot tell; all we know is that the creature is on a string, and its hopes and

---

which implies that the latter is mortal. But there they are still "parts" of the same soul. In the *Timaeus* they are usually spoken of as distinct "kinds" of soul; they have a different origin; and the lower "kinds" are shut away from the divine element lest they pollute it "beyond the unavoidable minimum" (69D). If we are meant to take this language literally, the unity of the personality is virtually abandoned. Cf., however, *Laws* 863B, where the question whether θυμός is a πάθος or a μέρος of the soul is left open, and *Ti.* 91E, where the term μέρη is used.

[33] Xen. *Cyr.* 6.1.41. Xenophon's imaginary Persian is no doubt a Mazdean dualist. But it is unnecessary to suppose that the psychology of the *Timaeus* (in which the irrational soul is conceived as educable, and therefore *not* incurably depraved) is borrowed from Mazdean sources. It has Greek antecedents in the archaic doctrine of the indwelling δαίμων, and in Empedocles' distinction between δαίμων and ψυχή; and Plato's adoption of it can be explained in terms of the development of his own thought. On the general question of Oriental influence on Plato's later thought I have said something in *JHS* 65 (1945). Since then, the problem has been fully discussed by Jula Kerschensteiner, *Plato u. d. Orient* (Diss. München, 1945); by Simone Pétrement, *Le Dualisme chez Platon;* and by Festugière in an important paper, "Platon et l'Orient," *Rev. de Phil.* 21 (1947), 5 ff. So far as concerns the suggestion of a Mazdean origin for Plato's dualism, the conclusions of all three writers are negative.

fears, pleasures and pains, jerk it about and make it dance.[34] In a
later passage the Athenian observes that it is a pity we have to take
human affairs seriously, and remarks that man is God's plaything,
"and that is really the best that can be said of him": men and
women should accordingly make this play as charming as possible,
sacrificing to the gods with music and dancing; "thus they will live
out their lives in accordance with their nature, being puppets
chiefly, and having in them only a small portion of reality." "You
are making out our human race very mean," says the Spartan.
And the Athenian apologises: "I thought of God, and I was moved
to speak as I did just now. Well, if you will have it so, let us say that
our race is not mean—that it is worth taking a little bit seriously
(σπουδῆς τινος ἄξιον)."[35]

Plato suggests here a religious origin for this way of thinking; and
we often meet it in later religious thinkers, from Marcus Aurelius to
Mr. T. S. Eliot—who has said in almost the same words, "Human
nature is able to endure only a very little reality." It agrees with
the drift of much else in the *Laws*—with the view that men are as
unfit to rule themselves as a flock of sheep,[36] that God, not man, is
the measure of things,[37] that man is the gods' property (κτῆμα,)[38]
and that if he wishes to be happy, he should be ταπεινός, "abject,"
before God—a word which nearly all pagan writers, and Plato
himself elsewhere, employ as a term of contempt.[39] Ought we to dis-
count all this as a senile aberration, the sour pessimism of a tired
and irritable old man? It might seem so: for it contrasts oddly with
the radiant picture of the soul's divine nature and destiny which
Plato painted in his middle dialogues and certainly never abjured.
But we may recall the philosopher of the *Republic*, to whom, as to

[34] *Laws* 644D–E. The germ of this idea may be seen already in the
Ion, where we are told that God, operating on the passions through the
"inspired" poets, ἔλκει τὴν ψυχὴν ὅποι ἂν βούληται τῶν ἀνθρώπων [draws
the soul of men in any direction he wishes] (536A), though the image
there is that of the magnet. Cf. also *Laws* 903D, where God is "the
gamester" (πεττευτής) and men are his pawns.

[35] *Laws*, 803B–804B.

[36] *Ibid.*, 713C–D.

[37] *Ibid.*, 716C.

[38] *Ibid.*, 902B, 906A; cf. *Critias*, 109B.

[39] *Ibid.*, 716A. For the implications of ταπεινός, cf., e.g., 774C
δουλεία ταπεινὴ καὶ ἀνελεύθερος. To be ταπεινός towards the gods was for
Plutarch a mark of superstition (*non posse suaviter*, 1101E), as it was also
for Maximus of Tyre (14.7 Hob.) and probably for most Greeks.

Aristotle's megalopsych, human life cannot appear important (μέγα τι);[40] we may remember that in the *Meno* the mass of men are likened to the shadows that flit in Homer's Hades, and that the conception of human beings as the chattels of a god appears already in the *Phaedo*.[41] We may think also of another passage in the *Phaedo*, where Plato predicts with undisguised relish the future of his fellow-men: in their next incarnation some of them will be donkeys, others wolves, while the μέτριοι, the respectable bourgeoisie, may look forward to becoming bees or ants.[42] No doubt this is partly Plato's fun; but it is the sort of fun which would have appealed to Jonathan Swift. It carries the implication that everybody except the philosopher is on the verge of becoming subhuman, which is (as ancient Platonists saw)[43] hard to reconcile with the view that every human soul is essentially rational.

In the light of these and other passages I think we have to recognise two strains or tendencies in Plato's thinking about the status of man. There is the faith and pride in human reason which he inherited from the fifth century, and for which he found religious sanction by equating the reason with the occult self of shamanistic tradition. And there is the bitter recognition of human worthlessness which was forced upon him by his experience of contemporary Athens and Syracuse. This too could be expressed in the language of religion, as a denial of all value to the activities and interests of this world in comparison with "the things Yonder." A psychologist might say that the relation between the two tendencies was not one of simple opposition, but that the first became a compensation—or overcompensation—for the second: the less Plato cared for actual humanity, the more nobly he thought of the soul. The tension between the two was resolved for a time in the dream of a new Rule of the Saints, an *élite* of purified men who should unite the incompatible virtues of (to use Mr. Koestler's terms) the Yogi and the Commissar, and thereby save not only themselves but society. But

[40] *Ibid.*, 486A; cf. *Tht.* 173C–E, Arist. *EN* 1123B32.

[41] *Meno* 100A, *Phaedo* 62B.

[42] *Phaedo* 81E–82B.

[43] Plot. *Enn.* 6.7.6: μεταλαβούσης δὲ θηρεῖον σῶμα θαυμάζεται πῶς, λόγος οὖσα ἀνθρώπου. Cf. *ibid.*, 1.1.11; Alex. Aphrod. *de Anima* p. 27 Br. (Suppl. Arist. II.i); Porphyry *apud* Aug. *Civ. Dei*, 10.30; Iamblichus *apud* Nemes. *nat. hom.* 2 (*PG* 40, 584A); Proclus, *in Ti.* III.294, 22 ff. The notion of reincarnation in animals was in fact transferred from the occult self of Pythagoreanism to the rational ψυχή which it did not fit: cf. Rostagni, *Il Verbo di Pitagora*, 118.

when that illusion faded, Plato's underlying despair came more and more to the surface, translating itself into religious terms, until it found its logical expression in his final proposals for a completely "closed" society,[44] to be ruled not by the illuminated reason, but (under God) by custom and religious law. The "Yogi," with his faith in the possibility and necessity of intellectual conversion, did not wholly vanish even now, but he certainly retreated before the "Commissar," whose problem is the conditioning of human cattle. On this interpretation the pessimism of the *Laws* is not a senile aberration: it is the fruit of Plato's personal experience of life, which in turn carried in it the seed of much later thought.[45]

It is in the light of this estimate of human nature that we must consider Plato's final proposals for stabilising the Conglomerate. But before turning to that, I must say a word about his opinions on another aspect of the irrational soul, namely, the importance traditionally ascribed to it as the source or channel of an intuitive insight. In this matter, it seems to me, Plato remained throughout his life faithful to the principles of his master. Knowledge, as distinct from true opinion, remained for him the affair of the intellect, which can justify its beliefs by rational argument. To the intuitions both of the seer and of the poet he consistently refused the title of knowledge, not because he thought them necessarily groundless, but because their grounds could not be produced.[46] Hence Greek custom was right, he thought, in giving the last word in military matters to the commander-in-chief, as a trained expert, and not to the seers who accompanied him on campaign; in general, it was the task of σωφροσύνη, rational judgement, to distinguish between the true seer and the charlatan.[47] In much

---

[44] *Laws* 942A–B: "The principal thing is that none, man or woman, should ever be without an officer set over him, and that none should get the mental habit of taking any step, whether in earnest or in jest, on his individual responsibility: in peace as in war he must live always with his eye on his superior officer, following his lead and guided by him in his smallest actions . . . in a word, we must train the mind not even to consider acting as an individual or know how to do it."

[45] On later developments of the theme of the unimportance of τὰ ἀνθρώπινα see Festugière in *Eranos* 44 (1946), 376 ff. For man as a puppet cf. M. Ant. 7.3 and Plot. *Enn.* 3.2.15 (I.290.54 A.-S.).

[46] *Ap.* 22C, poets and inspired seers λέγουσι μὲν πολλὰ καὶ καλά, ἴσασιν δ' οὐδὲν ὧν λέγουσι [say many admirable things, but understand nothing of what they say]. The same thing is said of *politicians* and seers, *Meno* 99C–D; of poets, *Ion* 533E–534D, *Laws* 719C; of seers, *Ti.* 72A.

[47] *Laches* 198E; *Chrm.* 173C.

the same way, the products of poetic intuition must be subject to the rational and moral censorship of the trained legislator. All that was in keeping with Socratic rationalism.[48] Nevertheless, Socrates had taken irrational intuition quite seriously, whether it expressed itself in dreams, in the inner voice of the "daemonion," or in the utterance of the Pythia.[49] And Plato makes a great show of taking it seriously too. Of the pseudo-sciences of augury and hepatoscopy he permits himself to speak with thinly veiled contempt;[50] but "the madness that comes by divine gift," the madness that inspires the prophet or the poet, or purges men in the Corybantic rite—this, is treated as if it were a real intrusion of the supernatural into human life.

How far did Plato intend this way of talking to be taken *au pied de la lettre?* In recent years the question has been often raised, and variously answered;[51] but unanimity has not been reached, nor is it likely to be. I should be inclined myself to say three things about it:

a) That Plato perceived what he took to be a real and significant analogy between mediumship, poetic creation, and certain pathological manifestations of the religious consciousness, all three of which have the appearance of being "given"[52] *ab extra;*

b) That the traditional religious explanations of these phenomena were, like much else in the Conglomerate, accepted by him

---

[48] The attack on poetry in the *Republic* is usually taken to be Platonic rather than Socratic: but the view of poetry as irrational, on which the attack depends, appears already in the *Apology* (n. 46 above).

[49] *Greeks and Irrat.*, chap. vi, p. 185.

[50] *Phaedrus* 244C–D; *Ti.* 72B.

[51] Cf. R. G. Collingwood, "Plato's Philosophy of Art," *Mind* N.S. 34 (1925), 154 ff.; E. Fascher, Προφήτης, 66 ff.; Jeanne Croissant, *Aristote et les mystères*, 14 ff., A. Delatte, *Les Conceptions de l'enthousiasme*, 57 ff.; P. Boyancé, *Le Culte des Muses*, 177 ff.; W. J. Verdenius, "L'*Ion* de Platon," *Mnem.* 1943, 233 ff., and "Platon et la poésie," *ibid.* 1944, 118 ff.; I. M. Linforth, "The Corybantic Rites in Plato," *Univ. Calif. Publ. Class. Philol.* 13 (1946), 160 ff. Some of these critics would divorce Plato's religious language from any sort of religious feeling: it is "no more than a pretty dress in which he clothes his thought" (Croissant); "to call art a divine force or an inspiration is simply to call it a *je ne sais quoi*" (Collingwood). This seems to me to miss part of Plato's meaning. On the other hand, those who, like Boyancé, take his language quite literally seem to overlook the ironical undertone which is evident in passages like *Meno* 99C–D and may be suspected elsewhere.

[52] *Phdr.* 244A: μανίας θείᾳ δόσει διδομένης [a madness given by a divine gift].

provisionally, not because he thought them finally adequate, but because no other language was available to express that mysterious "givenness";[53]

c) That while he thus accepted (with whatever ironical reservations) the poet, the prophet, and the "Corybantic" as being in some sense channels[54] of divine or daemonic[55] grace, he nevertheless rated their activities far below those of the rational self,[56] and held that they must be subject to the control and criticism of reason, since reason was for him no passive plaything of hidden forces, but an active manifestation of deity in man, a daemon in its own right. I suspect that, had Plato lived to-day, he would have been profoundly interested in the new depth-psychology, but appalled by the tendency to reduce the human reason to an instrument for rationalising unconscious impulses.

Much of what I have said applies also to Plato's fourth type of "divine madness," the madness of Eros. Here too was a "given," something which happens to a man without his choosing it or knowing why—the work, therefore, of a formidable daemon.[57] Here too—here, indeed, above all[58]—Plato recognised the operation of divine grace, and used the old religious language[59] to express that

[53] Cf. *Greeks and Irrat.*, chap. iii, p. 80.

[54] *Laws* 719C, the poet "resembles a fountain which gives free course to the rush of water."

[55] *Symp.* 202E.

[56] In the "rating of lives," *Phdr.* 248D, the μάντις or τελεστής and the poet are placed in the fifth and sixth classes respectively, below even the business man and the athlete. For Plato's opinion of μάντεις cf. also *Politicus* 290C–D; *Laws* 908D. Nevertheless both μάντεις and poets are assigned a function, though a subordinate one, in his final project for a reformed society (*Laws* 660A, 828B); and we hear of a μάντις who had studied under him in the Academy (Plut. *Dion.* 22).

[57] Cf. Taylor, *Plato*, 65: "In the Greek literature of the great period, Eros is a god to be dreaded for the havoc he makes of human life, not to be coveted for the blessings he bestows; a tiger, not a kitten to sport with."

[58] *Phdr.* 249E, the erotic madness is "the best of all *enthousiaseis*."

[59] This religious language does not, however, exclude for Plato an explanation of erotic attraction in mechanistic terms—suggested, perhaps, by Empedocles or Democritus—by postulating physical "emanations" from the eye of the beloved which are eventually reflected back upon their author (*Phdr.* 251B, 255C–D). Cf. the mechanistic explanation of the catharsis produced by Corybantic rites, *Laws* 791A (which is called Democritean by Delatte and Croissant, Pythagorean by Boyancé, but may quite possibly be Plato's own).

recognition. But Eros has a special importance in Plato's thought as being the one mode of experience which brings together the two natures of man, the divine self and the tethered beast.[60] For Eros is frankly rooted in what man shares with the animals,[61] the physiological impulse of sex (a fact which is unfortunately obscured by the persistent modern misuse of the term "Platonic love"); yet Eros also supplies the dynamic impulse which drives the soul forward in its quest of a satisfaction transcending earthly experience. It thus spans the whole compass of human personality, and makes the one empirical bridge between man as he is and man as he might be. Plato in fact comes very close here to the Freudian concept of *libido* and sublimation. But he never, as it seems to me, fully integrated this line of thought with the rest of his philosophy; had he done so, the notion of the intellect as a self-sufficient entity independent of the body might have been imperilled, and Plato was not going to risk that.[62]

I turn now to Plato's proposals for reforming and stabilising the Inherited Conglomerate.[63] They are set forth in his last work, the *Laws*, and may be briefly summarised as follows.

1. He would provide religious faith with a logical foundation by *proving* certain basic propositions.

2. He would give it a legal foundation by incorporating these propositions in an unalterable legal code, and imposing legal penalties on any person propagating disbelief in them.

3. He would give it an educational foundation by making the

[60] Eros as a δαίμων has the general function of linking the human with the divine (*Symp.* 202E). In conformity with that function, Plato sees the sexual and the nonsexual manifestations of Eros as expressions of the same basic impulse towards "birth in beauty"—a phrase which is for him the statement of a deep-seated organic law. Cf. I. Bruns, "Attische Liebestheorien," *NJbb* 1900, 17 ff., and Grube, *op. cit.*, 115.

[61] *Symp.* 207A–B.

[62] It is significant that the theme of immortality, in its usual Platonic sense, is completely missing from the *Symposium;* and that in the *Phaedrus*, where a sort of integration is attempted, this can be achieved only at the level of myth, and only at the cost of treating the irrational soul as persisting after death and retaining its carnal appetites in the discarnate state.

[63] In the following pages I am especially indebted to the excellent monograph of O. Reverdin, *La Religion de la cité platonicienne* (Travaux de l'Ecole Française d'Athènes, fasc. VI, 1945), which I have not found the less valuable because the writer's religious standpoint is very different from my own.

basic propositions a compulsory subject of instruction for all children.

4. He would give it a social foundation by promoting an intimate union of religious and civic life at all levels—as we should phrase it, a union of Church and State.

It may be said that most of these proposals were designed merely to strengthen and generalise existing Athenian practice. But when we take them together we see that they represent the first attempt to deal systematically with the problem of controlling religious belief. The problem itself was new: in an age of faith no one thinks of proving that gods exist or inventing techniques to induce belief in them. And some of the methods proposed were apparently new: in particular, no one before Plato seems to have realised the importance of early religious training as a means of conditioning the future adult. Moreover, when we look more closely at the proposals themselves, it becomes evident that Plato was trying not only to stabilise but also to reform, not only to buttress the traditional structure but also to discard so much of it as was plainly rotten and replace it by something more durable.

Plato's basic propositions are:

a) That gods exist;

b) That they are concerned with the fate of mankind;

c) That they cannot be bribed.

The arguments by which he attempted to prove these statements do not concern us here; they belong to the history of theology. But it is worth noticing some of the points on which he felt obliged to break with tradition, and some on which he compromised.

Who, in the first place, are the gods whose existence Plato sought to prove and whose worship he sought to enforce? The answer is not free from ambiguity. As regards worship, a passage in *Laws* iv provides a completely traditional list—gods of Olympus, gods of the city, gods of the underworld, local daemons and heroes.[64] These are the conventional figures of public cult, the gods who, as he puts it elsewhere in the *Laws*, "exist according to customary usage."[65] But are they the gods whose existence Plato thought he could prove? We have ground for doubting it. In the *Cratylus* he makes

[64] *Laws* 717A–B. Cf. 738D: every village is to have its local god, δαίμων, or hero, as every village in Attica probably in fact had (Ferguson, *Harv. Theol. Rev.* 37 [1944], 128 ff.).

[65] *Ibid.*, 904A, οἱ κατὰ νόμον ὄντες θεοί (cf. 885B and, if the text is sound, 891E).

Socrates say that we know nothing about these gods, not even their true names, and in the *Phaedrus*, that we *imagine* a god (πλάττομεν) without having seen one or formed any adequate idea of what he is like.[66] The reference in both passages is to mythological gods. And the implication seems to be that the cult of such gods has no rational basis, either empirical or metaphysical. Its level of validity is, at best, of the same order as that which Plato allows to the intuitions of the poet or the seer.

The supreme god of Plato's personal faith was, I take it, a very different sort of being, one whom (in the words of the *Timaeus*) "it is hard to find and impossible to describe to the masses."[67] Presumably Plato felt that such a god could not be introduced into the Conglomerate without destroying it; at any rate he abstained from the attempt. But there was one kind of god whom everyone could see, whose divinity could be recognised by the masses,[68] and about whom the philosopher could make, in Plato's opinion, logically valid statements. These "visible gods" were the heavenly bodies— or, more exactly, the divine minds by which those bodies were

[66] *Cra.* 400D, *Phdr.* 246C. Cf. also *Critias* 107A–B; *Epin.* 984D (which sounds definitely contemptuous). Those who, like Reverdin (*op. cit.*, 53), credit Plato with a wholehearted personal belief in the traditional gods, because he prescribes their cult and nowhere explicitly denies their existence, seem to me to make insufficient allowance for the compromises necessary to any practical scheme of religious reform. To detach the masses completely from their inherited beliefs, had it been possible, would in Plato's view have been disastrous; and no reformer can openly reject for himself what he would prescribe for others. See further my remarks in *JHS* 65 (1945), 22 f.

[67] *Ti.* 28C. On the much-debated question of Plato's God see especially Diès, *Autour de Platon*, 523 ff.; Festugière, *L'Idéal religieux des Grecs et l'Evangile*, 172 ff.; Hackforth, "Plato's Theism," *CQ* 30 (1936), 4 ff.; F. Solmsen, *Plato's Theology* (Cornell, 1942). I have stated my own tentative view, *JHS, loc. cit.*, 23.

[68] The heavenly bodies are everywhere the natural representatives or symbols of what Christopher Dawson calls "the transcendent element in external reality" (*Religion and Culture*, 29). Cf. *Ap.* 26D, where we are told that "everybody," including Socrates himself, believes the sun and the moon to be gods; and *Cra.* 397C–D, where the heavenly bodies are represented as the primitive gods of Greece. But in the fourth century, as we learn from the *Epinomis*, 982D, this belief was beginning to fade before the popularising of mechanistic explanations (cf. *Laws* 967A; *Epin.* 983C). Its revival in the Hellenistic Age was in no small degree due to Plato himself.

animated or controlled.[69] The great novelty in Plato's project for religious reform was the emphasis he laid, not merely on the divinity of sun, moon, and stars (for that was nothing new), but on their cult. In the *Laws*, not only are the stars described as "the gods in heaven," the sun and moon as "great gods," but Plato insists that prayer and sacrifice shall be made to them by all;[70] and the focal point of his new State Church is to be a joint cult of Apollo and the sun-god Helios, to which the High Priest will be attached and the highest political officers will be solemnly dedicated.[71] This

---

[69] On the question of animation *versus* external control see *Laws* 898E–899A, *Epin.* 983C. Animation was no doubt the popular theory, and was to prevail in the coming age; but Plato refuses to decide (the stars are either "gods" or "images of gods", *Epin.* 983E; for the latter view cf. *Ti.* 37C).

[70] *Laws* 821B–D. In itself, prayer to the sun was not foreign to Greek tradition: Socrates prays to him at sunrise (*Symp.* 220D), and a speaker in a lost play of Sophocles prays: ἥλιος, οἰκτείροιέ με, | ὃν οἱ σοφοὶ λέγουσι γεννητὴν θεῶν | καὶ πατέρα πάντων (fr. 752 P.). Elsewhere in the *Laws* (887D) Plato speaks of προκυλίσεις ἅμα καὶ προσκυνήσεις Ἑλλήνων τε καὶ βαρβάρων at the rising and setting of the sun and moon. Festugière has accused him of misrepresenting the facts here: "ni l'objet de culte ni le geste d'adoration ne sont grecs: ils sont barbares. Il s'agit de l'astrologie chaldéenne et de la προσκύνησις en usage à Babylone et chez les Perses" (*Rev. de Phil.* 21 [1947], 23). But while we may allow that the προκυλίσεις, and perhaps the moon-cult, are barbarian rather than Greek, Plato's statement seems sufficiently justified by Hesiod's rule of prayer and offerings at sunrise and sundown (*Erga* 338 f.) and by Ar. *Plut.* 771: καὶ προσκυνῶ γε πρῶτα μὲν τὸν ἥλιον, κτλ. Nevertheless, the proposals of the *Laws* do seem to give the heavenly bodies a religious importance which they lacked in ordinary Greek cult, though there may have been partial precedents in Pythagorean thought and usage. And in the *Epinomis*—which I am now inclined to regard either as Plato's own work or as put together from his "Nachlass"—we meet with something that is certainly Oriental, and is frankly presented as such, the proposal for *public* worship of the *planets*.

[71] *Laws* 946B–C, 947A. The dedication is not merely formal: the εὔθυνοι are to be actually housed in the τέμενος [sacred precinct] of the joint temple (946C–D). It should be added that the proposal to institute a High Priest (ἀρχιερεύς) appears to be an innovation; at any rate the title is nowhere attested before Hellenistic times (Reverdin, *op. cit.*, 61 f.). Presumably it reflects Plato's sense of the need for a tighter organisation of the religious life of Greek communities. The High Priest will be, however, like other priests, a layman, and will hold office only for a year; Plato did not conceive the idea of a professional clergy, and would certainly, I think, have disapproved it, as tending to impair the unity of "Church" and State, religious and political life.

joint cult—in place of the expected cult of Zeus—expresses the union of old and new, Apollo standing for the traditionalism of the masses, and Helios for the new "natural religion" of the philosophers;[72] it is Plato's last desperate attempt to build a bridge between the intellectuals and the people, and thereby save the unity of Greek belief and of Greek culture.　　　　　　　　　-

A similar mixture of necessary reform with necessary compromise may be observed in Plato's handling of his other basic propositions. In dealing with the traditional problem of divine justice, he firmly ignores not only the old belief in "jealous" gods,[73] but (with certain exceptions in religious law)[74] the old idea that the wicked man is punished in his descendants. That the doer shall suffer in person is for Plato a demonstrable law of the cosmos, which must be taught as an article of faith. The detailed working of the law is not, however, demonstrable: it belongs to the domain of "myth" or "incantation."[75] His own final belief in this matter is set forth in an impressive passage of *Laws* X:[76] the law of cosmic justice is a law of spiritual gravitation; in this life and in the whole series of lives every soul gravitates naturally to the company of its own kind, and therein lies its punishment or its reward; Hades, it is hinted, is not a place but a state of mind.[77] And to this Plato adds another warning, a warning which marks the transition from the classical to the Hellenistic outlook: if any man demands personal happiness from life,

[72] See Festugière, *Le Dieu cosmique* (= *La Révélation d'Hermès*, II, Paris, 1949).

[73] Divine φθόνος is explicitly rejected, *Phdr.* 247A, *Ti.* 29E (and Arist. *Metaph.* 983A2).

[74] See *Greeks and Irrat.*, chap. ii, n. 32.

[75] *Laws* 903B, ἐπῳδῶν μύθων: cf. 872E, where the doctrine of requital in future earthly lives is called μῦθος ἢ λόγος ἢ ὅ τι χρὴ προσαγορεύειν αὐτό, and L. Edelstein, "The Function of the Myth in Plato's Philosophy," *Journal of the History of Ideas*, 10 (1949), 463 ff.

[76] *Ibid.*, 904C–905D; cf. also 728B–C, and Plotinus' development of this idea, *Enn.* 4.3.24.

[77] 904D. Plato's language here (ὀνομάτων, ὀνειροπολοῦσιν) suggests that popular beliefs about the Underworld have no more than symbolic value. But the last words of the sentence are puzzling: they can hardly mean "when in sleep or trance" (England), since they are antithetic to ζῶντες, but seem to assert that the fear of Hades continues *after death*. Does Plato intend to hint that to experience this fear—the fruit of a guilty conscience—is already to *be* in Hades? That would accord with the general doctrine which he preached from the *Gorgias* onward, that wrongdoing is its own punishment.

let him remember that the cosmos does not exist for his sake, but he for the sake of the cosmos.[78] All this, however, was above the head of the common man, as Plato well knew; he does not, if I understand him rightly, propose to make it part of the compulsory official creed.

On the other hand, Plato's third proposition—that the gods cannot be bribed—implied a more drastic interference with traditional belief and practice. It involved rejecting the ordinary interpretation of sacrifice as an expression of gratitude for favours to come, "do ut des," a view which he had long ago stigmatised in the *Euthyphro* as the application to religion of a "commercial technique" (ἐμπορική τις τέχνη).[79] But it seems plain that the great emphasis he lays on this point both in the *Republic* and in the *Laws* is due not merely to theoretical considerations; he is attacking certain widespread practices which in his eyes constitute a threat to public morality. The "travelling priests and diviners" and purveyors of cathartic ritual who are denounced in a much-discussed passage of *Republic* ii, and again in the *Laws*,[80] are not, I think, merely those minor charlatans who in all societies prey upon the ignorant and superstitious. For they are said in both places to mislead whole cities,[81] an eminence that minor charlatans seldom achieve. The scope of Plato's criticism is in my view wider than some scholars have been willing to admit: he is attacking, I believe, the entire

---

[78] 903C–D, 905B. On the significance of this point of view see Festugière, *La Sainteté*, 60 ff., and V. Goldschmidt, *La Religion de Platon*, 101 f. It became one of the commonplaces of Stoicism, e.g., Chrysippus *apud* Plut. *Sto. rep.* 44, 1054F, M. Ant. 6.45, and reappears in Plotinus, e.g., *Enn.* 3.2.14. Men live in the cosmos like mice in a great house, enjoying splendours not designed for them (Cic. *nat. deor.* 2.17).

[79] *Euthyphro*, 14E. Cf. *Laws* 716E–717A.

[80] *R.* 364B–365A; *Laws* 909B (cf. 908D). The verbal similarities of the two passages are, I think, sufficient to show that Plato has in view the same class of persons (Thomas, Ἐπέκεινα, 30, Reverdin, *op. cit.*, 226).

[81] *R.* 364E: "persuading not only private persons but states as well," (cf. 366A–B, "the greatest states"); *Laws* 909B: "and try thus to wreck utterly not only individual persons but whole families and States for the sake of money." Plato may have in mind famous historical instances like the purification of Athens by Epimenides (mentioned at *Laws* 642D, where the respectful tone is in character for the Cretan speaker) or of Sparta by Thaletas: cf. Festugière, *REG* 51 (1938), 197. Boyancé, *REG* 55 (1942), 232, has objected that Epimenides was unconcerned with the Hereafter. But this is true only on Diels' assumption that the writings attributed to him were "Orphic" forgeries—an assumption which, whether it be correct or not, Plato is unlikely to have made.

tradition of ritual purification, so far as it was in the hands of private, "unlicensed" persons.[82]

This does not mean that he proposed to abolish ritual purification altogether. For Plato himself, the only truly effective catharsis was no doubt the practice of mental withdrawal and concentration which is described in the *Phaedo:*[83] the trained philosopher could cleanse his own soul without the help of ritual. But the common man could not, and the faith in ritual catharsis was far too deeply rooted in the popular mind for Plato to propose its complete elimination. He felt, however, the need for something like a Church, and a canon of authorised rituals, if religion was to be prevented from running off the rails and becoming a danger to public morality. In the field of religion, as in that of morals, the great enemy which had to be fought was antinomian individualism; and he looked to Delphi to organise the defence. We need not assume that Plato believed the Pythia to be verbally inspired. My own guess would be that his attitude to Delphi was more like that of a modern "political Catholic" towards the Vatican: he saw in Delphi a great conservative force which could be harnessed to the task of stabilising the Greek religious tradition and checking both the spread of materialism and the growth of aberrant tendencies within the tradition itself. Hence his insistence, both in the *Republic* and in the *Laws*, that the authority of Delphi is to be absolute in all religious matters.[84] Hence also the choice of Apollo to share with Helios the supreme position in the hierarchy of State cults: while Helios provides the few with a relatively rational form of worship, Apollo will dispense to the many, in regulated and harmless doses, the archaic ritual magic which they demand.[85]

---

[82] I find it hard to believe—as many still do, on the strength of "Musaeus and his son" (*R.* 363C)—that Plato intended to condemn the official Mysteries of Eleusis: cf. Nilsson, *Harv. Theol. Rev.* 28 (1935), 208 f., and Festugière, *loc. cit.* Certainly he cannot have meant to suggest in the *Laws* that the Eleusinian priesthood should be brought to trial for an offence which he regards as worse than atheism (907B). On the other hand, the *Republic* passage does not justify restricting Plato's condemnation to "Orphic" books and practices, though these are certainly included. The parallel passage in the *Laws* does not mention Orpheus at all.

[83] See above, n.6.

[84] *R.* 427B–C; *Laws* 738B–C, 759C.

[85] I do not intend to imply that for Plato Apolline religion is simply a pious lie, a fiction maintained for its social usefulness. Rather it reflects

Of such legalised magic the *Laws* provides many examples, some of them startlingly primitive. For instance, an animal, or even an inanimate object, which has caused the death of a man, is to be tried, condemned, and banished beyond the frontiers of the State, because it carries a "miasma" or pollution.[86] In this and many other matters Plato follows Athenian practice and Delphic authority. We need not suppose that he himself attached any value to proceedings of this kind; they were the price to be paid for harnessing Delphi and keeping superstition within bounds.

It remains to say a few words about the sanctions by which Plato proposes to enforce acceptance of his reformed version of the traditional beliefs. Those who offend against it by speech or act are to be denounced to the courts, and, if found guilty, are to be given not less than five years' solitary confinement in a reformatory, where they will be subjected to intensive religious propaganda, but denied all other human intercourse; if this fails to cure them, they will be put to death.[87] Plato in fact wishes to revive the fifth-century heresy trials (he makes it plain that he would condemn Anaxagoras unless he mended his opinions);[88] all that is new is the proposed psychological treatment of the guilty. That the fate of Socrates did not

---

or symbolises religious truth at the level of εἰκασία at which it can be assimilated by the people. Plato's universe was a graded one: as he believed in degrees of truth and reality, so he believed in degrees of religious insight. Cf. Reverdin, *op. cit.*, 243 ff.

[86] *Laws* 873E. Pollution is incurred in all cases of homicide, even involuntary (865C–D), or of suicide (873D), and requires a κάθαρσις [purification] which will be prescribed by the Delphic ἐξηγηταί [exegetes]. The infectiousness of μίασμα [pollution] is recognised within certain limits (881D–E, cf. 916C, and chap. ii, n. 43).

[87] *Laws* 907D–909D. Those whose irreligious teaching is aggravated by antisocial conduct are to suffer solitary confinement for life (909B–C) in hideous surroundings (908A)—a fate which Plato rightly regards as worse than death (908E). Grave *ritual* offences, such as sacrificing to a god when in a state of impurity, are to be punishable by death (910C–E), as they were at Athens: this is defended on the old ground that such acts bring the anger of the gods on the entire city (910B).

[88] *Ibid.*, 967B–C, "certain persons" who formerly got themselves into trouble through falsely asserting that the heavenly bodies were "a pack of stones and earth" had only themselves to blame for it. But the view that astronomy is a dangerous science is, thanks to modern discoveries, now out of date (967A); some smattering of it is indeed a necessary part of religious education (967D–968A).

warn Plato of the danger inherent in such measures may seem strange indeed.[89] But he apparently felt that freedom of thought in religious matters involved so grave a *threat to society* that the measures had to be taken. "Heresy" is perhaps a misleading word to use in this connection. Plato's proposed theocratic State does in certain respects foreshadow the mediaeval theocracy. But the mediaeval Inquisition was chiefly concerned lest people should suffer in the next world for having held false opinions in this one; overtly, at any rate, it was trying to save souls at the expense of bodies. Plato's concern was quite different. He was trying to save society from contamination by dangerous thoughts, which in his view were visibly destroying the springs of social conduct.[90] Any teaching which weakens the conviction that honesty is the best policy he feels obliged to prohibit as antisocial. The motives behind his legislation are thus practical and secular; in this respect the nearest historical analogue is not the Inquisition, but those trials of "intellectual deviationists" with which our own generation has become so familiar.

Such, then, in brief, were Plato's proposals for reforming the Conglomerate. They were not carried out, and the Conglomerate was not reformed.

[89] Cornford has drawn a striking parallel between Plato's position and that of the Grand Inquisitor in the story told in *The Brothers Karamazov* (*The Unwritten Philosophy*, 66 f.).

[90] Cf. *Laws*, 885D: "most of us, instead of seeking to avoid wrongdoing, do wrong and then try to patch it up," and 888B: . . . "most important of all . . . is to think rightly about the gods and so live well, or the opposite." For the wide diffusion of materialism see 891B.

Chapter VII of *The Greeks and the Irrational* by E. R. Dodds (The University of California Press, Berkeley, 1951). Reprinted by permission of The University of California Press and the author. [The opening sentence has been supplied by the editor, who is also responsible for omitting a few untranslated Greek phrases and for adding English translations of some others.]

15

PLATO'S VIEWS ON THE
NATURE OF THE SOUL

W. K. C. GUTHRIE

This subject [the teaching of Plato himself on a theme so important to religious philosophy as the nature and fate of the human soul] is certainly not one which has been neglected by scholars in the past. Yet although it has been subjected to repeated scrutiny, it remains true, as one of the most recent writers has remarked, that "the problem of the tripartite soul is among the thorniest of all Platonic problems, and in spite of a vast amount of discussion in recent years, it cannot be said to be solved."[1] The obvious truth of this statement, and the fact that, as it seems to me, one important point in particular has been overlooked in previous attempts at explanation, form my justification for raising the topic again.

The questions which I wish to reopen are these: What were Plato's beliefs about the nature of the human soul? In what sense did he believe it to be immortal? How far is he consistent in what he says about it in the dialogues? I take it that we should agree on two things, and in what follows I shall assume them to be true. Both have been well expressed by Professor Dodds. First, "Plato's philosophy did not spring forth fully mature, either from his own head or from the head of Socrates", but is "an organic thing which changed, partly in obedience to its inner law of growth, but partly also in response to external stimuli".[2] Second, Plato admitted two levels of truth, which may roughly be called truths of religion and truths of reason. There will always be some truths, and those the highest, which cannot be proved dialectically but must be conveyed in the form of myth, the details of which can claim only probability, not precise accuracy. At the same time he regarded it as the philosopher's duty to push back the frontiers of reason and win for it all possible ground from the domain of mythical im-

---

[1] R. Hackforth, *Plato's Phaedrus* (1952), p. 75.
[2] Dodds, *The Greeks and the Irrational* (1951), p. 208 [p. 207, this volume].

agery.³ As an example, we may say that immortality was for Plato a matter of rational proof, whereas what befell the immortal part of us after death could only be hinted at in a ἱερὸς λόγος [sacred story].

Having made these two points, I had better add that neverthe-less I shall be arguing for a greater measure of consistency in Plato's thought than is usually granted by his interpreters.

I have put some questions in general terms. The specific problem which they raise, and which has always been the centre of argu-ment, is this: Did Plato consider the soul as in its own essence simple or composite, and if the latter, did he believe that the whole of it was immortal, or only the highest part? (I use the English word 'soul', but it must be supposed in every case to stand for the Greek ψυχή.)

The mind and personality of Socrates formed the starting-point of Plato's philosophy, and remained its inspiration throughout his life. Where he went beyond Socrates, as of course he did, it was never (so I believe) with the intention of contradicting him, but rather of putting his simple, practical teaching on an unassailable theoretical basis. From him he would learn that the chief end of man is to look after the well-being of his soul, and that this θεραπεία ψυχῆς [tendance of soul] is a τέχνη [art] (*Laches* 185E) acquired by rigorous self-examination and an understanding of the meaning of ethical terms, which in turn is gained by the method of "common search", that is of question and answer between two people acting in a spirit of mutual helpfulness and friendship. Since full under-standing would inevitably reveal itself in right action, virtue is knowledge and no one sins willingly. For Socrates the "soul" that is to be cultivated is clearly the mind or understanding (νοῦς). The life extolled is the rational life, though this is no reason why he should not have said, as Xenophon makes him say (*Mem.* 4.3.14), that the soul of man has something divine in it. I think myself, with Erland Ehnmark,⁴ that he believed it destined for a blessed im-mortality, but for the present purpose we can leave this contro-versial question aside.

The *Phaedo* reads like a defence of this Socratic view, though a defence carried on by means of doctrines which go beyond any-thing that Socrates himself is likely to have said. The supremacy of

³ Compare Dodds, *Plato and the Irrational*, JHS 1945, pp. 23 f.
⁴ *Socrates and the Immortality of the Soul*, Eranus 1946, pp. 105–22.

the soul, its identity with the intellect, the need to cultivate it and render it as independent of the body as possible, all these are emphasized by every means at Plato's disposal. Moreover its immortality is made to depend on its singleness of nature, for nothing composite can be immune from destruction (78C). The idea of the composition of the soul out of several elements is worked out in the *Republic*, but more than hinted at in the *Gorgias* (503 ff.), where it is difficult to agree with Frutiger that "le principe de la simplicité de l'âme est encore maintenu".[5] Starting from his favourite analogy with the crafts, Plato's Socrates describes the making of an artefact as in every case a process of so arranging and fitting together a number of different parts or elements that they take their place in the structure of a new whole, which is to be a τεταγμένον καὶ κεκοσμημένον πρᾶγμα [regularly ordered product]. Trainers do the same for the body—κοσμοῦσι καὶ συντάττουσι [regulate and set it in order]—and the health of the soul depends similarly on its attainment of κόσμος [order] and τάξις [regulation], which must surely imply the presence of parts within it.

Here, however, no more is said, and the approach certainly seems tentative. *Rp.* iv gives us the full and explicit partition of the soul into reason, appetite and the intermediate element of θυμός [spirit]. Nor can we water down this doctrine by speaking loosely of "aspects" of an essentially unitary soul, instead of "parts" of a composite one. Not only are the words μέρη and εἶδος used as well as γένη, but such an interpretation is forbidden by Plato's appeal to a precise statement of the law of contradiction at 426B. With this, however, has to be compared the passage in Book x (611A ff.), where Plato reminds us that it is difficult for a σύνθετον [anything composite], such as we have just seen the soul to be, to be eternal, especially when, as in this case, it does not seem to be put together in the best possible manner. However, he adds, we must remember that soul in its truest nature is not like this—full of variety, dissimilarity and inconsistency (πολλῆς ποικιλίας τε καὶ ἀνομοιότητός τε καὶ διαφορᾶς γέμειν αὐτὸ πρὸς αὑτό). We see it like this now because it is damaged by its connexion with the body (λελωβημένον ... ὑπό τε τῆς τοῦ σώματος κοινωνίας καὶ ἄλλων κακῶν, ὥσπερ νῦν ἡμεῖς θεώμεθα), but ought to consider it in its purity (οἷόν ἐστι καθαρὸν γιγνόμενον). Then we should find it a much more beautiful thing (πολὺ κάλλιον). We must look only at its φιλοσοφία

[5] *Les Mythes de Platon* (1930), p. 85.

[love of wisdom], and understand that it is akin to the divine and immortal and everlasting (συγγενὴς οὖσα τῷ τε θείῳ καὶ ἀθανάτῳ καὶ τῷ ἀεὶ ὄντι: cf. *Phaedo* 79D, where the soul is spoken of in practically the same words as συγγενὴς οὖσα to τὸ καθαρόν τε καὶ ἀεὶ ὂν καὶ ἀθάνατον). Only then, if we see it stripped of its bodily associations, shall we behold its true nature, whether simple or composite (τὴν ἀληθῆ φύσιν εἴτε πολυειδὴς εἴτε μονοειδής).

The only reasonable conclusion from all this is that the soul for Plato is still in essence simple, and only appears composite as the result of its association with the body. I should not have taken up so much of your time with this well known passage were it not that an acute critic like Frutiger could still regard it not as confirming, but as correcting the insistence of the *Phaedo* on the simplicity of the soul. He thought that by saying it is *difficult* for a σύνθετον [anything composite] to be immortal, Plato meant that it is not impossible as it is said to be in the *Phaedo*. But this sort of tentative under-statement is of course characteristic of Plato. Even in the *Phaedo* he only says: οὐκοῦν ἅπερ ἀεὶ κατὰ ταὐτὰ καὶ ὡσαύτως ἔχει, ταῦτα μάλιστα εἰκὸς εἶναι τὰ ἀσύνθετα, τὰ δὲ ἄλλοτ' ἄλλως καὶ μηδέποτε κατὰ ταὐτά, ταῦτα δὲ σύνθετα [That which is always constant and invariable is *most likely to be* the incomposite, and what changes and is never constant to be composite]. So far as the words go, he is even there attributing probable, not certain mortality to the composite.[6]

In the *Meno*, as in the *Phaedo* and *Republic*, the immortality of the soul is brought into connexion with the theory that knowledge is recollection, but nothing is said as to its composition. The real difficulty begins with the *Phaedrus*. Before tackling it, we may note that the *Timaeus*, which was presumably written after all the dialogues so far mentioned, reproduces essentially the same scheme as the *Republic*. The soul is an immortal principle, but when it is incarnated in a mortal body, the θνητὸν εἶδος ψυχῆς [mortal form of soul] is "built on" to it (προσῳκοδόμουν 69C). This, subdivided as before into a nobler and a baser part, is located in the lower regions of the body. The head is the seat of that part which Plato calls divine (44D), and contrasts with the mortal. At 90A he says that God has given us this part as a *daimon*, and as proof of our kinship with heaven. Here too then, our soul in this life is tripartite, but only the highest part of it, namely the reason, is immortal.

---

[6] Frutiger *o.c.*, pp. 91–93; *Phaedo* 78C.

When he wrote the *Phaedo*, the twin currents of intellectualism and Puritanism still flowed so strongly in Plato that he assigned only reason to the soul, regarding all passion and emotion, as well as sheer physical appetite, as the work of the body trying to drag down the soul to its own level. These therefore must be repressed, and the soul cultivated as far as possible as if it were already disembodied, in that "practice for death" which is the philosophers' proper occupation. In the *Republic* he has advanced to a recognition that conflict occurs in the soul itself, and this figure of internal conflict (στάσις) is also developed in the *Sophist* (228B). It leads to a change of emphasis in practice as well as theory. The passions and appetites are acknowledged to have their place in human life. Attention is directed rather to their regulation than to their complete suppression. But Book x shows him still faithful to the conviction that the existence of these conflicting elements in the soul is only made possible by its association with the body, and that in its purity, its "truest nature", it is characterized by φιλοσοφία alone; and only this philosophic soul is immortal. This is the teaching of the *Timaeus* also, and I believe it to have been Plato's conviction throughout his life. That he should ever have brought himself to include the two lower parts of the soul in its purest and truest nature seems to me a psychological improbability far more difficult to swallow than any difficulty caused by their attachment to discarnate souls in the *Phaedrus*. Only the reason is immortal; or, since the word "reason" is too cold and dry to convey the full import of a philosophy based, like Plato's, on Eros (at its highest level, but still Eros), let us rather say: only that part of the soul which strives consistently after wisdom and knowledge can belong to the eternal world, for only that is συγγενὴς τῷ θείῳ. And after all, it is at least difficult to conceive how a completely disembodied soul could retain its appetite for food and drink, which are absorbed in bodily organs and serve the purposes of the body alone. Here however the real difficulties begin, and to appreciate them we must turn to the *Phaedrus*.

At the very beginning of what is said there about the soul (245C), we notice that its immortality is no longer made to depend on its simplicity, but a different proof from those in the *Phaedo* is offered, the proof from self-motion. Passing to its nature or form (ἰδέα, 246A), Plato emphasizes that what follows will be only a simile. It would be a superhuman task to describe it οἷόν ἐστι [as it is], but we may say ᾧ ἔοικε [what it resembles], and this means, as has been generally recognized, that "the myth will be in part an allegory, that is to say a description in symbolic terms which can be readily translated into what they stand for" (Hackforth, *Phaedrus* p. 72). Indeed the meaning of Plato's comparison of the soul to "the combined power of a team of winged horses and their charioteer" (246A) is transparent enough. It is the familiar tripartite soul, in which the charioteer represents the reason, the nobler horse the passionate element, and the baser horse the physical appetites.

Having said this, however, we have to admit that the composite nature of the soul is not, as it has appeared to be in the dialogues we have so far considered, dependent on its incarnation in a body. In the first place, the souls of the gods, equally with those of men, are likened to charioteer and horses; or to follow the simile more accurately, the god is said to be the charioteer who drives his winged team (246E). In the second place, souls that are destined for incarnation in mortal bodies have already their three elements— driver, obedient horse and unruly horse—before their fall from heaven, when they are still striving to follow in the train of the gods and get a glimpse of the vision of reality in the plain of truth.

We are in an obvious difficulty if we confront this picture of the soul with those in other dialogues. There, we said, it is only association with a body that imparts to the soul its lower elements. Here on the contrary they are ascribed to discarnate souls also. Scholars hitherto seem to have followed one of two courses. Either they say with Wilamowitz that the imagery in fact breaks down ("Das komplizierte Bild des Seelenwagens mit den zwei verschieden gemuteten Rossen ist allein für das Verhalten de Seele im Menschenleibe erfunden", *Platon* i p. 467; so also Taylor, *Plato* 307; we must not "press the details"); or else, like Professor Hackforth, they posit an unresolved contradiction in Plato's own mind. "Plato wavers to the end between the religious, Orphic-Pythagorean conception of a divine soul essentially ('in its true nature') divorced from all physical functions, all 'lower' activities, and a more secular and scientific conception of soul as essentially a source of motion both to itself and to τὰ ἄλλα." On this view "it can only move the body in virtue of itself possessing 'motions' over and above the reason which contemplates the eternal Forms." (*Phaedrus*, p. 76.)

I should like to suggest a different solution. The system of eschatology which Plato adopts in his myths is a complex one. In outline it was not original, for it appears in Empedocles, and is pretty clearly the system taught in the poems from which the verses were extracted that have been discovered on the famous gold plates from Italian graves. I like to call it Orphic, but in deference to the suspicion with which that name is generally greeted today, I am willing for the moment to regard this as no more than a personal whim. The name does not matter, but the system was there. It taught that essentially the soul is divine (the *daimon* common to Empedocles and *Timaeus* 90A; the θεός which the dead man is to become according to the tablets from Thurii), but has been compelled to undergo a series of incarnations as punishment for some not very clearly defined original sin or impurity. It may be the universal human impurity due to our origin from the Titans, sons of Earth and slayers of Dionysus. But since no classical authority says so explicitly, let us emulate Pindar's caution and speak of it as "requital for ancient grief." Empedocles specified the sins of flesh-eating and perjury, but why a divine being should commit these sins he does not say. Perhaps the sin as well as the punishment was "a decree of necessity."

Be that as it may, as soon as a soul has sinned, and is therefore doomed to the wheel of reincarnation, it has lost its purity. Thereafter, as for ten thousand years it makes the weary round of the wheel, now in and now out of a human or animal body, it is never free from the contamination of the sublunary world, exemplified in, *but not confined to* its direct association with a body.

This is the scheme of the *Phaedrus*. To the decree of necessity of Empedocles corresponds the "law of *Adrasteia*" of 248C. When one of the *daimones*, says Empedocles, has sinned, it must wander for thrice ten thousand seasons an exile from its native element, being born in all forms of mortality (fr. 115). In the language of Plato's myth, the soul which cannot follow the gods and get a full vision of the truth, falls to the earth and is born, first as a man, and afterwards, if its earthly life deserves it, as a beast. It cannot return "to the place whence it came" (248E) for ten thousand years, unless it succeeds in living the philosophic life three times in succession. Each circuit from one birth to the next lasts a thousand years, from which it follows that in the cycle of reincarnation much more time is spent out of the body than in it. How it is spent, we learn from the myth of Er in the *Republic*.

The point is this. For one who holds these beliefs, the essential contrast is not between an incarnate and a discarnate soul. Whether or not a soul is actually in the body or out of it is comparatively unimportant if it is caught in the wheel, and destined for incarnation or reincarnation. The essential difference is that between a soul that is in, or destined for, the κύκλος βαρυπένθης and one that has escaped from it and returned εἰς τὸ αὐτὸ ὅθεν ἥκει. Only after escape is immortality attained, for immortality does not simply mean an ability to outlast the body. It implies divinity and presupposes complete purity. Souls still in the wheel have the taint of the earthly still clinging to them, alike during incarnations and between them.

Here I would draw attention to something which is usually overlooked in this connection.[7] It is regularly said that the psychology of the *Phaedrus* is inconsistent with that of, for example, the *Phaedo*, because in the *Phaedrus* the lower parts of the soul survive when it is out of the body, but in the *Phaedo* they do not. This is not strictly true. It is said there, admittedly, that the passions and appetites are of the body and do not belong to the soul's true nature; but it is not said that the soul is immediately rid of them after death. On the contrary, we are told (81A ff.) that a soul that has given itself over to bodily desires and pleasures while in the body is, when it leaves it, still permeated by the corporeal. It must therefore wander about in the region of the corporeal until, "through the desires of that which follows about with it", it is again imprisoned in a body. To be immediately rid, at death, of the taint of the body (that is, of the lower parts of the soul) is a privilege reserved for the philosopher whose life has been a successful "practice for death". Similarly in the myth of the *Gorgias* it is said that every soul, just like every body, retains after death the blemishes which defaced it in life (524D–E). That is why Zeus decreed that judgment must be pronounced after death, lest the ugliness of the soul be hidden by the cloak of a fine body, or of wealth and power.

It is thus no contradiction of anything that Plato has ever said if in the *Phaedrus* he speaks of the lower parts of the soul outlasting its incarnation in a body. Even in the *Phaedrus*, I suggest, we may affirm that its composite nature is bound up, if not with actual inclusion in a body, at any rate with its involvement in the doom of repeated incarnation. The souls of the gods are in the simile compared to a charioteer and team of horses like the others, but with a significant difference. Driver and horses are at one, are alike good: "the horses and charioteers of the gods are all good themselves and of good stock, but the nature of the others is mixed" (246A). What

[7] I think for instance that it is missed by Professor Dodds in his remark about the *Phaedrus* in *The Greeks and the Irrational*, p. 231 n. 62.

can this mean except that essentially the souls of the gods are of one and the same nature, since they contain no possibility of evil?[8] This will apply also to the souls of those philosophic men who have made their final escape from the wheel of birth, for then their nature too will be wholly divine. "God shalt thou be instead of mortal" was the promise of the gold plates, which Empedocles knew had come true for him: "I tell you I am an immortal god, no longer mortal" (fr. 112.4). For Plato too the end of the philosophic life was ὁμοίωσις θεῷ [assimilation to god], for the immortal part of us, the reason, is so in virtue of being divine (*Ti.* 44D).

This is the conclusion to which we must come if we strip off the trappings of the myth to get at the truth of which for Plato it is the imperfect image (ᾧ ἔοικεν ἡ ψυχή [what the soul resembles], not οἷόν ἐστι [what it is]). Are we right to treat the imagery in this way? Yes, for Plato has made his meaning clear when he tells us that charioteer and horses of the gods are "good and of good origin", but that the nature of the others is mixed. For the gods the allegory of the chariot implies no plurality of nature. Its imagery was necessary in order to give an imaginative picture of a religious truth which Plato believes, but of which neither he nor any other man can give a rational explanation. It is a truth that can be stated in Christian as well as Platonic terms. How did sin first enter the world, if man is made by God and in God's own image? Plato's simile does not then explain (for that is impossible) but illustrates pictorially how the soul, which is in its pure essence simple and perfect, *could become* a mixture of good and bad. It is of one nature. That is represented by saying that horses and charioteer are alike good. But a soul may become contaminated, and this has actually happened to the souls of mortals who have been drawn into the wheel of birth. Having the horses and charioteer already in his picture, Plato can represent this without a change of imagery, by saying simply: "the nature of the others is mixed." Frutiger asks (p. 82): "Si durant leur vie céleste, les âmes n'avaient pas déjà en elles une force capable de vaincre la raison, par quoi pourraient-elles être entraînées au mal?" The question is pertinent, but one may meet it with another: "If the image of charioteer and horses

---

[8] Professor Hackforth (*Phaedrus*, p. 76) says: "One hesitates whether or not to 'translate' this statement", but decides after all to do so, and hence concludes that "even 'pure' soul is θυμοειδής and ἐπιθυμητικός as well as λογιστικός." It is this statement with which I find it particularly difficult to agree.

itself implies a mixture of forces in the soul, how is it that the gods are free from all danger of a fall?"

To any who may still think that on this explanation Plato does not seem to have made altogether clear how the fall of a soul is possible in the first place, I would answer that it would be most surprising if he had. Empedocles does not explain how a *daimon*, one of those "whose portion is length of life" (fr.115.5), first comes to follow Strife and take to bloodshed and perjury. He only tells us what happens when it does. As I have said, the fall of man, the origin of evil in the human soul, is scarcely susceptible to rational explanation by a religious teacher who believes that man is made in the image of God. How then did he fall? There is no answer, but since to such a man—Plato or the writer of *Genesis* ii and iii—there is no surer article of belief, he tells us not how it happened but how it might have happened. It is as if, said Plato, the souls of God and man alike were each a charioteer driving winged horses. Since the nature of God, as we know, is pure and simple, we must imagine that in his case driver and horses are completely at one; but in other souls a flaw appears, for the horses have not the perfection of the driver, and one of them brings the whole equipage to the ground.

Another passage has recently been adduced as evidence against the view that Plato consistently believed in the immortality and divinity of the highest part of soul alone—that which we call reason. Professor Hackforth sees "complete disagreement" between the *Laws*, his latest work, and the *Timaeus* in this respect. In *Laws* x, he writes, we find "attribution to the world-soul (*and by inference to the individual soul 'in its true nature'*) of much besides reason, viz. 'wish, reflection, forethought, counsel, opinion true and false, joy, grief, confidence, fear, hate, love, and all the motions akin to these'."[9]

Now "the individual soul in its true nature" is for Plato, or has been hitherto, the soul of the complete philosopher, which has cast off all the trammels of this world and won its way to the divine plane of reality where dwell the eternal Forms and the gods to which it is akin, being itself immortal and divine. For Plato to tell us that this soul, far from being εὐδαίμων [blessed, happy] is subject to grief and fear, would be a volte face so incredible that whatever be the explanation of this passage, I do not think it can be that.

[9] Hackforth, *Phaedrus*, p. 75 (my italics). The passage referred to is at 897A.

Moreover if we are going to take this to apply to the soul "in its true nature" we must account for the fact that Plato has not only included some activities which seem inappropriate, but omitted to mention those that most properly belong to it, namely any activities connected with the attainment of knowledge and wisdom for their own sakes. There is no mention of ἐπίστασθαι, γνῶναι, φιλοσοφεῖν or anything else which for Plato clearly *was* the function of the soul in its true nature. If we are to take the paragraph *au pied de la lettre*, it even seems that so far as we have quoted it, it describes the lower part of soul, excluding pure reason, for a little later on he speaks of it as "adding to itself *nous*", or else doing the opposite and consorting with folly. Could Plato ever have spoken of the soul "in its true nature" as "consorting with folly"?

To say that in this passage Plato is giving us his considered view of soul in its true nature is, I think, to forget the context and purpose of the argument. The *Laws* is still a political treatise, and by proving that in the government of the world as a whole psychical causes are prior to physical Plato has it in mind to combat the harmful effect which the opposite belief must have on the conduct of members of a *polis*. His reason for opposing those who say that nature is ruled by inanimate forces and not by design (τύχη not τέχνη), is to refute their low opinion of political activity (889D): "They say that statesmanship has little in common with nature but is largely an artificial affair, and so all legislation is not natural but artificial, and its tenets are not true." Naturally then when he has demonstrated the priority of soul, he emphasizes those aspects of it which link it with practical statesmanship. Deliberation, forethought, will, opinion, fear and confidence etc. are all of great importance to the statesman, and even on the psychology of the *Republic* or *Timaeus* they belong to the soul, not the body. It is the workings of soul in this world that interest Plato at present, not the behaviour of the philosophic soul that has died to the world, or the souls of the gods as they contemplate the reality beyond space and time. At 904A, he says that there is soul in every action both good and bad, and this is the kind of soul that he is primarily including in the statement under consideration (897A). Nor can it well be argued that because of this shift of interest he has actually changed his convictions and ceased to believe in the wheel of incarnation and the possibility of ultimate release, with all that that implies for the true nature of the soul. At 903D he speaks of the soul as being joined now to one body and now to another, and at 904D, in language which would not be out of place in the *Phaedo*, he tells how a soul by consorting with divine virtue becomes divine itself, and is then transported to another, better place. When this happens we can have no reason to think that it will be other than *nous* pure and simple, identical with the supremely good soul that guides the wheeling stars, in the perfect circularity of whose motion its nature as *nous* is revealed (νοῦ κίνησις, 897D).

There remains perhaps the difficulty mentioned by Professor Hackforth, that if the soul is to be the moving principle, it must itself possess motions "over and above the reason which contemplates the eternal forms" (p. 234 above). I do not know whether, when Plato defined the soul as ἀρχὴ κινήσεως [source of motion] in the *Phaedrus*, this was for his own philosophy a new development; but at least it represented an ancient view of soul which must always have been familiar to him, and it is impossible that he could have thought of it otherwise than as a source of energy. In the *Republic*, as Cornford has written,[10] the three parts of the soul are also to be thought of as "manifestations of a single fund of energy, called Eros, directed through divergent channels towards various ends". These channels seemed to Plato to be in the main three. Hence instead of defining *nous* (for which 'reason' is an inadequate translation) as the highest part of a tripartite soul, we can also describe it as the power of soul when all its energies are directed to the pursuit of wisdom, and every desire for the objects either of worldly ambition or of sensual gratification has lost its meaning. The highest manifestation is certainly as much of a motive force as are the other two. *Psyche* is the vital principle, it is the energy of life itself. The soul of the philosopher, or of God, does not lose that life when it turns to contemplate reality. On the contrary the philosophic souls "have life, and have it more abundantly", ἡ γὰρ νοῦ ἐνέργεια ζωή [for the activity of mind is life], as Aristotle wrote in a truly Platonic mood. But it would be a great distortion of Plato's words to say that they have θυμός [spirit] and ἐπιθυμία [appetite].

In this life, *nous* is characterized by the possession of philosophic *eros*. The lower manifestations of *eros* belong to the lower parts of the soul. God, and the soul that has attained divinity, can presumably no longer feel *eros* at all, for that is the intermediate state of one who has not yet fully attained. To ask: "What then is the

[10] *The Doctrine of Eros, The Unwritten Philosophy* (Cambridge, 1950), p. 71 [reprinted above, p. 121]. Cf. *R.* 485D.

nature of the 'motion' of God, and of souls absorbed into his being?" would be, for a man like Plato, to exceed the bounds of *logos*. Here mysticism steps in. The source of knowledge and of being cannot be looked at directly with the eye of the mind, any more than the sun, its earthly image, with the eye of the body.

Nevertheless this is just the sort of question that the irrepressible Aristotle did ask. In many fundamental things he remained the faithful pupil of Plato, and when they differed the reason was usually this: for Plato, however far dialectic might go, the veil between it and *mythos* must always remain, since it existed in the nature of things. For Aristotle, to take refuge in *mythos* at all was nothing but a confession of weakness. This final question therefore he tackled, and answered by drawing the distinction between κίνησις [movement] and ἐνέργεια [activity], and defining the former as ἐντελέχεια κινητοῦ ἀτελής [the incomplete actualization of the movable] (*Ph.* viii.257B 8). Where motion ends, we reach no state of passivity or ineffectiveness. On the contrary, it is only then that full and unimpeded activity begins.

And so I conclude that, once he had emerged from the purely Socratic phase of thought, Plato's views about the nature of the individual soul were fundamentally consistent. (How far these views were already inherent in the mind of Socrates is a question for another paper, if indeed it can be answered at all.) From the moment when they first incur the doom of pilgrimage through the cycle of *palingenesis*, souls are compounded of three main elements; or, if you like, three streams of energy directed to objects of different sorts. Of these, the lower two can only exist—they can only have meaning—in connexion with the possibility of contact with a body, that is, of existence within the cycle. The highest part, and that alone, is perfect and divine, and this at the same time is the soul in its true, or pure, nature. If there is inconsistency in this, it is an inconsistency inherent in the human situation, poised as we are uneasily between the worlds of beast and of god, a mixture of the two, divinely discontent. This also Aristotle saw. A man, he said, must live according to his highest part, and that is *nous*. In so far as he does this, he will indeed seem to be living "not *qua* man, but by virtue of a divinity which is in him". Yet at the same time "this part would seem to *be* each one of us, and it would be absurd to choose not one's own life but that of another" (*EN* x. 1177B 27 ff). Aristotle also maintained, even at a risk to the consistency of his own philosophy, which he valued above all else, that whereas soul as the principle of physical life must perish with its body, *nous* alone was different. It alone "comes in from outside" and is divine (*GA* 736B 28, *EN* 1177B 28), and it may outlast the death of the body (*Metaph.* 1070A 25), for it is something separate (*de An.* 430A 17). For "Pythagorean myths" about the migration of a soul into different bodies he felt nothing but contempt (*de An.* 407B 20 ff.), but the immortality and divinity of *nous*, and of *nous* alone, was a part of his Platonic heritage which he found it impossible to renounce.[11]

[11] I should like to draw attention to an excellent article on this subject which nowadays tends to be forgotten. It is *Plato and the Tripartite Soul*, by J. L. Stocks, in *Mind* vol. 24 (1915), pp. 207–21.

Published originally in *Recherches sur la Tradition Platonicienne, Entretiens*, Tome III, Fondation Hardt, *Pour l'Etude de l'Antiquité Classique* (Vandoeuvres-Genève, 1957), 2–19. Reprinted by permission of the Fondation Hardt and the author. [A parenthetical clause in the opening sentence has been added by the editor. Some Greek citations are accompanied, others replaced, by English translations supplied by the author.]

16

THE SOURCES OF EVIL
ACCORDING TO PLATO

HAROLD CHERNISS

The point of this paper is the plural in its title. My reason for making it is the persistent failure of scholars to understand how Plato, if he had a consistent theory of evil, could speak of the evil in this world as derivative from more than a single source. Some of them, consequently, stoutly maintain that he must have believed all evil to have one source only, though they disagree in identifying that source, while others deny that he ever achieved any coherent theory of evil at all.[1]

---

[1] Among those who maintain that the source of all evil according to Plato is matter or corporeality are Vlastos (1939: 80–82) [Cf. "References" at end of this selection], Festugière (1947: 36–42), and Pétrement (1947: 45–47 and 72–73); among those who contend that it is soul or an irrational element in soul are Wilamowitz-Moellendorff (1919: 320–321), Chilcott (1923: 29–31), Taylor (1928: 117; 1937: 455, n. 2, and 492), Cornford (1937: 209–210), and Morrow (1950: 163). For earlier exponents of the latter position, against which Hoffleit (1937) argued, cf. Zeller (1922: 765, n. 5), who for his part (1922: 973, n. 3 and 4) contends that in all dialogues before the *Laws* the source of all evil is matter but in the *Laws* is an evil world-soul and that this was a natural step in the development of Plato's theory. Greene (1944: 301) thinks it idle to seek in Plato for a single solution. According to him there are two solutions equally Platonic: "Plato identifies the source of moral evil at first chiefly with body or matter and then more and more with soul. . . . The unresolved residuum, or evil, in the world, as Plato sees it, may confidently be assigned to matter or 'Necessity,' once and once only . . . conceived as endowed with life (soul)" (*op. cit.*, 311). Sesemann (1912: 180) had already asserted that there are "zwei Grundauffassungen des Bösen, die in dem platonischen System unversöhnt einander gegenüber stehen." Meldrum (1950: 65) holds that "the discrepancies in what Plato says about evil . . . call attention to something obscure, perhaps incoherent, in his metaphysical thinking"; he argues (70) that "Plato's view of evil varies as νοῦς δημιουργικός or ψυχὴ ἀρχὴ κινήσεως predominates," and he concludes (74) that "there is no entity that we can call 'Plato's theology.'" Palas (1941: 52) goes even further and asserts that "the problem of evil never seriously concerned Plato at all," an assertion which Solmsen unwittingly contradicts (1942: 142) with the assurance that "the problem of evil . . .

This is not so strange as a similar lack of consensus concerning evidence would be in most fields of investigation. Plato did not collect all that he might have to say about various subjects and set down these doctrinal opinions in systematic arrangement under the rubrics that later became the conventional problems of philosophy. The form in which he chose to express his thought is the dialogue, and he always confined his treatment of any problem to such aspects of it as seemed to him to be pertinent to the particular context of the philosophical discussion which he was actually composing.[2] Because of this the interpretation of Plato is involved in peculiar difficulties, and there is a great temptation to treat the several dialogues as records of disconnected phases in the flux or—more courteously—in the development of Plato's thought.[3] One should, of course, beware of reading into the text what is not implied by it according to Plato's own standards; but one must be equally wary of neglecting the illumination that the different dialogues cast upon one another. Synoptic understanding is no less necessary in this modest field of investigation than Plato said it is to the philosopher in his larger sphere. Such a synoptic reading of the dialogues reveals, I believe, behind all the apparently diverse statements concerning the sources of evil a theory more complicated than any of the current interpretations has recognized but perfectly coherent in all its parts and consistent with Plato's fundamental theory of reality.

According to that theory the phenomenal world is a spatial reflection of the ideas, which alone are perfectly real entities.[4] Since

---

had an organic and important place in his thought." For the interpretations of Plato's theory of evil given by Aristotle, Theophrastus, and Eudemus and for the theories of Speusippus and Xenocrates *cf.* Cherniss, 1944: 95–97, n. 62, and 268–269, n. 176.

[2] The body of the *Timaeus* is not a dialogue; but dialogic characteristics are not entirely absent even from this exposition, just as they are present in the longer expository sections of the *Laws* (*cf.* Schaerer, 1938: 153–156). Moreover, the form of the *Timaeus* alone determines the treatment of important doctrinal factors there, e.g. the self-motion of soul (*cf.* Cherniss, 1944: 428–431).

[3] Stenzel (1931: 108, n. 1; 125; 133), who himself sought to trace Plato's development, issued a warning against the dangers of this temptation, a temptation to which British scholars have recently manifested a growing susceptibility.

[4] *Timaeus* 52A–C, *Politicus* 285D9–286B2 (*cf.* *Phaedrus* 250A–C), *Phaedo* 74D–75D.

no copy or reflection can be identical with its model or original, all phenomena must fall short of the reality of the ideas, and all must therefore be something less than perfect.[5] So all the phenomenal world is always involved in what may be called "negative evil," since it is a derogation of reality, the degree of deviation from the original which at the very least is implied in the existence of a copy or reflection.[6] It is evil in this sense that, as the contrary of good, is in the *Theaetetus* said to be ineradicable from this mortal world but absent from the divine;[7] and the same notion is implied by the statement in the *Philebus* that whatever fair things there are in this

---

[5] *Cf. Cratylus* 432C–D, *Sophist* 240A–B (*cf. Republic* 597A 4–7).

[6] Palas (1941: 50) says: "Letzten Endes aber beruht der axiologische Grundcharakter des empirischen Kosmos darin, dass der Kosmos das Abbild des Urbildes ist." This statement, which save for the first two words is literally correct, erroneously implies, however, that Plato meant to explain *all* evil in this way. It is Sesemann's similar neglect of Plato's distinctions that accounts for his formulation (1912: 174 and 176): the notion of the spatial-material principle as the source of all imperfection makes evil a positive force, whereas the notion of soul (through its ignorance) as the cause precludes all positive reality of evil, making it mere negation.

[7] *Theaetetus* 176A 5–8. This statement concerning the contrariety of good and evil was expanded into a theodicy by the Stoics (Aulus Gellius, VII, 2–3 [*S. V. F.* II, frag. 1169], where Chrysippus also uses *Phaedo* 60B–C); and Plotinus (III, ii, 5, 25–32) employs this passage as an appendix to a series of Stoical arguments, though he interprets it in a non-Stoical fashion. Sesemann (1912: 183) makes the passage say that "die Erhaltung des Guten fordert daher auch notwendig die Erhaltung des Bösen," supposes this to mean that evil is not only necessary but morally justified, and reads this conception into the *Lysis*, the *Timaeus*, and the *Laws*. But the ἀνάγκη of *Timaeus* 48A and the account of *Laws* 904B–D refer, as will be shown, to quite different matters; and *Lysis* 220D–221D is not parallel either, for its subject is the reason for man's desire of the good and it rejects the suggestion that the abolition of evil must involve the abolition of what is not evil (221B–D). As for *Theaetetus* 176A 5–8, the evils there in question, since they are said not to exist in the divine world and to be such as the soul can get free of, must be of a kind that is peculiar to phenomena as such, something implied in the nature of phenomenal existence and not in the nature of good itself. Nor is the good to which this evil is here said to be contrary the ideal or absolute good; it is the derivative good in the phenomenal world itself, as is shown by the remark of Theodorus (176A 3–4) which motivates Socrates' reply. The "expansion" of the passage by the Stoics and by Sesemann is therefore unwarranted, at least as an interpretation of Plato's meaning. (On this "expansion" and the Stoic paradox *cf.* also More [1921: 235]).

world are the result of a combination of the determinate and the indeterminate,[8] for indeterminateness characterizes phenomena as falling short of the complete reality of the ideas.[9]

Despite this negative evil, this deficiency which phenomenal existence as such implies, and despite the admission that for man at least there is more of evil in this world than good,[10] Plato in his myth of the creation declares that the Demiurge fashioned this universe because he was good and desired all things to be as nearly like himself in this respect as possible.[11] This myth expresses in the synthetic form of a cosmogony what is in fact an analysis of the constitutive factors of the universe which for Plato has neither beginning nor end,[12] and in the myth the Demiurge symbolizes the factor of rational causation in this universe. The Demiurge or god or gods or the class of causes so symbolized or represented[13] is wholly good and is responsible only for good;[14] and the cosmos fashioned by this cause is repeatedly declared to be good—good, that is, as a whole and as good as is possible considering the conditions on which it can exist at all.[15] Primary among these conditions is the nature of reflection or copy already mentioned. The Demiurge does not create either the ideas or space. Both of these are uncaused and ultimate factors;[16] and the immediate consequence of their existence, quite apart from any demiurgic causation, is the

---

[8] *Philebus* 26B 1–3 and 25E–26B generally.

[9] *Cf. Philebus* 16D7–E2 and *Amer. Jour. Philol.* 68: 233–234, 1947 with references *ibid.*, 234, n. 71.

[10] *Republic* 379C 4–5, *Laws* 906A2–B3 (*cf.* O. Apelt, *Platons Gesetze* 2: 541, n. 82).

[11] *Timaeus* 29D7–E3, 30A1–2.

[12] *Cf.* Cherniss, 1944: 421–431.

[13] *Cf.* Cherniss, 1944: 607–608 for the nature of the Demiurge in the *Timaeus*, the nature of "cause" in the *Philebus*, and Plato's use of "god" in the singular and plural.

[14] *Timaeus* 29E1, 30A6–7; *Republic* 379B–C (*cf.* 617E5 and *Timaeus* 42D3–4); *Laws* 900D2–3 and 900E6–8. *Cf.* the class of causes ὅσαι μετὰ νοῦ καλῶν καὶ ἀγαθῶν δημιουργοί (*Timaeus* 46E4).

[15] The last sentence of the *Timaeus* (92C4–9) solemnly declares the goodness of the phenomenal universe. That its goodness is limited, however, by the very conditions of its existence is indicated by the restrictive qualifications in such passages as *Timaeus* 29A5, 30B5–6, 46C8, 48A2–5, 53B5–6. That in many cases its partial aspects are good only by reference to the goodness of the whole is most clearly expressed in *Laws* 903B4–D3.

[16] *Timaeus* 52A1–4, 52A8–B2 (*cf.* 51A4–B2).

reflection of the immutable, non-spatial ideas in the unchanging and homogeneous mirror of space.[17] It is these spatial reflections upon which the demiurgic action is brought to bear, not to eliminate their character as reflections (for that is essential to their existence) and so not to annul the negative evil implicated in that character but by delimiting and organizing them to bring them nearer to conformity with the ideas, which are at once their originals and the models of this demiurgic activity.

These reflections, however, as consequences of the mere existence of space and the ideas, though they would be confused and indeterminate,[18] would still be static; and what is reduced to order by the Demiurge is said to have been not at rest but in erratic motion.[19] This precosmical chaotic motion of the myth is an isolated factor of the actually existing universe, random disorder which is only for the most part made subservient to the purposes of rational causation, for the phenomenal cosmos is the result of a combination of intelligent causation and "Necessity" or the "errant cause" that limits its effectiveness.[20] This erratic or random motion is, then, a source of evil different from the mere derogation of reality inherent in the nature of spatial reflection. The confusion of the errant cause with space to produce a Platonic matter which of its own nature is in disorderly motion is the chief reason why many interpreters have contended that in the *Timaeus* at least matter is the source of all evil.[21] According to Plato, however, nothing spatial

[17] *Cf.* Cherniss, 1944: 453–454.

[18] Since the spatial mirror is homogeneous and the ideas themselves are non-spatial, the reflections in space would not be locally distinct; and the Demiurge is conceived as delimiting them by geometrical configurations, thus representing spatially the "logical" distinctness of their non-spatial originals; *cf. Timaeus* 53A8–B5.

[19] *Timaeus* 30A3–6.

[20] *Timaeus* 46E3–6, 47E–48A, 56C3–7, 68E–69A; *cf.* Cherniss, 1944: 421–423 and 444.

[21] Vlastos (1939: 80–81): "Chaos . . . must, therefore, and for purely mechanical reasons, be in constant motion." Festugière (1946: 36, 40, 41) and most concisely in his later book (1949: 127): "la matière n'est pas seulement limite à l'Ordre, elle se trouve être par elle-même cause positive de désordre en ce qu'elle est mue, spontanément, de mouvements chaotiques." So Meldrum (1950: 66): "Νοῦς struggles to subdue ἀνάγκη. . . . The Demiurge does his best with these materials and succeeds on the whole, but to some extent they resist, and the evil of the world is simply this element of disorder that survives from chaos. So matter, τὸ σωματοειδές, is the κακοποιόν." In a note on this

statement Meldrum adds (*loc. cit.*, n. 10): " 'Necessity' is a name for τὸ σωματοειδές, more precisely for the causal powers of matter, for the αἰτίαι, ὅσαι μονωθεῖσαι φρονήσεως τὸ τυχὸν ἄτακτον ἑκάστοτε ἐξεργάζονται (*Timaeus* 46E)." The term, τὸ σωματοειδές in this context is apparently a reminiscence of the myth of the *Politicus* (273B4–C2), where in the absence of the Demiurge the increasing deviation of the cosmos from his instruction is charged to τὸ σωματοειδὲς τῆς συγκράσεως and it is said that ὅσα χαλεπὰ καὶ ἄδικα ἐν οὐρανῷ γίγνεται derive from the great disorder that prevailed before the Demiurge organized it into a cosmos. All interpretations such as the foregoing lean heavily upon this passage and upon the description of precosmical chaos in *Timaeus* 52D–53A, which they presume to be ultimate and unanalysable. What is referred to in this passage of the *Politicus* is undoubtedly the same as the errant cause of the *Timaeus* in operation; but the question is precisely whether erratic motion is an essential and irreducible characteristic of "corporeality" or is the resultant of "corporeality" and some other factor. In this connection it should be remembered, first, that "corporeality" itself is not for Plato an ultimate, unanalysable datum (*cf. Timaeus* 31B) and, second, that in the *Politicus* not only are the precosmical disorder and the retrograde motion mythical, i.e., factors of the actual phenomenal world isolated for the purpose of description, but the retrograde motion during the course of which this disorder finally comes again to predominance is represented as a reaction of the tension created by the motion which the Demiurge imposes upon the universe (*Politicus* 270A; see further note 44 *infra*).

A curious aspect of the interpretations that represent Platonic matter as thus self-moving is that they frequently represent it as the same time as "non-being" and, since it is the source of evil, represent evil therefore as somehow non-existent. So Festugière (1949: 129) says of what he calls Platonic Χώρα-matter: "Sous un premier aspect, elle apparaît comme une transposition physique de la notion dialectique de l'Autre: elle est un non-être relatif. ... Sous un second aspect, étant mue spontanément de mouvements désordonnés ..., la χώρα matière apparait comme un principe autonome de désordre...." *Cf.* Greene's statements (1944: 305): "Ananke ... is the negative substratum of phenomena" and (*ibid.*: 297) "... evil is somehow mere nonexistence (μὴ ὄν), or better, is otherness." In fact, Plato never suggests that evil is non-existence or "otherness"; and, far from calling space μὴ ὄν or θάτερον he says ταὐτὸν αὐτὴν ἀεὶ προσρητέον (*Timaeus* 50B6–7) and expressly refers to it as ὂν ἀεί (*Timaeus* 52A 8). The notion that space is a "transposition" or manifestation of the idea of otherness or non-being is entirely without foundation. The existence of space is for Plato a necessary inference from the analysis of phenomenal process (*Timaeus* 49A–51B), and in characterizing it as μετ' ἀναισθησίας ἁπτὸν λογισμῷ τινι νόθῳ, μόγις πιστόν (*Timaeus* 52B2) he shows that he did not consider it to be a dialectical inference from the nature of the ideas themselves. On Aristotle, *Physics* 192A6–8, which is Zeller's "evidence" (1922: 726, n. 3 and 733) for asserting that Platonic matter is non-being, *cf.* Cherniss, 1944: 92–96.

or corporeal can be the cause of its own motion; and, since every such motion requires as cause a motion beyond itself, the ultimate cause of all corporeal motion must be an incorporeal self-motion, which he identifies as soul.[22] This is primary causation, whereas the motions of corporeal entities induced by other corporeal entities in motion and themselves inducing motion in still others can be only secondary causes.[23] Erratic or random motion must therefore, as motion, have its primary source in soul just as much as orderly motion has; to suppose that Plato in the *Timaeus* meant to make it a characteristic of corporeality *per se* is to assume that he there temporarily forgot or abandoned a fundamental tenet which he not only emphatically maintained both before and afterwards but which in fact is implied in the *Timaeus* itself.[24]

Mindful of this and of Plato's explicit statements that soul is the principle of all motion and change in the phenomenal world,[25] some interpreters have concluded that the cause of the random, disorderly motions must be an irrational element in the soul that according to the *Timaeus* pervades the universe and moves the

---

[22] *Phaedrus* 245C5–246A2, *Laws* 894B8–896C4.

[23] *Laws* 895B, 897A; *Timaeus* 46D5–E2; *Phaedrus* 245C5–9.

[24] In the *Timaeus* the definition of soul is omitted as is all reference to self-motion in the *psychogonia* because to dwell upon it would have deprived the creation-myth of all literary plausibility (*cf.* Cherniss, 1944: 428–431, 455). Despite this, however, 37B5 is meant to be a reminder of the doctrine, for there soul is referred to (*pace* Cornford, 1937: 95, n. 2) by the phrase, "that which is moved by itself," as 37C3–5 plainly shows. Moreover, *Timaeus* 46D–E in making all corporeal motion secondary to the primary causation of soul assumes the doctrine that soul is self-motion, as is clear from *Phaedrus* 245C5–9 and *Laws* 895B, 897A, where this classification of primary and secondary causation is presented as a consequence of that doctrine; it is consequently impossible to eliminate this passage, as Owen (1953: 95) tries to do by suggesting that it "may well contain only the raw material" of the doctrine of soul as self-motion. This doctrine, moreover, whatever the relative chronology of the *Phaedrus* and the *Timaeus* may be, was certainly not a "new development" of Plato's thought when he wrote the *Phaedrus* (*cf.* Cherniss, 1944: 433–442); it is involved in the "final demonstration" of the *Phaedo*, and the concept of self-motion itself is at least as early as the *Charmides* (168E–169A), a dialogue in which it is explicitly asserted that soul is the source of all good and evil for the body (156E).

[25] *Phaedrus* 245C9, 246B6–7 (*cf.* *Laws* 896D10–E2); *Laws* 892A5–7, 896A5–B1.

heavenly bodies,[26] while others have ascribed this disorder to an evil world-soul opposed to this world-soul of the *Timaeus* and posited, they believe, in the *Laws*.[27] The text of the *Timaeus*, however, excludes the possibility of an irrational element in the world-soul there described,[28] while the existence of an evil world-soul as its adversary and the cause of the chaotic motions is not even mentioned in the *Timaeus* and is certainly not envisaged in the text of *Laws* to which its proponents appeal.[29]

[26] *Cf.* Robin, 1935: 228–229; Cornford, 1937: 176–177, 205–206, 209–210; Morrow, 1950: 162–163.

[27] *Cf.* Wilamowitz-Moellendorff, 1919: 320–321. Dodds (1947: 21), though rejecting the notion that there is in the *Laws* an evil soul in the sense of "the Devil," holds that evil soul there and Necessity or the Errant Cause in the *Timaeus* are "symbols" of the same thing, "irrationality, the element both in man and in the κόσμος which is incompletely mastered by a rational will."

[28] The motion of the world-soul *as a whole* is called "ceaseless and intelligent life" (*Timaeus* 36E). The Circle of the Different, which is sometimes taken to symbolize irrational motions in the world-soul (e.g. by Cornford, 1937: 76 and 208) has a constitution identical with that of the Circle of the Same (*Timaeus* 35B 2 ff.); and, since the intermediate Being, Sameness, and Difference that are blended to form the soul are equally present in all parts of it and are all necessary for its rational processes (*Timaeus* 35A, 37A2–C5), this constitutive Difference cannot be made the cause of irrational motions (as is done e.g. by Robin, 1935: 228) without attributing these motions to the rational soul qua rational. *Cf.* Cherniss, 1944: 410, n. 339, and 446, n. 387; Meldrum, 1950: 67–68.

[29] *Laws* 896D10–E6, according to which we cannot say that a single soul controls and inhabits all moving things and so must control the heavens too but must assume at least two, beneficent soul and soul capable of the contrary. What follows in 898C and 899B proves that this is meant to assert the existence not of two world-souls, one good and the other evil, but of two *kinds* or *aspects* of soul (*cf. Phaedrus* 246B6–C6). The question at issue is which kind of soul (πότερον ψυχῆς γένος [897B7]) controls the circuit of the heavens and the heavenly bodies; and, as the ἀριστὴ ψυχή of 897C7 and 898C4 means "the best *kind* of soul," so ἡ κακή of 897D1 and ἡ ἐναντία of 898C4–5 means "the bad kind." It is not even asserted here that there is a single good world-soul; on the contrary, in the conclusion that soul which is the cause of the heavenly circuits must be completely virtuous the question whether this kind of soul is itself one or more than one is expressly left open (898C6–8, *cf.* 899B5–6: "soul or souls are causes of all those things"). In 904A–E and 906A–C there is no mention of any good or evil world-soul either but only of good and bad kinds of soul (*cf.* 904B2–3: ὅσον ἀγαθὸν ψυχῆς ... τὸ δὲ κακόν) and a plurality of both kinds (*cf.* 904E5–7).

Nevertheless, Plato does categorically declare that soul is the cause of all good and evil in the phenomenal world.[30] It is recognized that this follows from the doctrine that soul is the cause of all motion in this world; but the contention that this is irreconcilable with the account of random and chaotic motion in the *Timaeus* as well as the attempts to reconcile the two by ascribing the chaotic motions to an irrational element in the world-soul or to an evil world-soul opposed to it both overlook the fact that these random, disorderly motions are expressly classified as secondary causes, which as secondary are to be regarded as somehow dependent upon the primary causality of psychical motion.[31]

It must first be observed, however, that some evil has its *immediate* source in such psychical motion, in other words that there are souls in the universe which produce evil effects because they are themselves evil.[32] Soul is good or bad according to its knowledge or ignorance, for soul is self-motion the mode or direction of which is determined by its knowledge, exact or erroneous, of the ideas and their relations to one another and which sets phenomena in motion in accordance with this knowledge or ignorance.[33] Among these objects of knowledge there are, moreover, ideas of certain phenomenal evils. Not of all, for much of what we term evil is merely negative, a phenomenal deficiency or deviation from the positive idea imperfectly reflected or imitated; but many such terms have a positive content too and as such must refer to real entities among the ideas. Of these latter, however, many again, though ideas of phenomenal evils, are not themselves evil. Such, for example, are the ideas of diseases which have constitutions of their own like living organisms; these are as ideas no more evil than are the ideas of man, of wolf, or of lion, but the phenomenal manifestations of all of these may by mutual inter-

---

[30] *Laws* 896D5–8; *cf. Charmides* 156E6–8.

[31] *Timaeus* 46D5–E6; *cf. Laws* 894E–895B, 896A–D.

[32] E.g. *Republic* 353E; *Laws* 904B–E, 906B. It is not disorder in human affairs alone that is caused by evil souls, as is sometimes asserted (*cf.* Festugière, 1949: 110–111, 130); the evils produced by soul ἀνοίᾳ συγγενομένη include merely physical change and disorder, just as *Timaeus* 48A5 ff. and 57E–58C show that the effects of the errant cause extend throughout the whole physical universe.

[33] *Cf. Laws* 896E8–897B5, where B1–4 gives the reason for the good and the evil effects of soul (*cf.* 898B5–8). *Phaedrus* 246B6–C6 expresses the same notion in mythical language, the vision of the ideas being the nourishment of the soul's plumage (*cf.* 248B5–C2).

ference in this world be evils relatively to one another. Similarly such ideas as pleasure, pain, and desire are not as ideas evil either; but their phenomenal manifestations, though they can be good, are frequently evil relatively to the circumstances and degree of their manifestation. Besides these, however, there are positive vices; of these the logic of Plato's doctrine requires that there be ideas, and the existence of such ideas he always, in consistency with that logic, maintained. Yet even these are not of themselves causes of evil in the phenomenal world. They are manifested as evil here only by soul which in ignorance mistakes their true nature and their relation to the Good, just as desire, pleasure, and pain have evil manifestations in this world only when the mode and direction of psychical motion is determined by error concerning their nature.[34]

What the ultimate cause of such error is, why soul should ever lapse from complete and accurate knowledge of the ideas, to this question Plato can, of course, give no adequate answer. He can

[34] See for ideas of diseases: *Phaedo* 105C and *Timaeus* 89B–C; of desire: *Philebus* 34E (*cf.* Aristotle, *Topics* 147A5–11); of positive vices: *Euthyphro* 5D, *Republic* 402C and 476A, *Theaetetus* 186A8, *Sophist* 251A, *Laws* 964C. On ideas of evil *cf.* Cherniss, 1944: 266 n. 175 (on p. 267) and for the opinions of later Platonists *ibid.*: 277, n. 176. The list of passages cited above refutes of itself Chilcott's statement (1923: 28) that, while ideas of evil appear in dialogues of "the middle period," this theory is criticized in the *Parmenides* and *Sophist* and that evil in the *Philebus* and *Timaeus* "has a purely negative existence." *Parmenides* 130C5–E4 far from being a criticism of such ideas emphasizes Plato's refusal to breach the logic of his theory by rejecting them, and the doctrine of the *Sophist* does not eliminate such ideas so long as they have *positive* meaning (*cf.* Cherniss, 1944; 265–266; Ross, 1951: 169). Like many others, Chilcott (*ibid.*: 28 and 29) feels that the existence of such ideas is incompatible with *Republic* 509B6–8, which he takes to mean that αὐτὸ τὸ ἀγαθόν is "the source of all existence." In fact, however, that passage need mean no more than that the ideas are what they are and are rightly known as such only in the light of the idea of good. This would be hard to reconcile with the existence of the ideas of positive evils that Plato clearly does posit only if by it he had meant, as Chilcott and many others under Neo-Platonic influence assume, that all ideas are derived from the Good or are created by it; but this the passage does not say, and that it was not so meant is shown by the interpretative summary at 517C3–5, where it is said not that the idea of good is the source or origin of the ideas but that in the intelligible world it provides truth and intelligence (ἀλήθειαν καὶ νοῦν). *Cf.* with this 508D4–6: when the soul fixes itself upon that which ἀλήθειά τε καὶ τὸ ὄν illuminate, ἐνόησέν τε καὶ ἔγνω αὐτὸ καὶ νοῦν ἔχειν φαίνεται.

only clothe in mythical language the assumption that this is so[35] or argue that epistemological considerations necessitate and justify the assumption.[36] But this assumption granted, it follows that soul, moving in ignorance or forgetfulness of the true nature of the ideas and especially of the relation obtaining between any of them and the idea of good, must cause evil in whatever part of the phenomenal world it affects by its motion, for it will misarrange the reflections of reality and may in its error even come to regard as real and take for the patterns of its action these spatial reflections themselves instead of their originals.[37] So positive evil in the world, both absolute and relative, is produced by the misguided motion of evil souls.[38] These, since they move in ignorance of truth, do not intend as evil the evil that they cause;[39] but the motions that they induce directly in phenomena are nevertheless induced deliberately and consequently cannot be the random motions of the errant cause, for these are motions transmitted by an object which has itself been set in motion by something else and are distinguished as secondary from the primary causality of soul.[40]

[35] As e.g., in *Phaedrus* 248C5–8 and in *Timaeus* 41D6–7, where the ingredients of the immortal part of the human soul are said to be the same as those of the world-soul "but no longer so pure."

[36] As in the *Meno* (85B–86B) where it is contended that the soul "recollects" knowledge the source of which could not have been sensible experience and which therefore it must have possessed outside of the sensible world and have "forgotten"; *cf. Phaedo* 72E–73A, 74A–76E.

[37] Hence the tendency of evil souls "to cleave to the corporeal": *cf. Phaedo* 81B–D (n.b. 81B3–8).

[38] That this is true of relative evils in the second sense above, e.g. evil desire, is obvious, for they are all manifested only in soul as modes of its motion (*cf. Laws* 897A1–4), the result of misjudging the true relation to the good of the ideas of desire, pleasure, pain, etc. It is true, however, of relative evils in the first sense also, e.g. diseases that are natural organic units. These are, in the first place, evil only in the mutual interference of their phenomenal manifestations, an interference caused by soul's maladministration of phenomena. Moreover, they are all living organisms, and so their phenomenal manifestations, being animate, are directly controlled by soul; and Plato goes so far as to suggest that the phenomenal manifestations of all animate beings lower than man is the direct result of successively greater degrees of depravity of soul: *cf. Phaedo* 81E–82A, *Timaeus* 91D–92C (*cf.* 42C), *Laws* 903D3–E1 and 904B6–E3; *Republic* 620A–D and *Phaedrus* 249B imply the same notion.

[39] *Laws* 860D1 and the passages listed by Shorey *ad loc.* (1933: 640); *cf.* More, 1921: 243–261.

[40] *Timaeus* 46E1–2, *Laws* 897A4–5. *Cf.* for the following account of

These random motions of secondary causality must have their ultimate source, however, in the primary causality of psychical self-motion; they do, in fact, follow inevitably the operation of this primary causality, whether it be good or evil. Consider the case of fully intelligent soul, the mode and direction of whose motion are in accord with its complete and constant knowledge of the ideas—the case, in short, of god or gods, for perfectly virtuous soul, that is fully intelligent soul, is what Plato means by god.[41] Soul of this kind in organizing phenomena moves them with a purpose perfectly good and sets them in motion proper to this end; but phenomena thus intentionally set in motion, since they are moved in a plenum of phenomenal reflections, must by their motions displace other phenomena, which in turn displace still others in directions unrelated to the intention of soul in moving the first directly. These secondary motions, as Plato calls them, the motions of phenomena

the errant cause Cherniss, 1944: 446–450. Morrow (1950: 153–154) holds that by "Necessity" in the *Timaeus* Plato means the dependable natures at the disposal of the Demiurge and the regularity of the effects that they produce upon one another: "the world on which the creator sets to work is characterized by necessity in the sense that specific effects follow regularly from specific causes." If this were true, Plato would hardly have described the mythical chaos on which the Demiurge sets to work as κινούμενον πλημμελῶς καὶ ἀτάκτως (*Timaeus* 30A4–5) and he certainly would not have called necessity in the sense in which he here uses it the πλανωμένη αἰτία (*Timaeus* 48A6–7) or identified it with the secondary causes which τὸ τυχὸν ἄτακτον ἑκάστοτε ἐξεργάζονται (*Timaeus* 46E5–6). This last passage, as Meldrum says (1950: 66, n. 10 *ad fin.*), "forbids us to interpret Necessity in terms of Regularity of Sequence or natural law." The nature of "errant" motion is well exemplified by the statement in *Timaeus* 43A7–B5: . . . βίᾳ δὲ ἐφέροντο καὶ ἔφερον, ὥστε τὸ μὲν ὅλον κινεῖσθαι ζῷον, ἀτάκτως μὴν ὅπῃ τύχοι προϊέναι καὶ ἀλόγως . . . καὶ πάντῃ κατὰ τοὺς ἓξ τόπους πλανώμενα προῄειν.

[41] For proof of this *cf.* Cherniss, 1944: 602–610, especially 606–609. Apparently under the influence of Hackforth's article, which I have there criticized (*op. cit.*: 606–608), Greene (1944: 292, n. 95; *cf.* 287, n. 50; 311 and n. 235) goes so far as to write: "Plato does not say that either kind of soul, good or evil, is a god." This is, in fact, just what he does say in *Laws* 899B5–8: "Since the causes of all these are soul or souls—and souls good in all virtue—, we shall say that they are gods. . . ." Virtuous soul is soul that has acquired intelligence (*Laws* 897B1–5 and 897B8–C2). In the *Timaeus* the work of the Demiurge is the work of intelligence (*Timaeus* 47E3–4, *cf. Laws* 966E4), and the only entity that can have intelligence is soul (*Timaeus* 46D5–6); and *Phaedrus* 249C5–6 (*cf.* 247D1–5) states that god's divinity is the result of constant contemplation of the ideas.

induced by the movement of other phenomena and necessarily moving others in turn, intelligent soul in its demiurgic action seeks to employ for its own good end by making them conform to the plan of organization.[42] This it does by inducing in these secondary motions an alteration of direction, thus persuading them to co-operate with its original purpose;[43] but in so doing the demiurgic action again indirectly sets up in other phenomena another series of motions unrelated to its intention, motions that are neither intelligent nor purposive but accidental, random, and erratic. This is the errant cause or necessity, which reason can at best organize "for the most part" because the very act of organizing it begets a random residue of motion. Hence there is disorder which is the necessary incidental result of the action of soul—even of perfectly good soul—in delimiting and ordering the confused and indeterminate spatial reflections of reality. Evil souls, in their ignorance mistaking such disorder for good, may augment it; but the general flux of phenomena is not attributable either to their purposive action or to any spontaneous motion inherent in corporeality. As the *Tiemaus* explains, it is the complex of secondary motions produced incidentally by the perfectly rational world-soul as it induces directly the rational motion of rotation in the spherical plenum of special figures, themselves delimited by reason.[44]

So, while all positive evil, both absolute and relative, in this world is caused directly by soul moving its objects intentionally but in ignorance of truth, soul, whether virtuous or evil, is also unintentionally and indirectly the source of evil that is necessarily

[42] *Timaeus* 68E1–6, *Laws* 896E8–897B4 (*cf. Timaeus* 46D1–E2).

[43] *Timaeus* 48A2–5 and 56C3–7.

[44] *Cf. Timaeus* 57D–58C; for the detailed interpretation of this passage and its implications see Cherniss, 1944: 444–445 and especially 448–450. In the myth of the *Politicus* the crucial passage, 273B–D, implies the same explanation of the errant cause, there regarded in abstraction from intelligent causation. When the demiurgic guidance has been withdrawn, the world, left to itself, at first remembers the instruction of the Demiurge fairly accurately but with gradually increasing vagueness as forgetfulness increases and its old disorder gains dominance. The corporeality of its constitution, the demiurgic guidance now abstracted from it, is the cause of this. In other words, the direction given to phenomena by the motion of intelligence persists, though with diminishing effect, through the series of secondary causes for a time even when no further intelligent impulse is being given; but the further from the impulse of intelligence these series of secondary motions proceed the more the effects of that impulse wane and the greater

incidental to its direct influence upon phenomena, whereas the negative evil inherent in the existence of the world as phenomenal is only the obverse of its goodness as a reflection—though only a *reflection* and therefore a derogation—of perfect reality. The question concerning the cause or source of evil is not the same, however, as the question of moral responsibility, with which it is often unconsciously confused. This confusion alone explains, I believe, such arguments as the one that it is grotesquely un-Platonic to make soul itself the cause of the instability of becoming and that therefore we must not take at its face value Plato's categorical assertion that soul is the cause of all motion and change.[45] For negative evil, whether the cause be considered the existence of space itself or the reflection that is an immediate consequence of its existence, nothing and no one is responsible; and for incidental evil, of which soul is certainly the ultimate cause though the necessary condition is the nature of phenomena once moved by soul to move one another, soul is not responsible either. There is moral responsibility only for the positive evil, of which soul is directly the cause, and for the ignorance of truth in which moving intentionally it produces such evil.

It may be said that this account fails to solve the "problem of evil," and so it does if evil is a problem to be solved only by demonstration of its nonexistence or by moral justification of it as the necessary condition for the existence of good.[46] Either of these "solutions" would have appeared to Plato to be an immoral falsification of the data of experience. Evil, like other phenomena, he regarded as something to be explained, not to be explained away; and all his remarks on the subject, when read in the light of this purpose, cohere to form a consistent account of evil which is a consequence of his analysis of the phenomenal world as a moving reflection in space of immutable, non-spatial reality.

Published originally in the *Proceedings of the American Philosophical Society* 98 (1954), 23–30. Reprinted by permission of the American Philosophical Society and the author. [The Greek phrase cited from *Laws* 889B5–6 has been replaced by English translation by the editor.]

in number become the merely random motions induced at each stage until at last the effect of the distant impulse of intelligence is virtually obliterated and the world is on the point of being nothing but the residual chaotic motions of secondary causality and of "running down" into "the limitless sea of dissimilarity."

[45] So Vlastos, 1939: 82. *Cf. Laws* 896B1.

[46] *Cf.* Greene, 1944: 298.

REFERENCES

Cherniss, Harold. 1944. Aristotle's criticism of Plato and the Academy I. Baltimore, The Johns Hopkins Press.

Chilcott, C. M. 1923. The Platonic theory of evil. *Class. Quart.* **17**: 27–34.

Cornford, F. M. 1937. Plato's cosmology. London, Kegan Paul.

Dodds, E. R. 1947. Plato and the irrational. *Jour. Hellenic. Stud.* **45**: 16–25.

Festugière, A. J. 1947. Platon et l'Orient. *Rev. de Philologie* **73**: 1–45.

———. 1949. La Révélation d'Hermès Trismégiste II: Le Dieu Cosmique. Paris, J. Gabalda et Cie.

Greene, W. C. 1944. Moira: Fate, good, and evil in Greek thought. Cambridge, Harvard Univ. Press.

Hoffleit, H. B. 1937. An un-Platonic theory of evil in Plato. *Amer. Jour. Philol.* **58**: 45–58.

Meldrum, M. 1950. Plato and the ΑΡΧΗ ΚΑΚΩΝ. *Jour. Hellenic. Stud.* **70**: 65–74.

More, Paul Elmer. 1921. The religion of Plato. Princeton, Princeton Univ. Press.

Morrow, Glenn R. 1950. Necessity and persuasion in Plato's *Timaeus*. *Philos. Rev.* **59**: 147–163.

Owen, G. E. L. 1953. The place of the *Timaeus* in Plato's dialogues. *Class. Quarterly* **47** = N.S.3: 79–95.

Palas, Reino. 1941. Die Bewertung der Sinnenwelt bei Platon. Helsinki, Druckerei-A.G. der Finnischen Literaturgesellschaft.

Pétrement, Simone. 1947. Le Dualisme chez Platon, les Gnostiques et les Manichéens. Paris, Presses Universitaires de France.

Robin, Leon. 1935. Platon. Paris, Alcan.

Ross, Sir David. 1951. Plato's theory of ideas. Oxford, Clarendon Press.

Schaerer, René. 1938. La question platonicienne. Neuchatel, Secrétariat de l'Université.

Sesemann, Wilhelm. 1912. Die Ethik Platos und das Problem des Bösen. Philosophische Abhandlungen Hermann Cohen zum 70 sten Geburtstag Dargebracht: 170–189. Berlin, Bruno Cassirer.

Shorey, Paul. 1933. What Plato said. Chicago, Univ. of Chicago Press.

Solmsen, Friedrich. 1942. Plato's theology. Ithaca, Cornell Univ. Press.

Stenzel, J. 1931. Studien zur Entwicklung der Platonischen Dialektik von Sokrates zu Aristoteles. Leipzig-Berlin, Teubner.

Taylor, A. E. 1928. A commentary on Plato's *Timaeus*. Oxford, Clarendon Press.

———. 1937. Plato, the man and his work. London, Methuen.

Vlastos, Gregory. 1939. The disorderly motion in the *Timaeus*. *Class. Quart.* **33**: 71–83.

Wilamowitz-Moellendorff, Ulrich von. 1919. Platon II. Berlin, Weidmann.

Zeller, Eduard. 1922. Die Philosophie der Griechen, II, 1⁵, Leipzig, Reisland.

17

PLATO'S DOCTRINE OF ARTISTIC IMITATION

W. J. VERDENIUS

It is well known that Plato made imitation the general principle of art. Even music and dance are regarded by him as essentially imitative arts[1]. Aristotle adopted the idea of imitation from his master, and though he modified it in some respects it retained the same fundamental importance in his theory of art. The concept of imitation deeply influenced the aesthetic theories of the Hellenistic and Roman worlds, and it remained the basis for many theories of art as late as the eighteenth century. Afterwards, under the influence of Romanticism, it became discredited, and this reaction was so strong that at present it still determines the general estimation of Plato's aesthetics. According to Wilamowitz[2], Plato, in speaking of imitation, "rapped out a fatal word". Many scholars have repeated this condemnation in similar terms. Otto Apelt, for instance, fails to regard the idea of imitation as anything more than "a systematic violation of art", "a hunger-cure", "depriving it of all its charms"[3].

All modern objections against Plato's theory of art centre in the assertion that his rationalism precluded him from recognizing the specific character of artistic creation. He is accused of fashioning art after the pattern of science, which has to copy nature as truly as possible. He is said to have forgotten that true art does not copy an existing reality, but that it creates a new reality arising from the artist's own phantasy, and that it is the spontaneous character of this expression which guarantees the independent value of purely aesthetic qualities.

However, it may be asked whether this criticism is justifiable from a historical as well as a systematical point of view. In this case

---

[1] Cf. *Cra.* 423C–D, *R.* 399A–C, 401A, *Plt.* 306D, *Laws* 655D, 668A, 795E, 798D, 814E.

[2] *Platon* I[2] (Berlin, 1920), 479.

[3] *Platonische Aufsätze* (Leipzig-Berlin, 1912), 68–70.

two questions arise, firstly, whether Plato really intended imitation to mean a slavish copy, and secondly, whether modern aestheticians are right in disregarding the imitative elements in art and in considering phantasy and self-expression to be its fundamental principles. The first question has an important bearing on the second: for if it should turn out that Plato's concept of imitation is not to be taken in the popular sense, modern aesthetics would seem somewhat rash in proclaiming "that its breaking with the classical doctrine of imitation is irrevocable"[4]. It is to be admitted that this doctrine in the course of history has given rise to many positions now definitively abandoned. Yet this very fact should induce us to remount to the source of this tradition and to ask ourselves whether the principle in its original enunciation does not deserve some reconsideration.

Such a reconsideration has to be based on a careful examination of the texts. Plato's writings have been called "a veritable poison for chimerical and revolutionary spirits who overlook the qualifications and limitations"[5]. However, for the same reason complacent and conservative spirits are apt to dispose of Plato's thoughts too easily. So let us turn to his own words, with an open mind and attending to their qualifications and limitations.

"Whenever a poet is seated on the Muses' tripod, he is not in his senses, but resembles a fountain, which gives free course to the upward rush of water; and, since his art consists in imitation, he is compelled often to contradict himself, when he creates characters of contradictory moods; and he knows not which of these contradictory utterances is true" (*Laws* 719C)[6].

These words were written down by Plato to illustrate the true nature of the lawgiver by contrasting it with the nature of the artist. So they may create the impression of being no more than a casual remark. However, comparing this passage with Plato's other utterances on the same subject we seem to be entitled to take it as a starting-point for our discussion, because it can be shown to present the problem in its most radical form.

In his masterly picture of poetic inspiration which is given in the *Ion* Plato says: "God takes away the mind of these men, and uses

[4] F. Leander, *Lessing als ästhetischer Denker*, Göteborgs Högskolas Årsskrift 48: 3 (1942), 3.

[5] P. Shorey, *Platonism Ancient and Modern* (Berkeley, 1938), 164.

[6] Quotations from Plato are given in the translations of the Loeb Library.

them as his ministers, just as he does soothsayers and godly seers, in order that we who hear them may know that it is not they who utter these words of great price, when they are out of their wits, but that it is God himself who speaks and addresses us through them" (534C–D). Evidently inspiration is not a gift freely to be used by the poet, but a compelling force blindly to be followed. Accordingly, the poet's art seems to be completely withdrawn from his will and control. This induces us to interpret his sitting on the tripod of the Muse mentioned above in a more literal sense than our modern outlook might be inclined to do. Exactly like the Delphic priestess he opens himself so fully to his Muse that her inspiration pervades him entirely and takes complete possession of him.

However, if it is the Muse herself who speaks through his mouth, it seems strange that the poet should involve himself in contradictions. There is no room for assuming a malignant intent on the part of the Muse, for Plato expressly assures that "from every point of view the divine and the divinity are free from falsehood", and that "God is altogether simple and true in deed and word, and neither changes himself nor deceives others by visions or words or the sending of signs in waking or in dreams" (*R.* 382E). We can only conclude that the artist himself is to blame for confusing the inspiration of the Muse. This means that his state of being possessed is not absolute: the Muse does not completely direct his tongue and he does not completely lose his human character. Plato stresses the poet's dependence, but he certainly did not mean to represent him as no more than a speaking-tube in the mouth of the Muse. After all, he calls the poet her interpreter (*Ion* 534E). Divine inspiration cannot reach the human world but through the poet's interpretation. Accordingly, a poem, though its origin lies beyond human control, does not mechanically reproduce a divine message, but it is the result of a contact in which divine as well as human activities are involved. Interpretation, the human aspect of the process of artistic creation, is easily attended by misunderstanding. The poet is a less able "maker" than his Muse (*Laws* 669C). So if a work of art shows contradictions, this is an imperfection to be imputed to human weakness.

It might be asked whether the occurrence of contradictions in a poem necessarily proves the poet to be confused and his work to be imperfect. Plato says: "The poet contradicts himself, when he creates characters of contradictory moods". If this restriction is taken into account, the poet seems to be free from all blame. In fact, the contradictions between the characters of a piece of literature not only need not impair the unity and the harmony of the whole, but they may even be regarded as necessary means to lend some variety to the work.

However, this argument overlooks an important fact[7]. The Greeks were inclined to regard their great poets as reliable sources and infallible authorities for all kinds of practical wisdom. They isolated the words and deeds of the epic and tragic characters from their contexts and used them as general maxims. For instance, the Athenians claimed the high command of an expedition against the Persians by referring to the *Iliad* (2, 552–554), where the Athenian Menestheus is said to be unequalled in drawing up horses and soldiers (*Hdt.* VII 161). Mythological examples were also adduced to excuse actual wrongdoing, and this practice must have been rather common, because it is parodied by Aristophanes (*Nub.* 1079–82) and sharply criticized by Plato (*R.* 377E–378B, 391D–392A, *Laws* 941B).

In the light of this criticism we can understand Plato's stressing the contradictory character of poetical variety. He opposes the Greek inclination towards a pragmatical interpretation of literature by exposing the poet's lack of well-founded knowledge. "The poet does not know what he is saying" (*Ap.* 22B–C, *Meno* 99C–D, *Ti.* 72A, *Laws* 801B–C), i.e., the same ecstasy which enables him to enter into contact with the Muse does not allow him fully to realize the purport of his own words. Being absorbed in a flow of successive impressions he is unaware of their general connections and implications, for his state of possession precludes him from passing an independent judgment on the images which present themselves to his mind. He can only register these images without deliberately arranging them into a well-considered whole. So the relative character of their contradictions is not sufficiently brought out, and the hearer is left entangled in a multitude of conflicting views. This situation is likely to back up his sceptical attitude of mind, tempting him to choose his poetical pretexts according to his own interests. It must be admitted that the poet may at times hit upon a valuable thought (*R.* 377A, *Laws* 682A). Yet his work as a whole cannot be relied upon as a faithful image of truth (*R.* 600E).

---

[7] For a fuller discussion of this problem, see my papers, *L'Ion de Platon*, Mnemos. III 11 (1943), 233–62, and *Platon et la poésie*, *ib.* 12 (1944), 118–50.

Even the greatest poetry remains enigmatic (*Alc.* II 147B, *R.* 332B, *Tht.* 194C), for owing to the irrational origin of his wisdom it is impossible to call the poet to account about the real meaning of his words (*Hp. Mi.* 365D, *Prt.* 347E). So it seems wisest to abstain from definite interpretations (*Ly.* 214B, *Phdr.* 252B, *R.* 331E).

This conclusion might seem surprising to the Christian point of view. A Muse who condescends to so completely taking possession of her servant should be expected in some way to guarantee a correct understanding of her revelations. It would be difficult to give a generally accepted definition of Christian revelation. Yet the Christian ideas of revelation may be said to have a common feature in being based upon the principle of divine love. The love of God would not be absolute, if it did not to a certain extent embrace our understanding of its manifestations. In this respect it is interesting to compare the inspiration of the Platonic poet with that of the Old-Testamentary prophets. These men, too, were seized and overwhelmed by a divine message and felt themselves under a compelling force. But this force at the same time makes a moral demand, which appeals to the deepest layers of their personality. This appeal does not have an abstract character, but it is supported by a personal care: the prophet feels his God to be near to him saying: "Do not fear, for I am with you to protect you" (*Jerem.* I, 8). Thus divine revelation takes the form of a personal meeting, and this deeply affects the character of human understanding. The nearness of God is answered by the confidence of the prophet, who does not waver about the meaning of his inspirations, but simply puts his trust in them. Neither need his audience be troubled by epistemological doubts: the prophet is an elected being and as such infallible, though his words may have a further-reaching, e.g., a messianic, tenor which he did not fully realize himself[8].

The Platonic Muse, however, being a true Greek god, does not know about love. Having touched the poet's mind in its ecstasy, she does not care about the further adventures of her message. The poet can only meet his god when being in an abnormal state, and this god leaves him as soon as he returns to sanity. So he is not only entirely left to himself as to the real meaning of the revelation, but his interpretation is a mere guess, because it refers to something fundamentally inaccessible to rational understanding.

[8] Cf. J. Hessen, *Platonismus und Prophetismus* (Munich[2], 1955), 52 ff. See further W. J. Verdenius, "Plato and Christianity", *Ratio* 5 (1963), 15–32.

Accordingly, Plato admonishes his readers to distrust any interpretation of poetry. However, it has already been noted that this
warning is mainly directed against the practice of eliciting paradig-
matical truths from the great poets. Consequently, it must not be
supposed that Plato should have utterly despaired of understanding
anything of a poem. The question arises how far his doubts upon
the possibility of a pragmatical interpretation are counter-balanced
by a belief in the possibility of an aesthetical interpretation. Plato
likes to disguise his theoretical views by his pedagogical zeal, and
so his theory of art is continually coloured by his solicitude for the
mental health of his contemporaries. This fact has caused serious
misunderstandings. It has often been denied that Plato held a
doctrine, i.e., a systematical opinion, of art, and that his discussion
of the cultural function of art is based on a theoretical interpretation. However, doubts upon this fact have mainly arisen from the
modern point of view that systematical knowledge should also be
enunciated in a systematical form. Plato does not expound his
aesthetics in a systematical form, but the same applies to the whole
of his philosophy.

For instance, a recent discussion of Plato's theology has taken the
form of "a variety of approaches", and the author rightly observes
that (1) "Plato approaches the problem of the nature and activities
of the Deity in a variety of ways", (2) "Strictly speaking, however,
he did not in the passages which we have examined "approach"
the religious problem as such. He discussed other subjects, such as
the nature of Being, the nature of the Universe, the status of Soul",
(3) "No attempt is discernible to coordinate the different aspects
of the theological problem in a comprehensive and unified theory",
(4) "We should overstate our case, however, if we refused to find
any continuity at all in Plato's successive attacks on the problem"[9].
The same applies to Plato's aesthetics. His approaches to the problem of art are seldom concerned with art as such and his educational interest is seldom absent. But it does not follow that his
criticisms should not also have a philosophical aim. This aim is
mostly hidden by other arguments and it can only be reconstructed
by combining many scattered passages.

[9] F. Solmsen, *Plato's Theology* (Ithaca, N.Y., 1942), 131, 161. See
further W. J. Verdenius, *Platons Gottesbegriff*, in H. J. Rose a.o., *La
notion du divin depuis Homére jusqu' a Platon* (Vandoeuvres-Genève, 1945),
241–93.

What is the aesthetical meaning of Plato's conception of inspirational knowledge? In the *Ion* it is only said that the poet is out of his senses, that he is in an ecstasy, and that he is possessed by the Muse (533E–534D), but Plato does not go into a psychological examination of this mental state. He probably adhered to the traditional belief in the divine character of inspiration. He only states that ecstasy is a prerequisite for artistic quality and that it cannot be replaced by a rational method: "All the good epic poets utter all those fine poems not from art, but as inspired and possessed, and the good lyric poets likewise". "For a poet is a light and winged and sacred thing, and is unable ever to indite until he has been inspired and put out of his senses, and his mind is no longer in him: every man, whilst he retains possession of that, is powerless to indite a verse or chant an oracle" (*Ion* 533E, 534B). The same view is expressed in the *Phaedrus* (245A): "He who without the divine madness comes to the door of the Muses, confident that he will be a good poet by art, meets with no success, and the poetry of the sane man vanishes into nothingness before that of the inspired madman". Accordingly, Plato stresses the fact that a true poet should not compose "arguments", but "tales" (*Phd.* 61B).

These passages are important, because they show that Plato knew how to distinguish good poetry from bad poetry, i.e., that he knew how to conceive of poetry in purely aesthetic terms. This is borne out by many other facts: his writing verse in youth, his many quotations from Greek poetry, the poetical quality of his prose, his avowal of "a certain love and reverence for Homer that has possessed me from a boy" (*R.* 595B), and his admission of "being under the spell of poetry" (*R.* 607C)[10].

Now, if Plato was able to judge a poem from an aesthetical point of view, he is not likely to have confined himself to emphasizing the irrational origin of inspiration; we also expect him to have explained the character of poetical expression. However, instead of an explanation he presents us with a paradox. In the passage which formed our starting-point the poet is said to contradict himself,

[10] Further evidence of Plato's appreciation of poetry is given in my paper *Platon et la poésie*, Mnemos. III 12 (1944), 122–23. In this paper I have tried to show (1) that Plato's personal appreciation of art is compatible with his criticism of its cultural function, and (2) that both this appreciation and this criticism are in accordance with his general philosophy. The present discussion is intended as a corroboration of this view.

"since his art consists in imitation". Would it not be much more natural, if he contradicted himself in spite of the fact that he uses the method of imitation? However, we have seen that (1) these contradictions arise from the fact that the poet's interpretation necessarily confuses the Muse's inspiration, and (2) imitation is the basis of art. It follows that confusion does not take place in spite of imitation, but that it forms an essential characteristic of imitation.

If our assumption that Plato held a systematical doctrine of art is true, it must be possible to give a further definition of this confused character of imitation. The degree of confusion obviously depends upon the artist's familiarity with his object. "It is plain to all that the imitative tribe will imitate with most ease and success the things amidst which it has been reared, whereas it is hard for any man to imitate well in action what lies outside the range of his rearing, and still harder in speech" (*Ti.* 19D). This is a simple thought, but it has important consequences. The poet imitates human characters and he is guided by the Muse. Why this guidance? Obviously because the Muse wants him to express something more than the facts of everyday life in their casual succession. If this were the only aim of his art, imitation would never fail. That it does fail, is an indication that it also refers to something not directly observable and describable, to a more general aspect of reality. Evidently it is the task of the poet to represent these general values through the medium of human life. Imitating characters and actions he must at the same time try to evoke an idea of their ultimate principles. These lie so far from his natural range of thought that he needs the help of divine inspiration. Unfortunately, the ecstatical condition which brings him into contact with the Muse also precludes him from fully understanding her intentions. He can only register his impressions, or in other words, imitate the images which present themselves to his mind. Consequently, his representations are lacking in articulateness: they remain tentative suggestions, in which the general and the particular, the abstract and the concrete, the essential and the accidental are blended so much that the work taken as a whole appears to be inconsistent.

It follows that poetical imitation cannot be a copy true to nature. It remains confused and defective, because it refers to an object with which it is only partly familiar. Imitation implies transformation, and transformation implies confusion, if it is determined by a sphere of reality (in this case, the poetical mind) inferior to its object. This conception has its roots in the general spirit of Plato's philosophy. The world is called a divine work of art (*Ti.* 28A–29A, 37C). As such it is an "image" of something else (29B, 92C), an imitation of a superior model (48E). From these passages it is apparent that the concept of imitation has a metaphysical foundation. This foundation is explained in the tenth book of the *Republic*, where reality is divided into three levels, viz. the ideal Forms, visible objects, and images. A painter is unable to contribute anything to the creation of ideal Being, for he is a human being and bound to the laws of relative reality. Neither may he construct a material object after an ideal pattern, for this is the task of the craftsman. He is forced to descend another step from the realm of ideal Being and to use the visible objects as models for his images. Thus these images are situated on the lowest level of reality, and they are two grades away from the essential nature of things (*R.* 596A–597E).

This conclusion does not seem very edifying. Would it really have been Plato's intention to appoint no other task to the painter than copying domestic utensils? Is it conceivable that he, who expresses his admiration for the idealistic art of Phidias (*Meno* 91D) and who is so far from adopting a flat realism in his own literary work, should have refused to painting admittance to the realm of ideal values?

Fortunately, Plato strikes a different note. The true artist tries to trace the essence of beauty and grace (*R.* 401C), and when he has depicted a pattern of the most beautiful man, such an image refers to an ideal the actual occurrence of which is irrelevant (*R.* 472D). According to P. Shorey[11], Plato is here speaking from the point of view of ordinary opinion, and many similar attempts have been made to deny to Plato a sense of idealistic art[12]. The following interpretation is intended to show that Plato's idealistic conception of art is compatible with his conviction that painting cannot be a direct reflection of ideal Being.

We have already seen that poetry tries to translate a divine message into human language. Similarly, painting both refers to an

[11] Cf. the note to his translation of *R.* 472D in the Loeb Library.

[12] The main passage referred to in this connection is *R.* 598A, where painting is said not to imitate the true nature of the thing itself but the works of the craftsmen. But from the fact that art is no *direct* imitation of the ideal Forms it does not follow that it could not reveal them indirectly. Similarly, in *Pl.* 286A Plato says that the ideal Forms can only be *clearly* revealed by argument, which does not exclude the possibility of another, though a less ideal, approach.

ideal pattern and a phenomenal image. Though Plato does not explain the relation between the divine character of inspiration and the ideal character of patterns[13], he expressly declares poetry and painting to be of a similar nature in so far as both are two removes from true reality (*R.* 597E, 598E ff.). So their characteristics are to a certain extent mutually applicable. Poetry is said to "imitate human beings acting under compulsion or voluntarily, and as a result of their actions supposing themselves to have fared well or ill and in all this feeling either grief or joy" (*R.* 603C), i.e., poetry just like painting, uses visual reality as a model. But a poet can also be an "imitator of the good" (*R.* 397D), and in that case his art obviously gets an idealistic character.

How are we to reconcile these two points of view? It has been suggested that in Plato's own soul idealism and realism fought an unconscious struggle, so that now one power emerged and now the other, and he imperceptibly involved himself in contradictions[14]. Such a psychological explanation might on the face of it seem attractive, because the contradictions, once they are stowed away in the depth of the soul, are removed from our field of vision and easily forgotten. However, this solution of the paradox will hardly satisfy anyone who is convinced of Plato's having a well-balanced personality. This conviction induces us to seek for another interpretation and to validate the importance of Plato's idealistic view of art by connecting it with his general sphere of thought.

The clue to a correct understanding of Plato's philosophy lies in his conception of a hierarchical structure of reality[15]. There are different planes of being, each of them (except the Good, which is absolutely real) trying, within its own limits, to express the values superior to it. Consequently, the degree of reality of anything is dependent upon its degree of approximation to eternal Being. The empirical world does not represent true reality, but is only an approximation to it, "something that resembles real being but is not that" (*R.* 597A), it "yearns" to be like the ideal Forms but "falls short" of them (*Phd.* 74D, 75AB), "with difficulty" it reveals something of the superior world of which it is an "image" (*Phdr.* 250B).

[13] An extension of the doctrine of inspiration to painting does not originate until the Hellenistic period, cf. B. Schweitzer, *Der bildende Künstler und der Begriff des Künstlerischen in der Antike*, Neue Heidelb. Jbb. (1925), 28–132.

[14] O. Apelt, *Platonische Aufsätze*, 67.

[15] *Cf.* R. Schaerer, *La question platonicienne* (Neuchatel, 1938), especially 157 ff.; *Dieu, l'homme et la vie d'après Platon* (Neuchatel, 1944).

The term "image" shows that Plato's doctrine of imitation is closely related to his hierarchical conception of reality. In fact, "the idea of imitation is at the centre of his philosophy"[16]). Our thoughts and arguments are imitations of reality (*Ti.* 47B–C, *Criti.* 107B–C), words are imitations of things (*Cra.* 423E–424B), sounds are imitations of divine harmony (*Ti.* 80B), time imitates eternity (*Ti.* 38A), laws imitate truth (*Plt.* 300C), human governments are imitations of true government (*Plt.* 293E, 297C), devout men try to imitate their gods (*Phdr.* 252C–D, 253B, *Laws* 713E), visible figures are imitations of eternal ones (*Ti.* 50C), etc.

This is sufficient proof that Platonic imitation is bound up with the idea of approximation and does not mean a true copy. Plato himself has warned us against this interpretation: "The image must not by any means reproduce all the qualities of that which it imitates, if it is to be an image". Do you not perceive how far images are from possessing the same qualities as the originals which they imitate? Yes, I do" (*Cra.* 432B–D). In other words, imitation can never be more than suggestion or evocation.

We can now proceed to the question what is the character of artistic suggestion. It cannot directly refer to the ideal values, for art is separated from the plane of real Being by the domain of phenomenal reality. So it must content itself with representing visual objects, it must even humble itself before material reality, in so far as it cannot produce anything but bloodless images. Yet we have seen that true art is inspired by a divine voice and that it refers to an ideal pattern of beauty. Now the hierarchical structure of reality prevents the ideal Forms from directly manifesting themselves in visual bodies. Beauty itself will not be found "presented in the guise of a face or of hands or of any other portion of the body, nor as a particular description or piece of knowledge, nor as existing somewhere in another substance, such as an animal or the earth or sky or any other thing; but existing ever in singularity of form independent by itself" (*Symp.* 211A–B). Correspondingly, the Muse never completely descends to the human level, but to a certain extent she keeps her secret. To a certain extent, for Platonic transcendence is mitigated by the idea of exemplariness. The Demiurge "being devoid of envy desired that all should be, so far as possible, like unto Himself" (*Ti.* 29E). So a gradually fading sheen of eternal radiance may be said to pervade all stages of reality.

[16] A. Diès, *Autour de Platon* (Paris, 1927), 594.

Accordingly, art is not confined to the limits of its visual models. True art does not lapse into flat realism, but it strives to transcend the material world; in its poor images it tries to evocate something of that higher realm of being which also glimmers through phenomenal reality. It is true that Plato attaches much value to the likeness of a work of art, but this idea should not be interpreted in modern terms. In true art likeness does not refer to commonplace reality, but to ideal Beauty[17].

This carries us back to the confused character of poetical imitation. The above discussion will have shown that the deficiencies of poetry, though they are exaggerated by Plato for his pedagogical purpose, are closely bound up with the ontological status of art in general. Like painting, poetical imitation lies on a lower level of reality than its object, of which it can only produce an adumbration. It tries to transcend itself, but is hampered by the inadequacy of its means. This incommensurability of means and ends causes poetry to approach to divination. But the same holds good of art in general; music, for instance, is said to be full of "guessing" (*Phlb.* 56A, 62C).

Art, therefore, has a double aspect: in its visible manifestation it is a thing of the most inferior value, a shadow; yet it has an indirect relation to the essential nature of things. The intensity of this relation depends upon the degree to which the artist succeeds in illuminating the higher aspects of the intermediate plane, viz. of visual reality. Thus imitation, when viewed in the light of a hierarchical conception of reality, may constitute a reconciliation of realism and idealism in art.

This doctrine is well illustrated by the spirit of Greek art. It has been argued that the Greek artist only aimed at deceptive imitation of nature, but that his inner being unconsciously and against his own prejudice bestowed an idealistic character on his work. In this respect, it is said, the practice of art was in advance of the theory of art; the Greek mind, in spite of its gift for idealistic art, remained unconscious of the fact that true idealism should abandon given reality.

However, the term "abandon" is out of place here. It is true that the Greek artist followed nature, but he did not stick to its casual aspects; he rather tried to detect its deeper meanings. He was well

[17] Cf. *Laws* 668B2. I take this much disputed phrase to mean: "which gets its likeness from its being a representation of Beauty".

aware of the fact that the essential nature of things is not identical with their visual appearance, but that it must still be represented in natural forms. He also knew that suggesting a deeper meaning is not to be achieved through deforming nature but through clarifying its fundamental structure. So there is no reason to assume a contrast between artistic production and aesthetic consciousness. The masters of Greek idealistic art would have subscribed to Plato's aesthetics.

Greek art in Plato's time, however, was showing an increasing tendency towards realism, and it is not to be wondered at that he had serious worries about it. He sharply criticizes illusionistic art, which through a skilful use of perspective and polychromy tries to create the impression of a second original. This kind of imitation is denounced as imposture and jugglery (*R.* 598D, 602D), because it claims to produce a doublet of its object. Only a god could make a doublet of a living being (*Cra.* 432B–C). Man cannot extend the existing whole of things and so is unable to create anything. Accordingly, true artistic representation does not aim at a deceptive reproduction of the outer appearance of its object, but it is based on a profound study of the real proportions and colours (*Sph.* 233E–236C, *Laws* 668D–E).

It may be concluded that there are two points differentiating good art from mere trickery: its truthfulness and its modesty. The artist should not content himself with a superficial glance at his object, but he must try to penetrate its inner structure. His task is faithful interpretation, not slavish imitation. Secondly, he should have the honesty to admit the poorness of his means and not try to overstep the limitations they lay upon him. His work should clearly show that its representation of reality, in spite of, or rather, on account of, its very faithfulness, is fundamentally different from reality itself. It should present itself, not as a copy, but as a transposition on a different level and as obedient to the laws of this medium[18].

We are now able to understand what it means when art is called

[18] On the distinction of two kinds of imitation *cf.* Schaerer, *La question platonicienne*, 161–65.

It has often been maintained that there is a contradiction between *R.* III, where imitation is allowed and even encouraged (398B, 401B), and *R.* X, where imitative poetry is said not to be admitted into the ideal state (595A). However, in the latter passage the term imitation is meant in the popular sense of slavish copy.

a "play" (e.g., *R.* 602B, *Sph.* 234A–B, *Plt.* 288C, *Laws* 796B, 889D–E). In Plato's thought this term does not refer to an arbitrary pastime or a mere discharge of surplus energy, but it denotes "every activity which is exercised with a view to something more important"[19]. Accordingly, art does not have its end in itself, but it is only relatively important, in so far as its suggestive power refers to a higher plane of reality. The illusionistic artist is not contented with such a subservient role, he attempts "seriously to imitate all things" (*R.* 397A) and he is "eager to abandon himself to the fashioning of phantoms and sets this in the forefront of his life as the best thing he has" (*R.* 599A).

It should be remembered that Plato does not level his criticism at contemporary art as such, but in so far as it exemplifies a danger resident in art in general[20]. In a sense every artist is unable to recognize the "playing" and relative character of his works. The reason lies in the fact that "he has nothing more valuable than the things he has composed or written" (*Phdr.* 278D), i.e., he does not know a standard of true being which might point out to him the real place of his products in the order of things. Art is called by Plato a "waking dream" (*Sph.* 266C). The nature of the dream state, "whether the man is asleep or awake", lies in "the mistaking of resemblance for identity" (*R.* 476C). The artist, who so intensely absorbs himself in his subject matter that "his soul supposes herself to be among the scenes he is describing" (*Ion* 535B), is likely to forget the cleavage which separates him from reality and to claim a greater independence for his images than they deserve. Even if he should deliberately reject a slavish realism and should sincerely attempt to evocate the deeper background of things, his very need of self-transcendence makes him run the risk of taking himself too seriously. The ideal artist, though bestowing serious labours on his work, would not attach much value to his imitations. In fact, "if he had genuine knowledge of the things he imitates he would far rather devote himself to real things than to the imitation of them" (*R.* 599B). So he would frankly admit the deficiencies of his knowledge and his means and would give his products for what they are: images which, by interpreting the real nature of their objects, try to suggest something of the world of ideal Being, but which never belie their irrational origin and the limitations of their medium.

[19] Schaerer, *op. cit.*, 22 n. 1.
[20] Cf. Schaerer, *op. cit.*, 208.

However, Plato realizes very well that such a combination of self-transcendence and humbleness must be a rare thing. Hence he warns his readers to keep a guarded attitude against all art (*R.* 608A–B, *Laws* 669B–C). The spell of imitation may easily overtake us, so that we abandon ourselves to unreliable authorities. This risk is taken by Plato very seriously: "What shall it profit a man if he gain the whole world of poetry and art, and lose his own soul?" (*R.* 607D). For art "seems to be a corruption of the mind of all those who do not possess as an antidote a knowledge of its real nature" (*R.* 595B).

Chapter I of *Mimesis* by W. J. Verdenius (E. J. Brill, Leiden, 1949). Reprinted by permission of E. J. Brill and the author. [Some additional references have been supplied by the author.]

NOTES ON CONTRIBUTORS

Renford Bambrough, Fellow and Dean of St. John's College and Lecturer in Philosophy in the University of Cambridge.

Harold Cherniss, member of the permanent faculty at the Institute for Advanced Study, Princeton, New Jersey. Previously he had taught Greek at Cornell, Johns Hopkins, and Berkeley.

Francis M. Cornford, late Laurence Professor of Ancient Philosophy and Fellow of Trinity College in the University of Cambridge.

Raphael Demos, late Professor of Philosophy at Harvard University.

E. R. Dodds, Hon. Fellow of University College, Oxford; Hon. Student of Christ Church, Oxford.

W. K. C. Guthrie, Master of Downing College and Laurence Professor of Ancient Philosophy in the University of Cambridge.

Wayne A. R. Leys, Professor of Philosophy at Southern Illinois University.

J. D. Mabbott, former President of St. John's College in Oxford University.

R. A. Markus, Senior Lecturer in Medieval History at the University of Liverpool.

Glenn R. Morrow, Professor of Philosophy, Emeritus, at the University of Pennsylvania.

Terry Penner, Assistant Professor of Philosophy at Princeton University.

David Sachs, Professor of Philosophy at The Johns Hopkins University.

Paul Shorey, late Professor of Greek at the University of Chicago.

F. E. Sparshott, Professor of Ethics at Victoria College in the University of Toronto.

W. J. Verdenius, Professor of Greek at the University of Utrecht, Holland.

Gregory Vlastos, Stuart Professor of Philosophy at Princeton University.

SELECTED BIBLIOGRAPHY OF RECENT BOOKS AND ARTICLES IN ENGLISH ON PLATO'S ETHICS, POLITICS, PHILOSOPHY OF RELIGION, and AESTHETICS.

I. Books and Articles by Contributors to this Volume.

Cornford, F. M. *Before and After Socrates* (Cambridge, England, 1932). Chapter 3 on Plato.

From Religion to Philosophy (London, 1912), pp. 242 ff. on "Plato: the Socratic and Mystic Dialogues."

"Psychology and Social Structure in the *Republic* of Plato," *Classical Quarterly* 6 (1912), 246–65.

The Unwritten Philosophy, edited by W. K. C. Guthrie (Cambridge, 1949). "Plato's Commonwealth." "The Doctrine of Eros in Plato's *Symposium*." "The Marxist View of Ancient Philosophy."

Demos, R. "Paradoxes in Plato's Doctrine of the Ideal State," *Classical Quarterly* 7 (1957), 164–74.

"Plato on Moral Principles," *Mind* 76 (1967), 125–26.

Dodds, E. R. *The Greeks and the Irrational* (Berkeley, 1951).

"Plato and the Irrational," *Journal of Hellenic Studies* 65 (1945), 16 ff.

Plato's Gorgias: Revised Text, with Introduction and Commentary (Oxford, 1959).

Morrow, G. R. "The Demiurge in Politics," *Proceedings of the American Philosophical Association* 27 (1954), 5–23.

"Plato's Conception of Persuasion," *Philosophical Review* 62 (1953), 234–50.

Plato's Law of Slavery in Its Relation to Greek Law. Illinois Studies in Language and Literature, Vol. 25, No. 3 (Urbana, Illinois, 1939).

"Plato and Greek Slavery," *Mind* 48 (1939), 186–201.

"Plato and the Law of Nature," in *Studies in Political Theory Presented to G. H. Sabine*, ed. by M. Konvitz and A. E. Murphy (Ithaca, N.Y., 1948).

Plato's Cretan City (Princeton, 1960).

Shorey, P. "The Idea of Good in Plato's *Republic*," *Studies in Classical Philology* 1 (1895), 188–239.

"The Idea of Justice in Plato's *Republic*," *Ethical Record* 2 (1890), 185–99.

What Plato Said (Chicago, 1933; 6th Impression, 1965).

Plato: The Republic, I and II (London and Cambridge, Mass.: 1930 and 1935).

Sparshott, F. E. "Socrates and Thrasymachus," *Monist* 50 (1966), 421–59.

Verdenius, W. J. "Plato and Christianity," *Ratio* 5 (1963), 15–32.

Mimesis: Plato's Doctrine of Artistic Imitation and Its Meaning for Us (Leiden, 1949).

Vlastos, G. "Slavery in Plato's Thought," *Philos. Rev.* 50 (1941), 289–304.

"Socratic Knowledge and Platonic 'Pessimism'," *Philos. Rev.* 66 (1957), 226–38.

"Does Slavery Exist in Plato's *Republic?*" *Class. Philology* 63 (1968), 291–95.

II. Books by Other Authors.

Adkins, A. W. H. *Merit and Responsibility: A Study in Greek Values* (Oxford, 1960). Chapters 13 and 14 on Plato.

Barker, E. *Greek Political Theory* (London, 1947). Extensive treatment of Plato's political theory.

Crombie, I. M. *Examination of Plato's Doctrines*, Vol. I: *Plato on Man and Society* (London, 1962).

Cross, R. C. and A. D. Woozley *Plato's Republic: A Philosophical Commentary* (London, 1964).

Foster, M. B. *Political Philosophies of Plato and Hegel* (Oxford, 1935).

Gould, J. *The Development of Plato's Ethics* (Cambridge, England, 1955).

Gould, T. *Platonic Love* (London, 1963).

Gouldner, A. W. *Enter Plato* (New York, 1965).

Grote, G. *Plato and the Other Companions of Socrates*. 4 vols. (London, 1888).

Hackforth, R. *Plato's Examination of Pleasure* (Cambridge, England, 1945).

Plato's Phaedrus (Cambridge, England, 1952).

Jaeger, W. *Paideia*, English translation, Vols. 2 and 3 (New York, 1943).

Joseph, H. W. B. *Essays in Ancient and Modern Philosophy* (Oxford, 1935).

Knowledge and the Good in Plato's Republic (Oxford, 1948).

Levinson, R. *In Defense of Plato* (Cambridge, Mass., 1953).

MacIntyre, A. *Short History of Ethics* (London, 1966). Chapters 4 and 5 on Plato.

Murphy, N. R. *Interpretation of Plato's Republic* (Oxford, 1951).

North, Helen *Sophrōsynē* (Ithaca, N.Y., 1966). Chapter V on Plato.

Pieper, J. *Enthusiasm and Divine Madness: The Platonic Dialogue Phaedrus*, English translation by R. and C. Winston (New York, 1964).

Popper, K. *The Open Society and Its Enemies*, Vol. I: *The Spell of Plato*, Fourth Edition Revised (Princeton, 1962).

Rau, Catherine *Art and Society: A Reconsideration of Plato* (New York, 1951).

Rosen, S. *Plato's Symposium* (New Haven, 1968).

Sabine, G. H. *History of Political Theory*, Revised Edition (New York, 1950). Chapters 3 and 4 on Plato.

Sinclair, T. A. *History of Greek Political Theory* (London, 1951). Chapters 7 to 10 on Plato.

Singer, I. *Nature of Love from Plato to Luther* (New York, 1966). Chapter 4 on "Platonic Eros."

Solmsen, F. *Plato's Theology* (Ithaca, N.Y., 1942).

Strauss, Leo *Natural Right and History* (Chicago, 1953). Extensive discussion of Plato in Chapters 3 and 4.

Taylor, A. E. *Plato*, Fourth Edition Revised (London, 1937).

Warry, J. G. *Greek Aesthetic Theory* (London, 1962). Chapters 1 to 4 on Plato.

Wild, J. *Plato's Modern Enemies and the Theory of Natural Law* (Chicago, 1953).

Plato's Theory of Man (Cambridge, Mass., 1946).

Wolin, S. *Politics and Vision* (Boston, 1960). Chapter 2 on Plato.

III. Articles by Other Authors.

Armstrong, A. H. "Platonic Mysticism," *Dublin Review* 216 (1945), 130–42.

Bluck, R. S. "Plato, Pindar, and Metempsychosis," *American Journal of Philology* 79 (1958), 405–14.

Bury, R. G. "The Theory of Education in Plato's *Laws*," *Révue des Etudes Grecques* 50 (1937), 304–20.

Cooper, N. "Pleasure and Goodness in Plato's *Philebus*," *Philosophical Quarterly* 70 (1968), 12–15.

Ehnmark, E. "Transmigration in Plato," *Harvard Theological Review* 50 (1957), 1–20.

Faris, J. A. "Is Plato's Caste State Based on Racial Differences?" *Classical Quarterly* 44 (1950), 38–43.

Ferguson, A. S. "The Platonic Choice of Lives," *Philosophical Quarterly* 1 (1950), 5–34.

Foster, M. B. "Plato's Concept of Justice in the *Republic*," *Philosophical Quarterly* 1 (1950), 206–17.

Gallop, D. "True and False Pleasures," *Philosophical Quarterly* 10 (1960), 331–41.

Gosling, J. "False Pleasures: *Philebus* 35C–41B," *Phronesis* 4 (1959), 44–53.

"Father Kenny on False Pleasures," *Phronesis* 6 (1961), 41–45.

Grey, D. R. "Art in the *Republic*," *Philosophy* 27 (1952), 291–310.

Hackforth, R. "Moral Evil and Ignorance in Plato's Ethics," *Classical Quarterly* 40 (1946), 118–20.

"Plato's Theism," *Classical Quarterly* 30 (1936), 4–9.

Hall, R. M. "Justice and the Individual in the *Republic*," *Phronesis* 4 (1959), 149–58.

"Plato's Just Man," *New Scholasticism* 43 (1968), 202–25.

Hartland-Swann, J. "Plato as Poet," *Philosophy* 26 (1951), 3–18 and 131–41.

Hoerber, R. G. "More on Justice in the *Republic*," *Phronesis* 5 (1960), 32–34.

Hyland, D. A. "*Eros, Epithymia*, and *Philia* in Plato," *Phronesis* 13 (1968), 32–46.

Kelsen, H. "Platonic Justice," in *What Is Justice?* (Berkeley, 1960).

Kenny, A. "False Pleasures in the Philebus: Reply to Mr. Gosling," *Phronesis* 5 (1960), 45–52.

Kirwan, C. "Glaucon's Challenge," *Phronesis* 5 (1960), 45–52.

Larson, C. W. R. "The Platonic Synonyms, *Dikaiosyne* and *Sophrosyne*," *American Journal of Philology* 72 (1951), 395–414.

Maguire, J. P. "Plato's Theory of Natural Law," *Yale Classical Studies* 10 (1947), 151 ff.

Morris, C. R. "Plato's Theory of the Good Man's Motive," *Proceedings of the Aristotelian Society* N.S. 34 (1933/34), 129–42.

Mulgan, R. G. "Individual and Collective Virtues in the *Republic*," *Phronesis* 13 (1968), 84–85.

Rudberg, G. "Plato's Belief in God," in *Platonica Selecta* (Stockholm, 1956).

Schiller, J. "Just Man and Just Acts in Plato's *Republic*," *Journal of the History of Philosophy* 6 (1968), 1–14.

Skemp, J. B. "Comment on Communal and Individual Interest in the *Republic*," *Phronesis* 6 (1960), 35–38.

"The Development of Plato's Political Thought" in *Plato's Statesman: a Translation with Introductory Essays and Footnotes* (London, 1952), 26–66.

Strauss, L. "Plato," in *History of Political Philosophy*, ed. by L. Strauss and J. Cropsey (Chicago, 1964).

Symonds, J. A. "A Problem in Greek Ethics" (first published 1883), reprinted in *Studies in Sexual Inversion* (London, 1928, privately printed).

Taylor, A. E. "Decline and Fall of the State in *Republic* VIII," *Mind* 48 (1939), 23–38.

Thayer, H. S. "Plato: The Theory and Language of Function," *Philosophical Quarterly* 14 (1964), 303–18.

Unger, E. "Contemporary Anti-Platonism," *Cambridge Journal* 2 (1949), 643–59.

Weingartner, R. "Vulgar Justice and Platonic Justice," *Philosophy and Phenomenological Research* 25 (1964/65), 248–52.

Wilford, A. "The Status of Reason in *Plato's Psychology*," *Phronesis* 4 (1959), 54–58.

INDEX LOCORUM

ARISTOTLE

ISOCRATES

PLATO

Gorgias	491–94	176
Gorgias	492D–E	27
Gorgias	492E	30
Gorgias	493A	214
Gorgias	493A–C	208
Gorgias	493B	30
Gorgias	493B7	208
Gorgias	493C	209
Gorgias	493D	209
Gorgias	493E	29, 30
Gorgias	494C	29
Gorgias	495A	27
Gorgias	495C	28
Gorgias	498C	32
Gorgias	499B	14, 28
Gorgias	499D	26
Gorgias	499D–E	27
Gorgias	500A	28
Gorgias	501A–B	20
Gorgias	501C	21
Gorgias	503 ff.	232
Gorgias	503D ff.	69
Gorgias	503E	21
Gorgias	504B–D	69
Gorgias	507	31
Gorgias	507A	8
Gorgias	507E	30, 208
Gorgias	509A	31
Gorgias	510D	31
Gorgias	511B	31
Gorgias	512	31
Gorgias	512A	33
Gorgias	512A–B	69
Gorgias	513	31
Gorgias	517	21
Gorgias	518	21
Gorgias	521–22	176, 183
Gorgias	521D	9, 14
Gorgias	521E	197